easy

Microsoft® Windows® 7

Mark Edward Soper

que®

800 East 96th Street
Indianapolis, Indiana 46240

CONTENTS

EASY MICROSOFT® WINDOWS® 7

ISBN-13: 978-0-7897-3994-0
ISBN-10: 0-7897-3994-1

UK ISBN-13: 978-0-7897-4217-9
UK ISBN-10: 0-7897-4217-9

Library of Congress Cataloging-in-Publication Data:
Soper, Mark Edward.
  Easy Microsoft Windows 7 / Mark Edward Soper.
    p. cm.
  ISBN 978-0-7897-3994-0
  1. Microsoft Windows (Computer file) 2. Operating systems (Computers) I. Title.
  QA76.76.O63S6542 2009
  005.4'46--dc22

                          2009025527

Printed in the United States of America

First Printing: September 2009

TRADEMARKS

WARNING AND DISCLAIMER

BULK SALES

Que Publishing offers excellent discounts on this book when ordered in quantity for bulk purchases or special sales. For more information, please contact

U.S. Corporate and Government Sales
1-800-382-3419
corpsales@pearsontechgroup.com

For sales outside of the U.S., please contact

International Sales
international@pearson.com

Associate Publisher
Greg Wiegand

Acquisitions Editor
Michelle Newcomb

Development Editor
Kevin Howard

Managing Editor
Kristy Hart

Project Editor
Andy Beaster

Copy Editor
Water Crest Publishing

Indexer
Lisa Stumpf

Proofreader
Dan Knott

Technical Editor
Vince Averello

Publishing Coordinator
Cindy Teeters

Designer
Anne Jones

Compositor
Nonie Ratcliff

ABOUT THE AUTHOR

Mark Edward Soper has been using Microsoft Windows ever since version 1.0, and since 1992, he's taught thousands of computer troubleshooting and network students across the country how to use Windows as part of their work and everyday lives. Mark has contributed to Que's *Special Edition Using* series on Windows Me, Windows XP, and Windows Vista; *Easy Windows Vista; Windows 7 in Depth*, and has written two books about Windows Vista, including *Maximum PC Microsoft Windows Vista Exposed* and *Unleashing Microsoft Windows Vista Media Center*.

When he's not teaching, learning, or writing about Microsoft Windows, Mark stays busy with many other technology-related activities. He is a long-time contributor to *Upgrading and Repairing PCs*, working on the 11th through 18th editions, co-authored *Upgrading and Repairing Networks, 5th Edition*, written two books on A+ Certification (with a third in process), and written two books about digital photography, *Easy Digital Cameras* and *The Shot Doctor: The Amateur's Guide to Taking Great Digital Photos*. Mark also stays busy on the web, posting many blog entries and articles at MaximumPC.com, as well as articles for *Maximum PC* magazine. He also teaches Windows, digital photography, and digital imaging at Ivy Tech State College's Evansville, Indiana campus.

DEDICATION

For Cheryl—always.

ACKNOWLEDGMENTS

I've been using Windows since its beginnings as a toy-like front end for MS-DOS, but I've had plenty of help along the way in reaching this point.

Thanks first and always to God, who showed me my life's work (with much help from my wife Cheryl's encouragement) and has been with me in good times and bad.

I also want to thank the many people who helped me learn about Windows 7 and its many predecessors, including Jim Peck and Mayer Rubin, who gave me the opportunity to teach thousands of students about earlier versions of Windows; magazine editors Edie Rockwood and Ron Kobler, for assigning me to dig deeper into Windows; Ed Bott, who provided my first opportunity to contribute to a major Windows book; Ivy Tech State College, Bob Cowart, and Brian Knittel, who have continued my real-world Windows education. And, of course, the Microsoft family.

Thanks also to my family, both for their encouragement over the years and for the opportunity to explain various Windows features and to fix things that go wrong. Even though some of them have joined the "dark side" (they have Macs), we all still love each other.

I also want to thank the editorial and design team that Que put together for this book: Many thanks to Michelle Newcomb for bringing me back for another *Easy* series book, and thanks to Kevin Howard, Vince Averello, and Andy Beaster for overseeing their respective parts of the publishing process. Thanks also to Cindy Teeters for keeping track of invoices and making sure payments were timely. And I also want to thank Sarah, Dan, Lisa, and Nonie for the nuts and bolts work they do to make sure you have an outstanding book. This is my tenth year working with Que Publishing, and it's the best yet. May there be many more!

WE WANT TO HEAR FROM YOU!

As the reader of this book, *you* are our most important critic and commentator. We value your opinion and want to know what we're doing right, what we could do better, what areas you'd like to see us publish in, and any other words of wisdom you're willing to pass our way.

As an associate publisher for Que Publishing, I welcome your comments. You can email or write me directly to let me know what you did or didn't like about this book—as well as what we can do to make our books better.

Please note that I cannot help you with technical problems related to the topic of this book. We do have a User Services group, however, where I will forward specific technical questions related to the book.

When you write, please be sure to include this book's title and author as well as your name, email address, and phone number. I will carefully review your comments and share them with the author and editors who worked on the book.

Email: feedback@quepublishing.com

Mail: Greg Wiegand
Associate Publisher
Que Publishing
800 East 96th Street
Indianapolis, IN 46240 USA

READER SERVICES

Visit our website and register this book at www.informit.com/title/9780789739940 for convenient access to any updates, downloads, or errata that might be available for this book.

INTRODUCTION

WHY THIS BOOK WAS CREATED

The Que Publishing *Easy* series has always been known for accurate, simple, step-by-step instructions for using popular software. This book is no exception. Whether you're a veteran Windows user who is upgrading from Windows Vista, are making the jump from Windows XP or an older version, or are new to computers and Windows, Windows 7 has a lot to offer—and a lot for you to learn if you want to get the most out of it.

Easy Windows 7 is designed to make the learning process as painless as possible. We've looked hard at all the new and improved features in Windows 7, as well as the fundamentals of any operating system, and boiled them down into an easy-to-read visual guide that gets you familiar with this newest Microsoft creation in a hurry.

We won't waste your time discussing obscure operations that not even help desk workers or Windows geniuses ever use. Instead, our objective with *Easy Windows 7* is to give you a solid grounding in the everyday features you need to make your computing life better, more productive, and even more fun.

HOW TO READ EASY WINDOWS 7

Much as I'd like to write the "great American novel" someday, *Easy Windows 7* isn't that book: If you found it in the fiction section by mistake, please keep in mind that, although compelling, this book is not only "based on fact"—but *is* factual. Though it's no thriller, we hope that *Easy Windows 7* will be a "page-turner" because you're having such a good time learning more about Windows 7, you can't put this book down (except to reach for your keyboard and mouse).

Where to begin? There are several ways to use this book to learn more about Windows 7, as follows:

- Start at Chapter 1, "What's New in Windows 7," and work your way through.

- Go straight to the chapters that look the most interesting.

- Hit the table of contents or the index and go directly to the sections that tell you stuff you don't know already.

They'll all work—and to help you get a better feel for what's inside, here's a closer look at what's in each chapter.

BEYOND THE TABLE OF CONTENTS— WHAT'S INSIDE

Chapter 1, "What's New in Windows 7," provides a quick overview of Windows 7's most important new features. If you're reading this book mainly to brush up on what's new and different, start here and follow the references to the chapters with more information.

Chapter 2, "Getting Started with Windows 7," is designed for users who aren't quite sure what to do once the system starts. This chapter covers how to log into Windows 7, what the Getting Started menu does, how to use special Windows keys, and some of the most important keyboard shortcuts.

Chapter 3, "Using the Windows 7 Desktop," helps you understand the new (and actually improved) features that Windows 7 has added to the desktop. Learn how to view, manage, and cycle through program windows faster than before and how to add gadgets to make your desktop work harder for you.

Chapter 4, "Working with Your Folders," and Chapter 5, "Working with Your Files," should be read together, as many file operations are also folder operations (such as moving, renaming, and deleting). In addition, you will want to learn how to use Windows 7's new Libraries feature—it makes working with multiple folders of photos or other content easier than ever before.

Chapter 6, "Printing," helps you print smarter by covering not only how to use traditional features such as default printer, print preview, and printer setup, but also new device stage and font management features.

Chapter 7, "Using Windows Media Player," shows you how to enjoy all types of media on your desktop.

Chapter 8, "Windows Media Center," introduces you to the way to enjoy your photos, music, videos, and TV on your desktop or through your home theater system.

Chapter 9, "Gaming," helps you understand how Games Explorer keeps your games organized and helps you choose games that are appropriate for your family and your computer's performance levels.

Chapter 10, "Browsing the Internet," provides step-by-step instructions on using Internet Explorer 8's new features, including the Favorites Bar, InPrivate Browsing, Compatibility View, and Accelerators.

Chapter 11, "User Accounts and System Security," helps you keep your data and your family safe from Internet intruders by showing you how to use Parental Controls, check for spyware, and use Windows Defender.

Chapter 12, "Personalizing Windows 7," helps you make your Windows 7 PC truly personal by setting the desktop wallpaper, color scheme, screen saver, mouse pointers, and sounds the way you like.

Chapter 13, "System Maintenance and Performance," helps you keep Windows running at peak efficiency and shows you how to solve problems and keep your information safe.

Chapter 14, "Setting Up Programs," helps you manage your programs. From installing to uninstalling, adding shortcuts, to taming AutoPlay and toolbars,

this chapter is the one your programs want you to read.

Chapter 15, "Windows Accessories," helps you work with the new features in the most commonly-used accessories (Calculator, WordPad, NotePad, Paint, and Windows Photo Viewer).

Chapter 16, "Networking Your Home," introduces you to Windows 7's new HomeGroup feature for easy and secure home networking. This chapter also shows you how to build a network with older Windows desktops and even how to transfer files from your old PC to your new Windows 7 PC.

Chapter 17, "Using Windows Live Essentials," helps you get up to speed on this optional, yet highly recommended, part of the Windows 7 family. From photo organizing to email and burning CDs and DVDs to share with others, Windows Live Essentials helps you stay in touch—and we show you how it works.

Baffled by PC and Windows terminology? Check out the Glossary!

Also be sure to check out the additional tasks available online in PDF format at www.informit.com/title/9780789739940.

Enjoy!

Chapter 1

WHAT'S NEW IN WINDOWS 7

Microsoft Windows 7 is the seventh generation of the world's most popular computer operating system. Although the general look of Windows 7 resembles Windows Vista, Windows 7 offers many new and improved features to make computing on any type of PC easier. Whether you use a laptop, desktop, or a standard or small-sized notebook computer, Windows 7 is designed to make life easier for you. From printing to working with photos and other types of media, from using the Internet to solving problems, Windows 7 provides you with tremendous new tools.

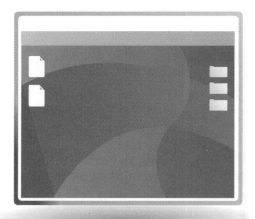

The Getting Started menu helps new
Window 7 users find links to important
tasks in a single location

Windows Live Photo Gallery is one of
the Windows Live Essentials you can
download using Getting Started

GETTING STARTED

When you first start using Windows 7, the features you need are located in the Getting Started menu. Use this menu to learn more about Windows 7, personalize the operating system's visual and audio features, transfer files from your old computer, add users, and more.

Click **Start**.

Click **Getting Started**.

Select the option you want to use.

NOTE

To learn more about these options, see "Using Getting Started" in Chapter 2, "Getting Started with Windows 7. ■

AERO PEEK

Aero Peek enables you to instantly view the desktop without minimizing or closing programs. After you view the desktop, you can instantly bring program windows back to their original positions.

1 Normal desktop with program windows open.

2 Aero Peek displays transparent frames in place of program windows.

End

NOTE

To learn more about Aero Peek, see "Using Aero Peek to View the Desktop" in Chapter 3, "Using the Windows 7 Desktop." ■

AERO SNAP

Aero Snap enables you to control the window size and location of any program running on your desktop without lifting your hands off the keyboard. You can move a program window to the left or right of your desktop, maximize it, or minimize it.

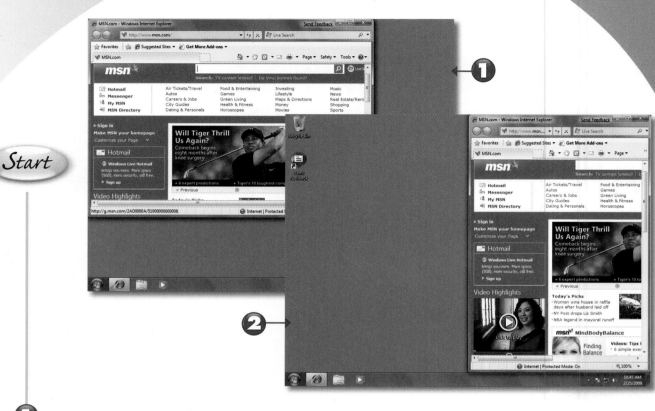

Start

1 Program running in window.

2 Aero Snap moves program window to right.

End

NOTE

To learn more about Aero Snap, see "Using Aero Snap to Manage Windows" in Chapter 3. ■

LIBRARIES

The new Libraries feature enables you to view the contents of all folders you use for a particular type of file by selecting the corresponding library link in the Start menu. For example, if you have digital photos in your Pictures folder as well as on an external hard disk and a network folder, adding the other locations to the Pictures library will enable you to view and work with all of your photos at the same time.

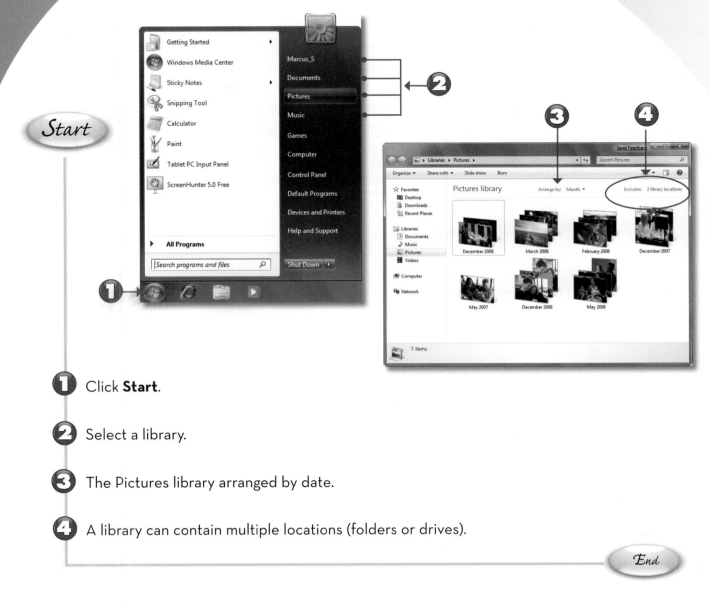

1 Click **Start**.

2 Select a library.

3 The Pictures library arranged by date.

4 A library can contain multiple locations (folders or drives).

NOTE

To learn more about using libraries, see "Using Libraries" in Chapter 4, "Working with Your Folders." ∎

NOTE

Windows 7's libraries include Documents, Music, Pictures, and Videos. ∎

INTERNET EXPLORER 8

Windows 7 includes Microsoft's newest browser, Internet Explorer 8. Internet Explorer 8 makes surfing the web even easier with new features like suggested websites and an easy-to-access library of add-ons you can use to customize your web-browsing experience, such as a visual search for eBay items, various web radio add-ons, and much more.

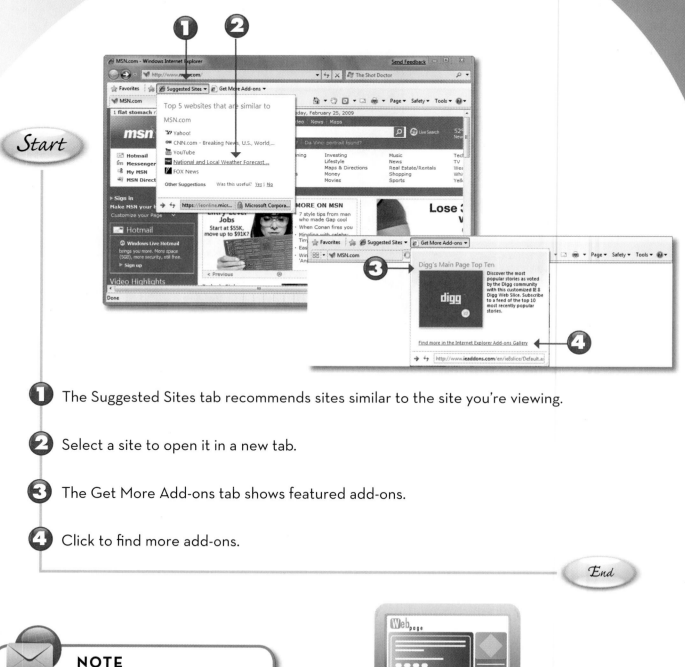

Start

1. The Suggested Sites tab recommends sites similar to the site you're viewing.

2. Select a site to open it in a new tab.

3. The Get More Add-ons tab shows featured add-ons.

4. Click to find more add-ons.

End

NOTE

To learn more about using Internet Explorer 8, see Chapter 10, "Browsing the Internet." ■

WINDOWS ACTION CENTER

Wondering if your system is as secure as it should be? Need to fix a problem with your system? The new Windows Action Center combines access to security and maintenance warnings and solutions into a single window.

Start

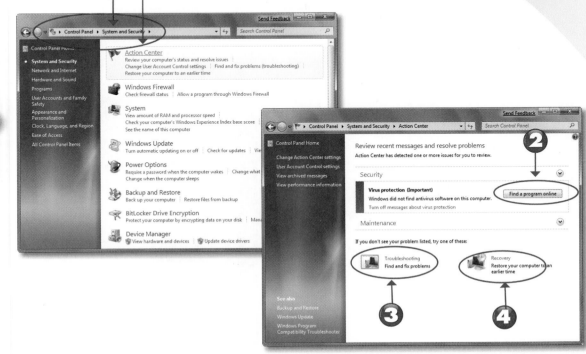

① Action Center is the first option in the System and Security section of the Control Panel.

② Click to solve listed problems with your system's security.

③ Click to find and solve problems with your system.

④ Click to restore your system's configuration to an earlier time with System Restore.

End

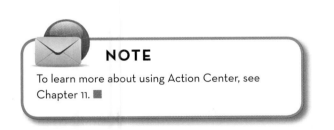

NOTE

To learn more about using Action Center, see Chapter 11. ■

WINDOWS LIVE ESSENTIALS

Windows Live Essentials is an optional part of Windows 7. If you take pictures, write blogs, send and receive email, use social-networking sites, work with video files, or use instant messaging, Windows Live Essentials has the programs you need to get started.

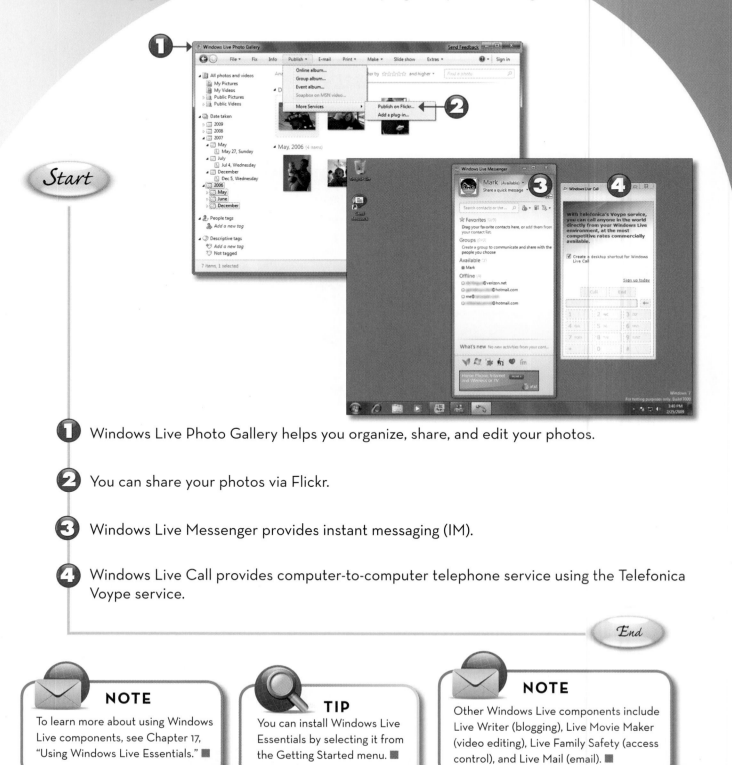

Start

End

1. Windows Live Photo Gallery helps you organize, share, and edit your photos.

2. You can share your photos via Flickr.

3. Windows Live Messenger provides instant messaging (IM).

4. Windows Live Call provides computer-to-computer telephone service using the Telefonica Voype service.

NOTE

To learn more about using Windows Live components, see Chapter 17, "Using Windows Live Essentials." ■

TIP

You can install Windows Live Essentials by selecting it from the Getting Started menu. ■

NOTE

Other Windows Live components include Live Writer (blogging), Live Movie Maker (video editing), Live Family Safety (access control), and Live Mail (email). ■

DEVICE STAGE

Device Stage takes managing multifunction peripherals to a whole new level. With a multi-function printer, smartphone, or another device that supports Device Stage, you can control all of its functions from a single window.

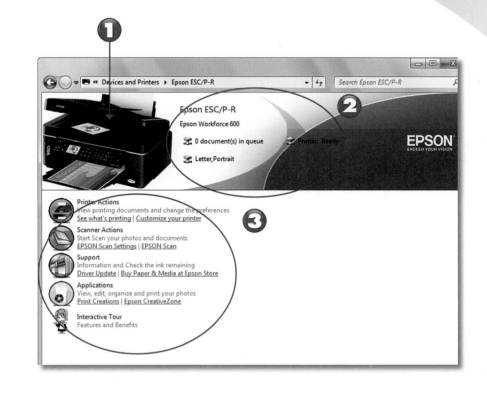

Start

Device Stage displays an accurate illustration of the device.

Device-specific setup and configuration information.

Device-specific functions and support features.

End

NOTE

To learn more about using Device Stage, see Chapter 6, "Printing."

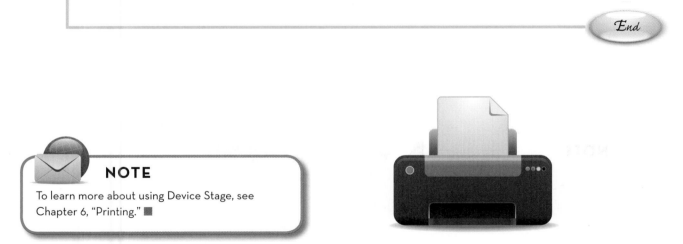

Chapter 2

GETTING STARTED WITH WINDOWS 7

Whether you're a newcomer to Windows or an experienced user of older versions, Windows 7's improvements start as soon as you log onto the system. In this chapter, you learn how to log on, how to adjust User Account Control (UAC), and how to interact with Windows through a mouse or a keyboard.

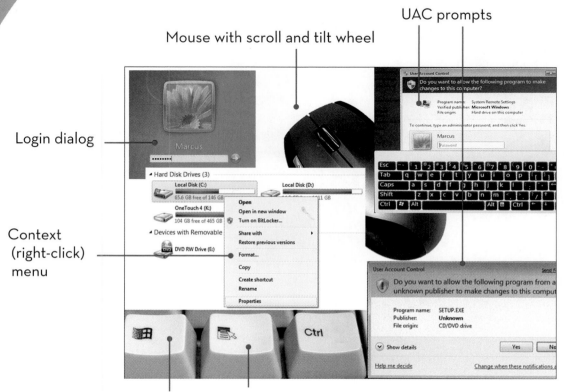

UAC prompts

Mouse with scroll and tilt wheel

Login dialog

Context (right-click) menu

Windows key   Context menu key

LOGGING INTO WINDOWS 7

If you are using a preinstalled copy of Windows 7, you might not need to log in. However, if you have set up different users, or if you have installed Windows 7 as an upgrade to a previous version of Windows that had multiple user accounts, you will need to log in.

To log into Windows 7, you must know the user name and password (if any) set up for your account. If you installed Windows 7 yourself, be sure to make note of this information when you are prompted to provide it during the installation process.

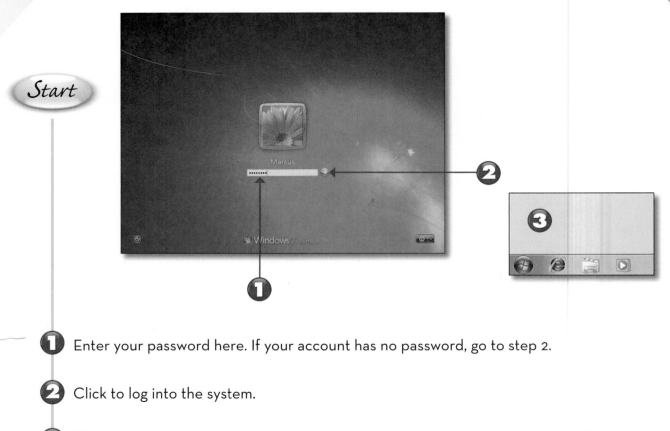

Start

1 Enter your password here. If your account has no password, go to step 2.

2 Click to log into the system.

3 If you have provided the correct password (or if your account has no password), the Windows desktop appears.

End

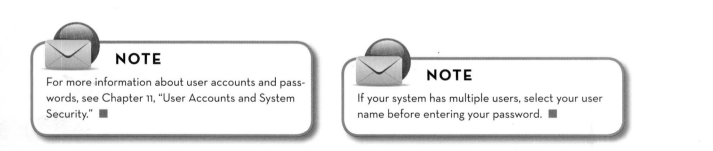

NOTE

For more information about user accounts and passwords, see Chapter 11, "User Accounts and System Security." ∎

NOTE

If your system has multiple users, select your user name before entering your password. ∎

DEALING WITH A FAILED LOGIN

What happens if you cannot log into your system? Windows 7 helps you by providing a password reminder, as you see in this tutorial.

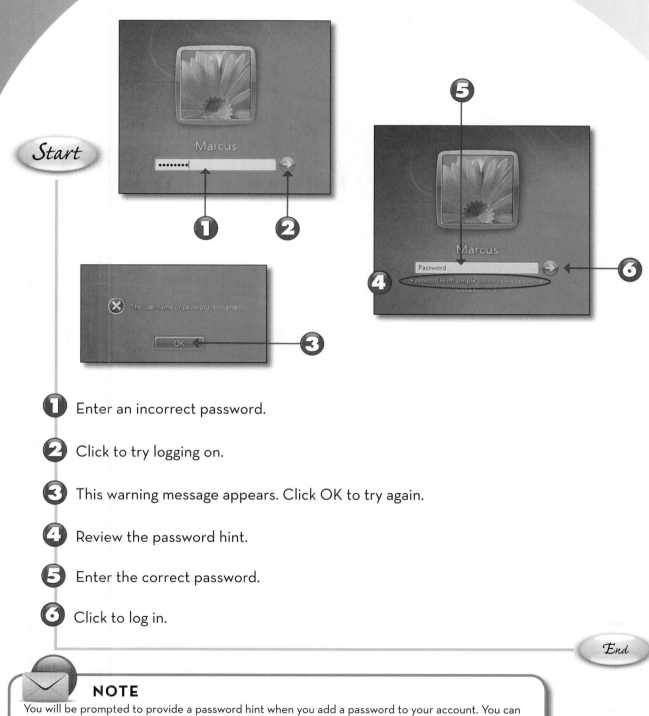

1 Enter an incorrect password.

2 Click to try logging on.

3 This warning message appears. Click OK to try again.

4 Review the password hint.

5 Enter the correct password.

6 Click to log in.

NOTE

You will be prompted to provide a password hint when you add a password to your account. You can also create a password reset disk. See Chapter 11, " User Accounts and System Security," for details. ■

USING THE MOUSE

Most users will work with Windows 7 by using a mouse or equivalent pointing device. This tutorial shows you what the buttons and other major controls do.

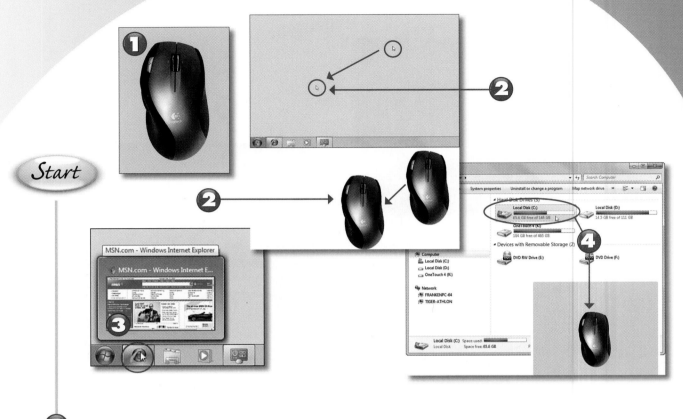

Start

Continued

1. Place the mouse on a solid surface or mousepad.

2. As you move the mouse, a mouse pointer appears on-screen and moves as the mouse moves.

3. Hover the mouse over an icon in the taskbar to see a live thumbnail of the program.

4. Click the left button to select a menu item, shortcut, or other object.

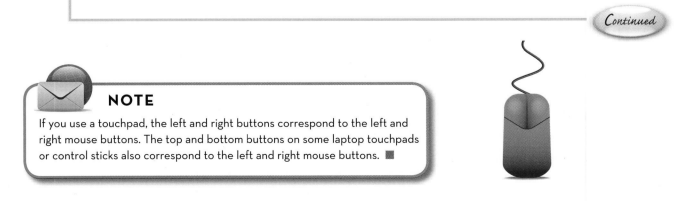

NOTE

If you use a touchpad, the left and right buttons correspond to the left and right mouse buttons. The top and bottom buttons on some laptop touchpads or control sticks also correspond to the left and right mouse buttons. ■

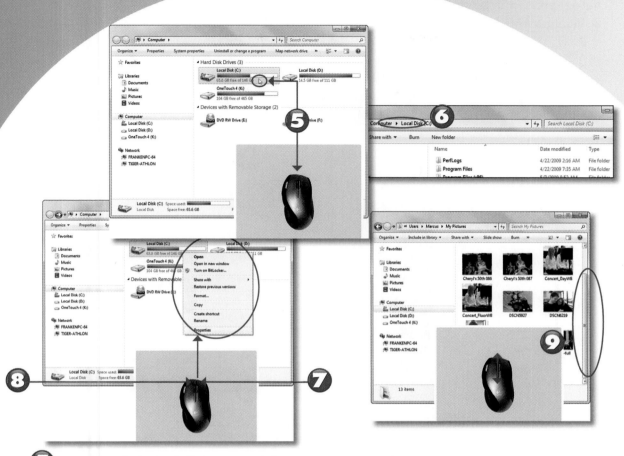

5 Double-click the left button while pointing at an object.

6 The object opens.

7 Right-click an object to display its context menu.

8 Click an item from the menu to use it.

9 Scroll up and down the page with the scroll wheel.

End

NOTE

You can also scroll from side to side with some mice by pushing the scroll wheel from side to side. ∎

USING THE KEYBOARD

Although most Windows users work with the mouse to move around the desktop or activate menus, don't overlook the keyboard. This tutorial helps you understand how to use the special buttons and functions of a typical keyboard.

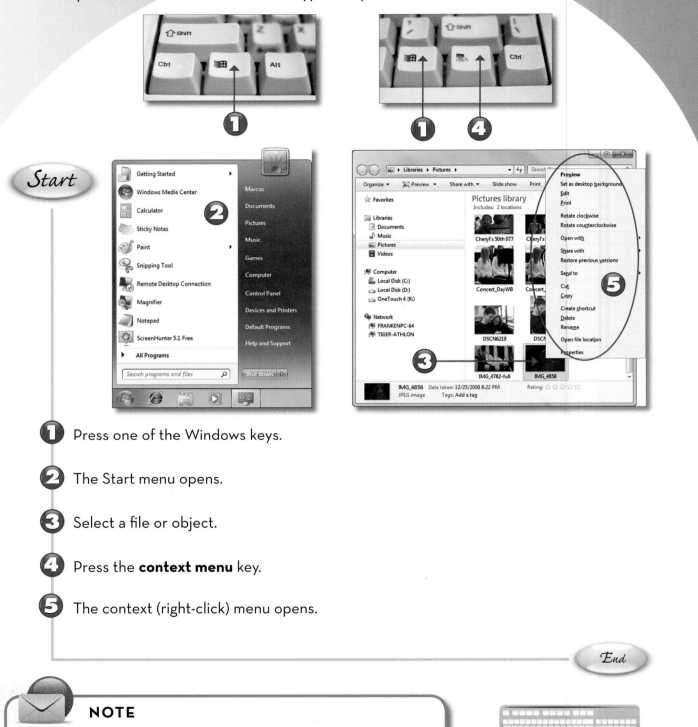

1 Press one of the Windows keys.

2 The Start menu opens.

3 Select a file or object.

4 Press the **context menu** key.

5 The context (right-click) menu opens.

NOTE

Windows also includes many keyboard shortcuts. To learn about them, open Help and Support from the Start menu and search for "keyboard shortcuts." ■

USER ACCOUNT CONTROL (UAC) FOR ADMINISTRATORS

User Account Control (UAC) is a feature that helps protect you from programs and events that could harm your system. If a change to your system is protected by UAC, a UAC prompt appears in front of a dimmed desktop, and you must approve the change before the operation continues.

With the default UAC settings in Windows, an administrator will seldom see a UAC prompt unless he or she attempts to run a program that is not identified with a digital signature. Such programs might be older Windows applications, downloaded programs, or websites trying to run a program without your permission. This tutorial shows you how UAC works for an administrator.

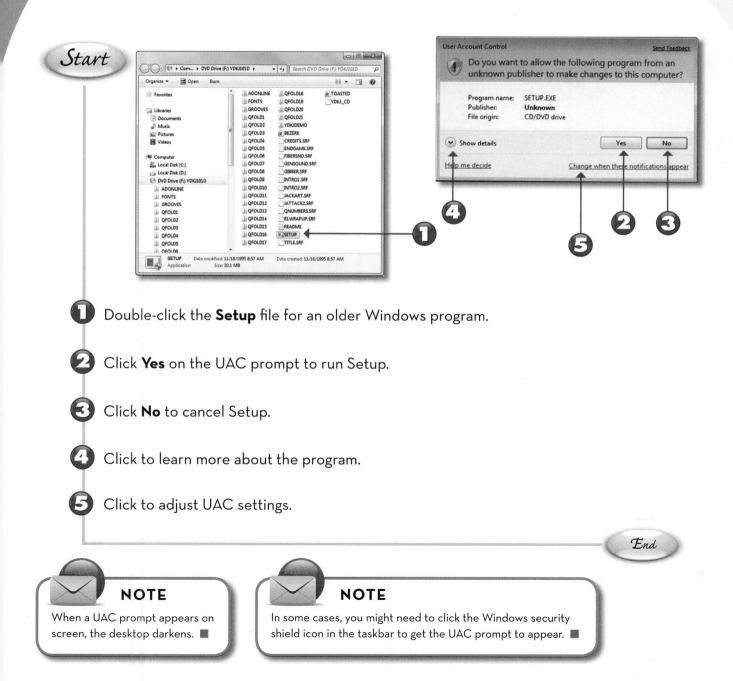

① Double-click the **Setup** file for an older Windows program.

② Click **Yes** on the UAC prompt to run Setup.

③ Click **No** to cancel Setup.

④ Click to learn more about the program.

⑤ Click to adjust UAC settings.

NOTE

When a UAC prompt appears on screen, the desktop darkens. ■

NOTE

In some cases, you might need to click the Windows security shield icon in the taskbar to get the UAC prompt to appear. ■

USER ACCOUNT CONTROL FOR STANDARD USERS

Standard users are likely to see UAC prompts much more often than administrators. If a standard user tries to install a program, or tries to open a Windows 7 feature that is marked with the blue and yellow Windows security shield, a UAC prompt is often displayed. As you see in this tutorial, standard users must provide the password for the system's administrator when prompted before the selected operation can continue.

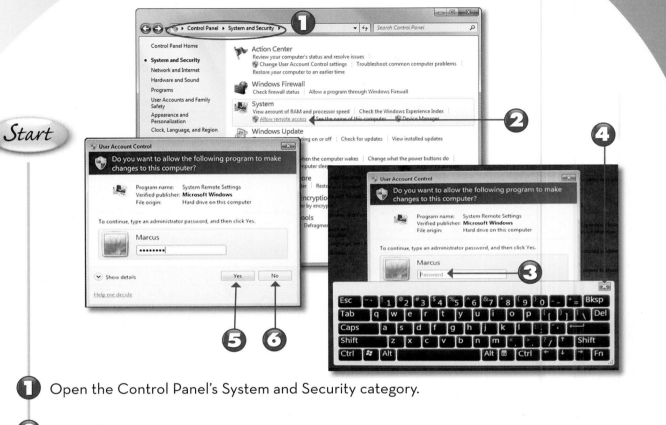

1 Open the Control Panel's System and Security category.

2 Click **Allow Remote Access**.

3 A UAC prompt appears. Enter the administrator's password with the on-screen or physical keyboard.

4 Click to close the on-screen keyboard.

5 Click **Yes** to continue.

6 Click **No** to cancel.

NOTE

To enter text using the on-screen keyboard, click the letter or number you want with the mouse. ■

ADJUSTING USER ACCOUNT CONTROL (UAC)

If you find that UAC's default settings are too obtrusive, or do not provide enough protection, you can fine-tune how UAC works from the Getting Started menu.

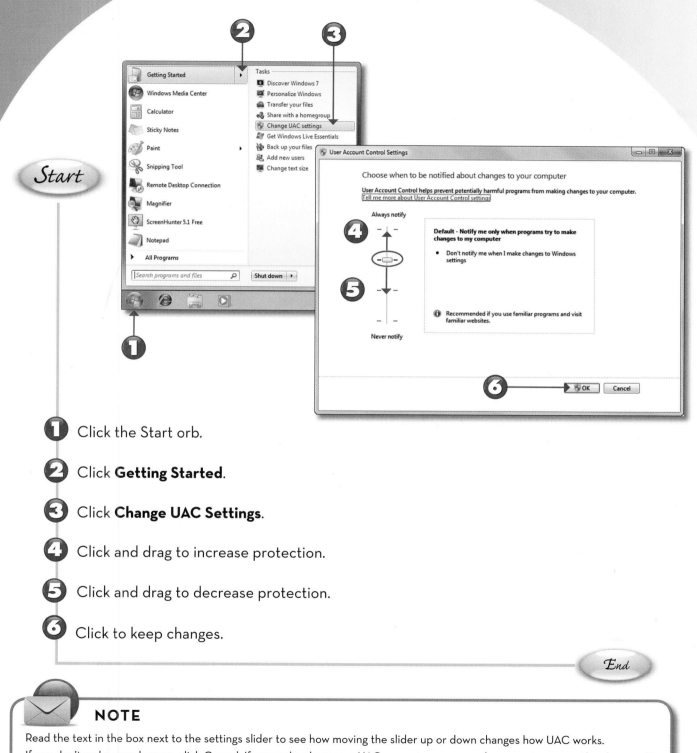

1 Click the Start orb.

2 Click **Getting Started**.

3 Click **Change UAC Settings**.

4 Click and drag to increase protection.

5 Click and drag to decrease protection.

6 Click to keep changes.

NOTE

Read the text in the box next to the settings slider to see how moving the slider up or down changes how UAC works.

If you don't make any changes, click Cancel. If you make changes, a UAC prompt appears, and you must approve the change. ■

USING THE WINDOWS 7 DESKTOP

Although the Windows 7 desktop still has a taskbar across the bottom of the screen, it represents a huge departure from previous Windows desktops. The new desktop makes it easier to manage programs, switch between program windows, and find the window you want to work with now.

Hover over a taskbar icon to see a jump list of recently opened documents or dialogs

Gadgets can now be placed anywhere on the desktop

STARTING A PROGRAM FROM THE START MENU

You can start a program from a desktop shortcut, but you're more likely to start a program from the Start menu.

1 Click the Start orb.

2 If the program is listed on the left pane, click it to start it.

3 If the program is not listed on the left pane, hover the mouse over **All Programs**.

4 Scroll to the program listing.

5 Click the program listing to start it.

NOTE

If the program is within a folder on the Start menu, click the folder to open it; then click the program name to start the program. ■

OPENING A NEW PROGRAM WINDOW

Windows 7's taskbar also makes it easy to create a new program window for a currently running program.

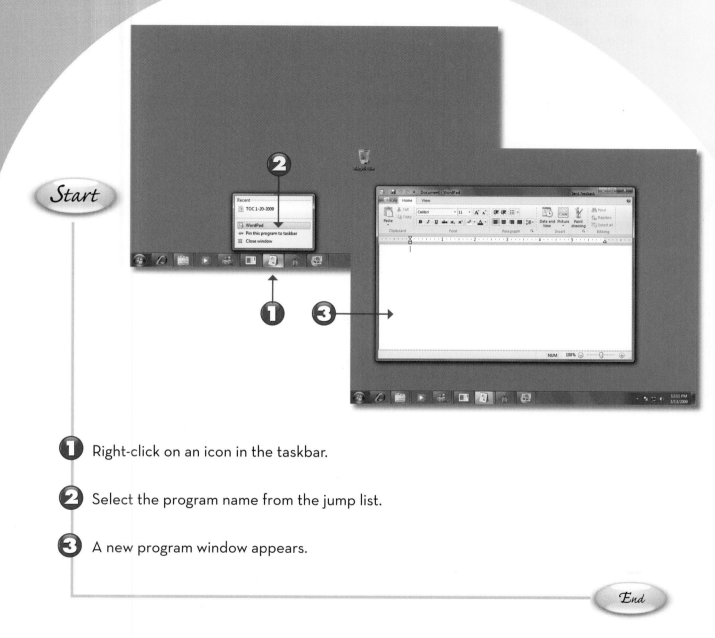

 Right-click on an icon in the taskbar.

2 Select the program name from the jump list.

3 A new program window appears.

TIP

Use the Recent submenu to open a recently used document. Use Pin This Program to Taskbar to keep programs you use frequently on the taskbar at all times. Use Close Window or Close All Windows to close open program windows. ■

MAXIMIZING, MINIMIZING, RESTORING, AND RESIZING A WINDOW

Windows 7 provides a variety of ways to control the size and position of program windows. In this section, you learn how to use your mouse to adjust window size and position. You can also use Aero Snap (this chapter, p. 28) to adjust window position from the keyboard.

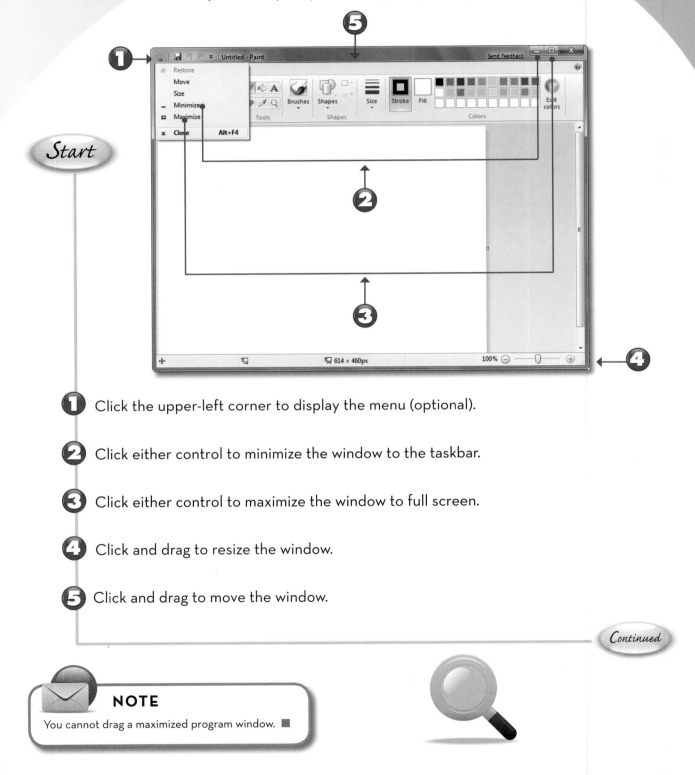

Start

1 Click the upper-left corner to display the menu (optional).

2 Click either control to minimize the window to the taskbar.

3 Click either control to maximize the window to full screen.

4 Click and drag to resize the window.

5 Click and drag to move the window.

Continued

NOTE

You cannot drag a maximized program window. ■

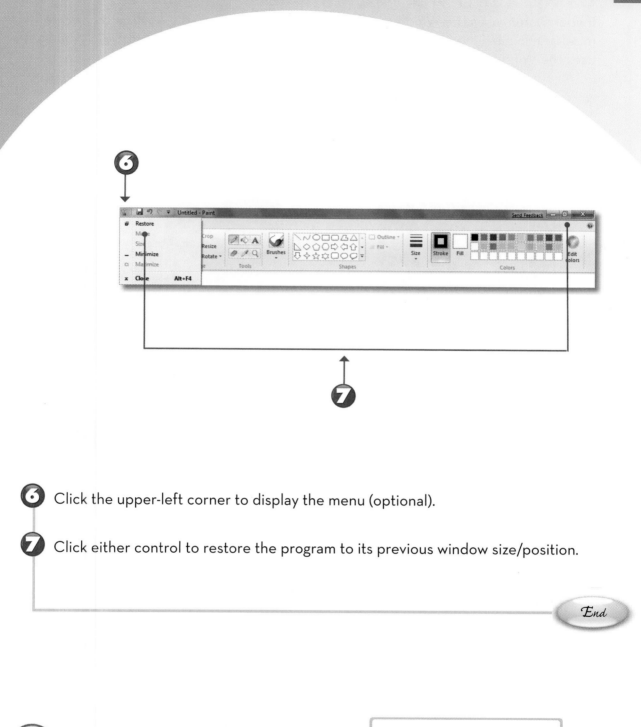

6 Click the upper-left corner to display the menu (optional).

7 Click either control to restore the program to its previous window size/position.

End

NOTE

As you can see from this tutorial, you do not need to open the upper-left corner menu to work with window sizing. ■

USING AERO SNAP TO MANAGE WINDOWS

If your system uses the Windows Aero desktop, you can use your keyboard to move, maximize, or minimize the active window by using a new feature called Aero Snap. Aero Snap uses the Windows key along with the arrow keys to adjust window position.

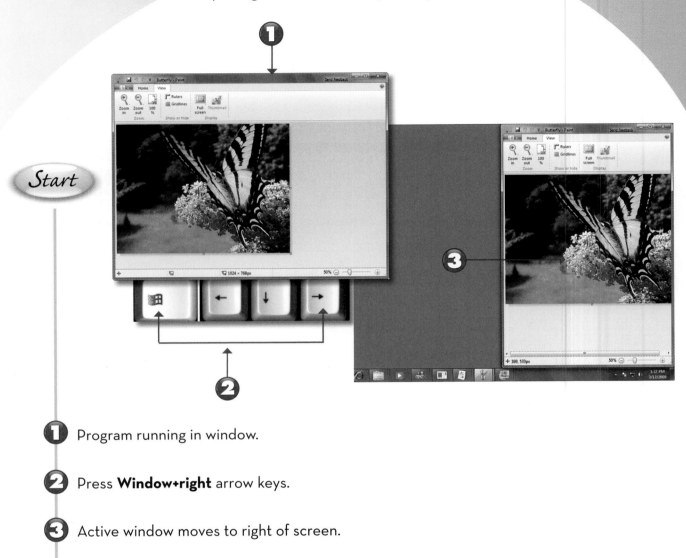

Start

1 Program running in window.

2 Press **Window+right** arrow keys.

3 Active window moves to right of screen.

Continued

NOTE

If you are using a built-in keyboard on a portable computer, the Window key might be located away from the arrow keys. ■

4 Press **Window+up** arrow.

5 Active window is maximized.

6 Press **Window+left** arrow.

7 Active window moves to left of screen.

End

NOTE
Press Window+down arrow to minimize active window to toolbar. ■

NOTE
To learn more about Windows Aero, see Chapter 12, "Personalizing Windows 7." ■

USING AERO PEEK TO VIEW THE DESKTOP

If your system supports the Windows Aero desktop (the title bar of the active window is translucent when it is not maximized), you can use a new feature called Aero Peek to see your desktop, even if you have many program windows open.

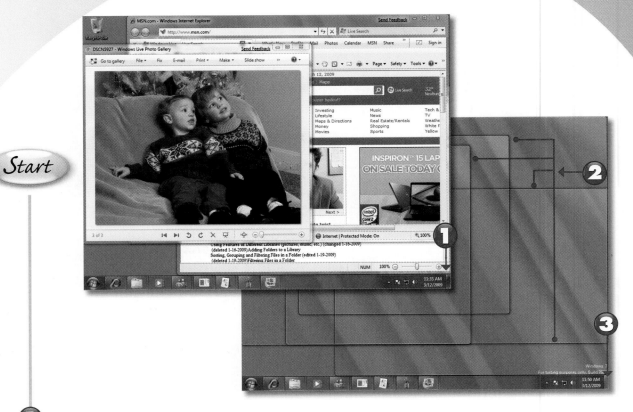

Start

1 The Aero Peek control box. Hover the mouse over the box to view the desktop.

2 Aero Peek displays only the outlines of open windows.

3 Click the control box to toggle window display on and off.

End

NOTE

Windows 7 Starter Edition does not support Windows Aero. ■

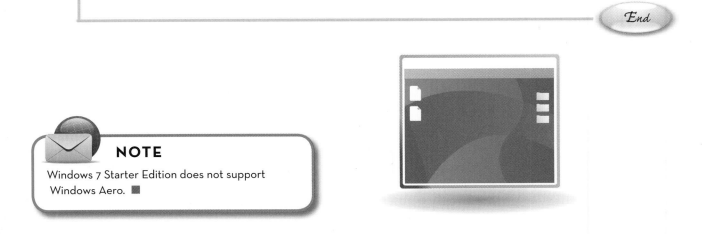

USING ALT-TAB TO CYCLE THROUGH PROGRAMS

Use the Alt-Tab keys (also known as "cool switching") to select which program you want to make active. In Windows 7, pressing Alt-Tab cycles through live thumbnails of each running program.

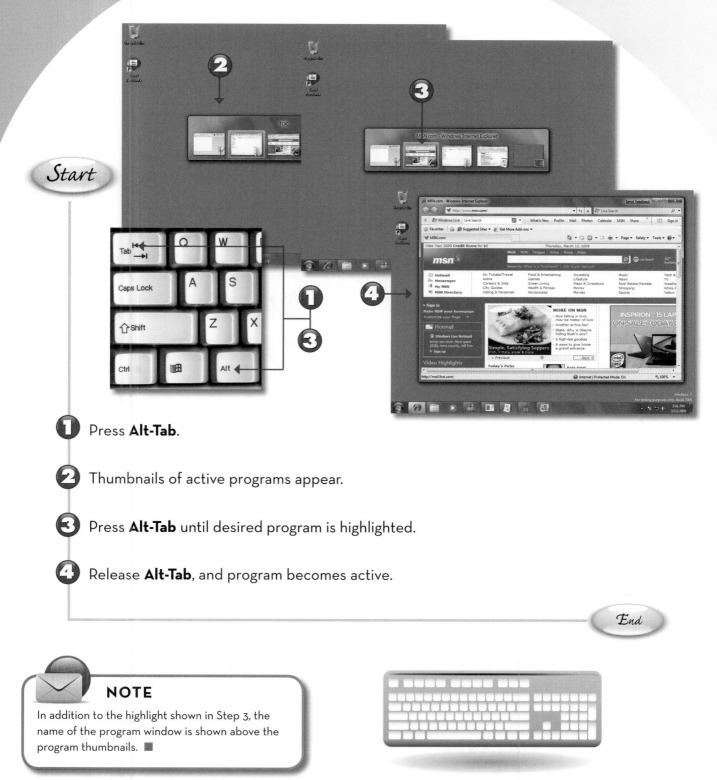

1 Press **Alt-Tab**.

2 Thumbnails of active programs appear.

3 Press **Alt-Tab** until desired program is highlighted.

4 Release **Alt-Tab**, and program becomes active.

NOTE

In addition to the highlight shown in Step 3, the name of the program window is shown above the program thumbnails. ■

USING WINDOWS FLIP (WIN-TAB) TO CYCLE THROUGH PROGRAMS

Systems running the Windows Aero desktop can use Windows Flip to cycle through running programs and select the one they want to make active. Windows Flip uses the Windows and Tab keys.

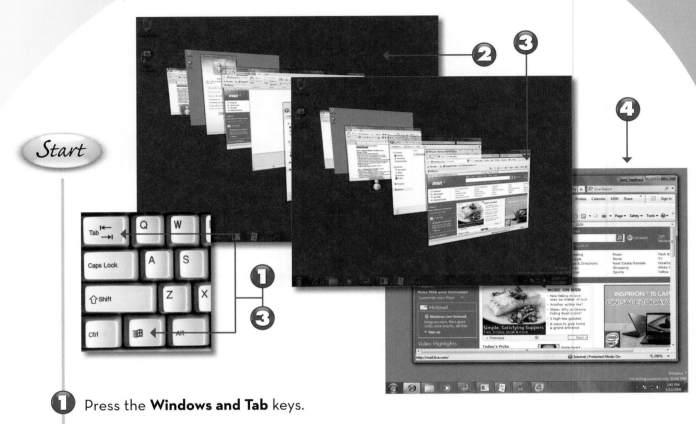

Start

1 Press the **Windows and Tab** keys.

2 Running programs are displayed in an overlapping arc across the screen.

3 Continue to press the **Windows and Tab** keys until the program you want to make active is at the front of the stack.

4 Release the keys, and the program becomes active.

End

NOTE

You might see icons for minimized programs as well as program windows appear in Steps 2 and 3. ■

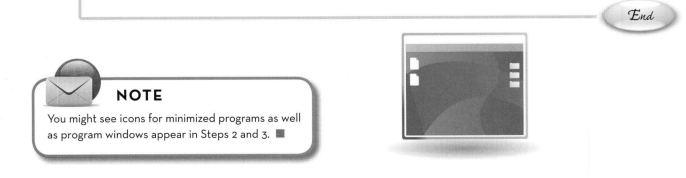

USING THE TASKBAR TO VIEW AND SELECT RUNNING PROGRAMS

The Windows 7 taskbar not only looks different than the one in previous versions of Windows (it uses icons, not text, by default), but it makes it easier than ever to choose the program you want to make active.

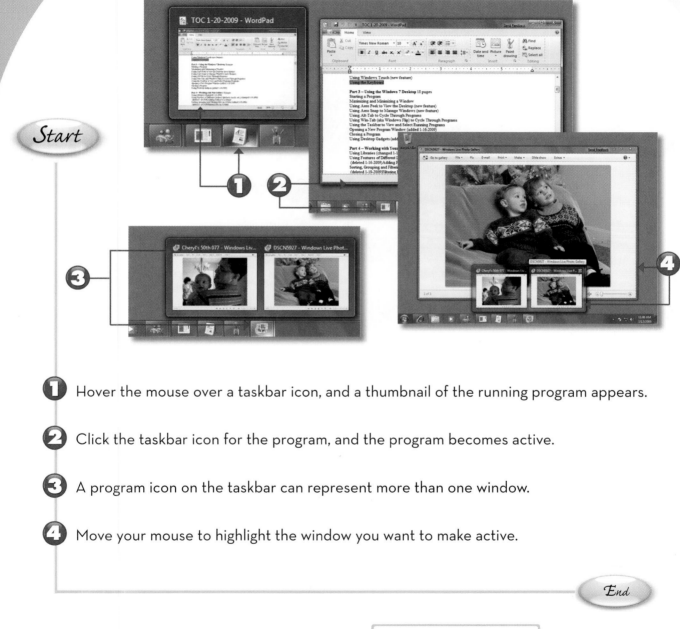

Start

1 Hover the mouse over a taskbar icon, and a thumbnail of the running program appears.

2 Click the taskbar icon for the program, and the program becomes active.

3 A program icon on the taskbar can represent more than one window.

4 Move your mouse to highlight the window you want to make active.

End

NOTE

This feature requires Windows Aero. ■

CLOSING A PROGRAM

Windows 7 offers several ways to close a program, so you can select the method that's best for a given situation.

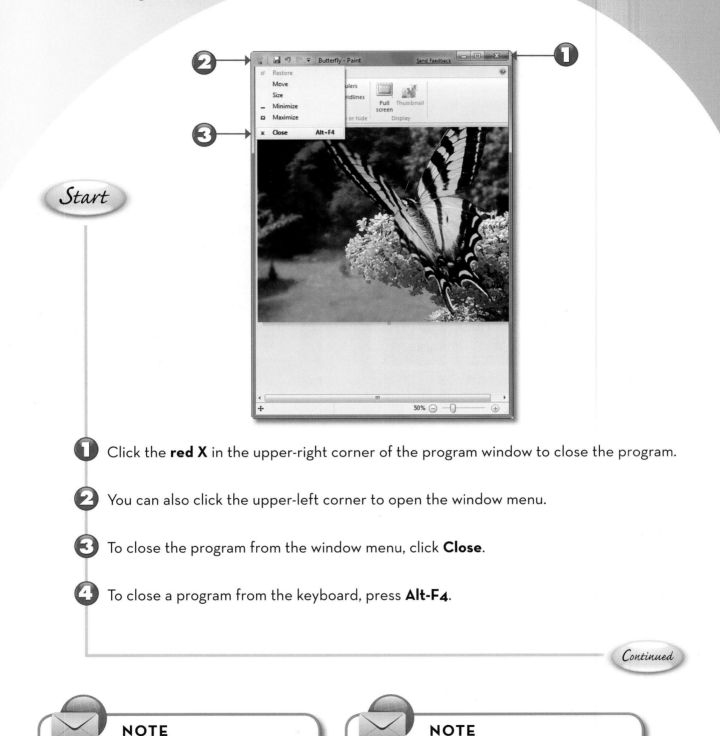

Start

1. Click the **red X** in the upper-right corner of the program window to close the program.

2. You can also click the upper-left corner to open the window menu.

3. To close the program from the window menu, click **Close**.

4. To close a program from the keyboard, press **Alt-F4**.

Continued

NOTE

You don't need to open the window menu to use Alt-F4 to close the program window. ■

NOTE

The right-click menu shown in Step 6 also allows you to pin the program to the Taskbar for faster access. ■

5 To close a program in the taskbar, right-click the program icon and select Close Window.

6 To close all windows for a particular program from the taskbar, right-click the program icon and select **Close All Windows**.

End

USING DESKTOP GADGETS

Windows 7 improves Windows Vista's use of gadgets (small desktop programs) by freeing them from the side of the monitor. In Windows 7, you can place desktop gadgets wherever you'd like on the desktop, and you can use gadgets developed for Windows Vista as well as those developed for Windows 7.

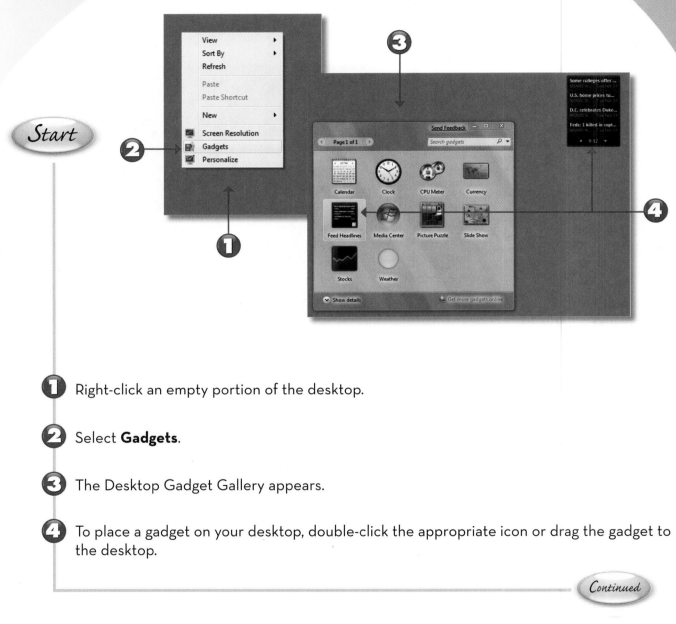

1 Right-click an empty portion of the desktop.

2 Select **Gadgets**.

3 The Desktop Gadget Gallery appears.

4 To place a gadget on your desktop, double-click the appropriate icon or drag the gadget to the desktop.

Continued

NOTE
You can also open the Desktop Gadget Gallery from the Start menu. ■

NOTE
Repeat step 4 until you have added all the gadgets you want to add to your desktop. ■

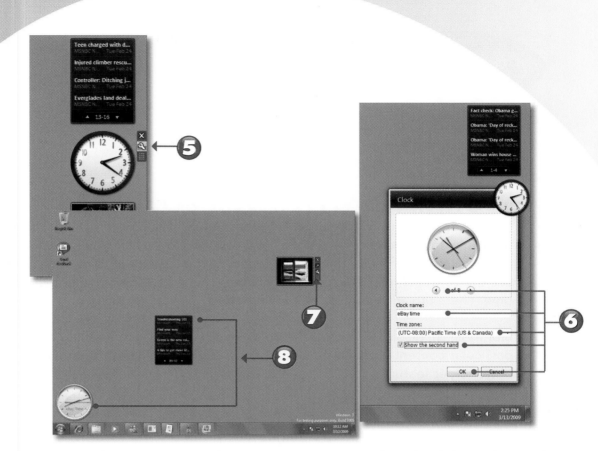

5 To adjust settings for any gadget, move your mouse to the right side of the gadget and select the setup (wrench) icon.

6 Select or enter the desired options and click **OK** when finished.

7 To drag a gadget, move the mouse to the right of the gadget and click **Drag Gadget**.

8 Move the gadget as desired, and release the left mouse button to place the gadget.

End

NOTE

Use the Get More Gadgets Online link to download additional gadgets. ■

NOTE

Select a gadget; then click Show Details to learn more about the gadget. ■

WORKING WITH YOUR FOLDERS

Folders enable you to store different types of files (such as documents, music, photos, videos, and others) in different locations. However, if you have files of a particular type in more than one location, it would be great to have a way to see the contents of all the folders containing the same type of file at the same time. That's the advantage of Windows 7's new libraries feature.

Libraries can display all the local hard disk and network folders that contain any particular content type. This chapter shows you how to use libraries as well as other folder features.

The new Libraries feature enables you to view the contents of multiple folders at the same time

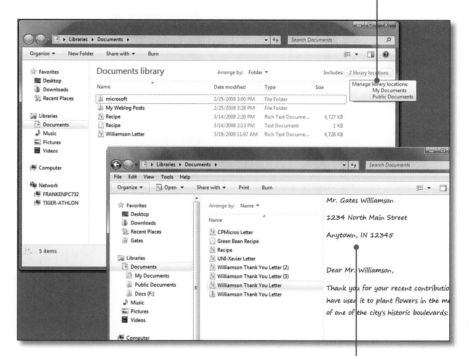

Use the Preview Pane option to view a document in a library before you open it

USING LIBRARIES

When you click on Documents, Pictures, Music, or Recorded TV links on the Start menu, you are opening Windows 7's new Libraries view. Libraries enable you to see the contents of multiple folders on hard disk or network shares as a single logical folder.

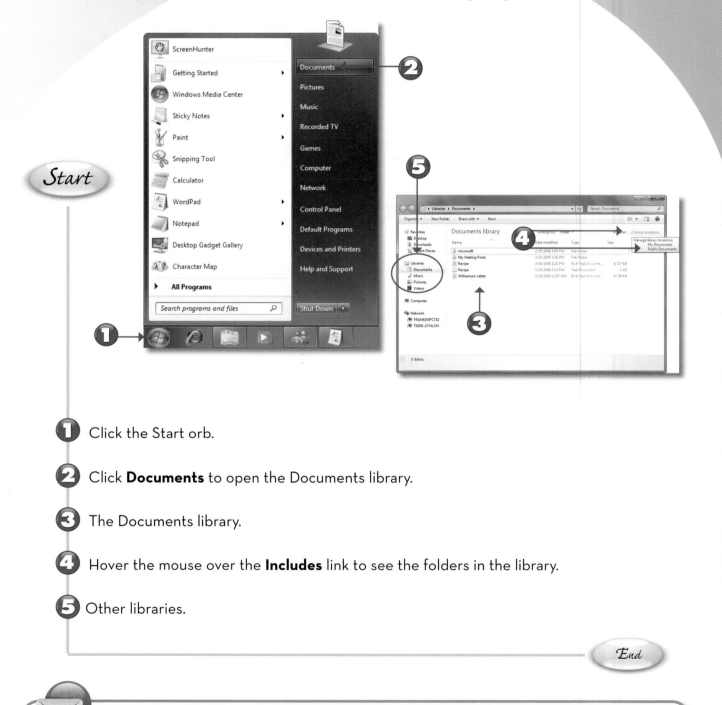

1 Click the Start orb.

2 Click **Documents** to open the Documents library.

3 The Documents library.

4 Hover the mouse over the **Includes** link to see the folders in the library.

5 Other libraries.

End

NOTE

By default, each user's libraries include their personal documents, music, pictures, and videos folders, as well as the corresponding public folders. The Recorded TV library is an exception. By default, it includes only the Public Recorded TV folder. ■

ENABLING THE MENU PANE

By default, libraries do not use the standard Windows menu bar. However, it's a good idea to enable the Windows menu bar, as it enables you to perform more tasks than you can with the right-click context menu alone.

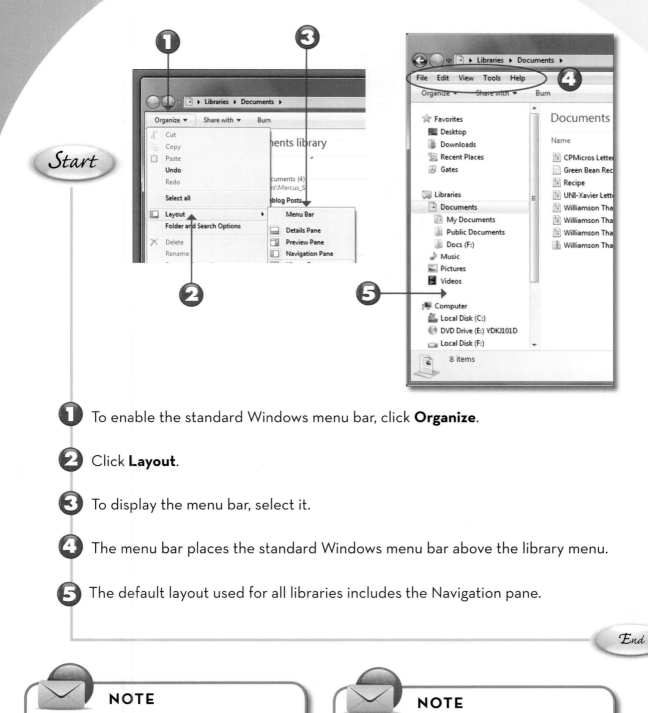

1 To enable the standard Windows menu bar, click **Organize**.

2 Click **Layout**.

3 To display the menu bar, select it.

4 The menu bar places the standard Windows menu bar above the library menu.

5 The default layout used for all libraries includes the Navigation pane.

NOTE

The Windows menu bar also provides easier ways to navigate to different locations. ∎

NOTE

The Navigation pane lists other locations available to your system. ∎

ADDING FOLDERS TO A LIBRARY

If you want to make accessing files in other folders or on a network share easier, add the folders or shares to the appropriate library. Here's how.

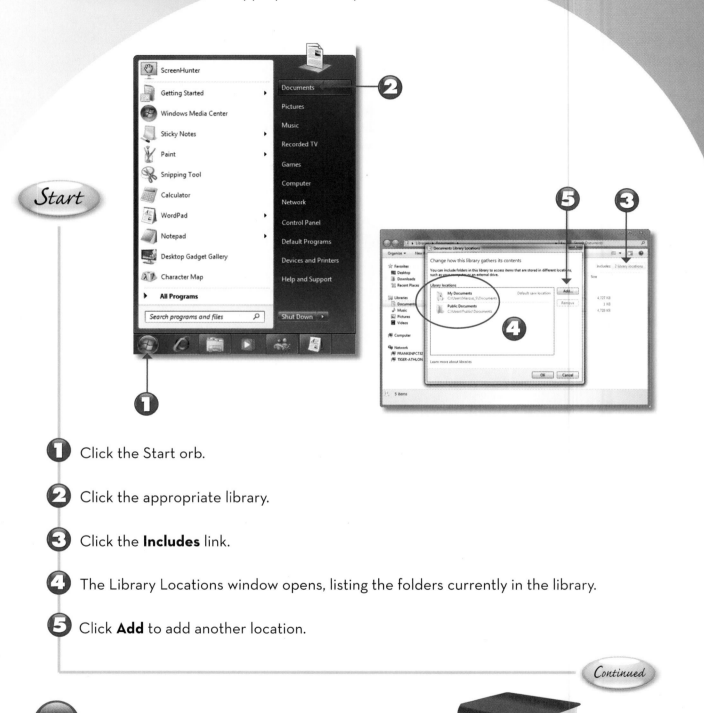

1 Click the Start orb.

2 Click the appropriate library.

3 Click the **Includes** link.

4 The Library Locations window opens, listing the folders currently in the library.

5 Click **Add** to add another location.

Continued

NOTE

Libraries can include local hard disk and network share folders, but not folders on removable-media drives such as CD, DVD, or USB flash memory drives. ■

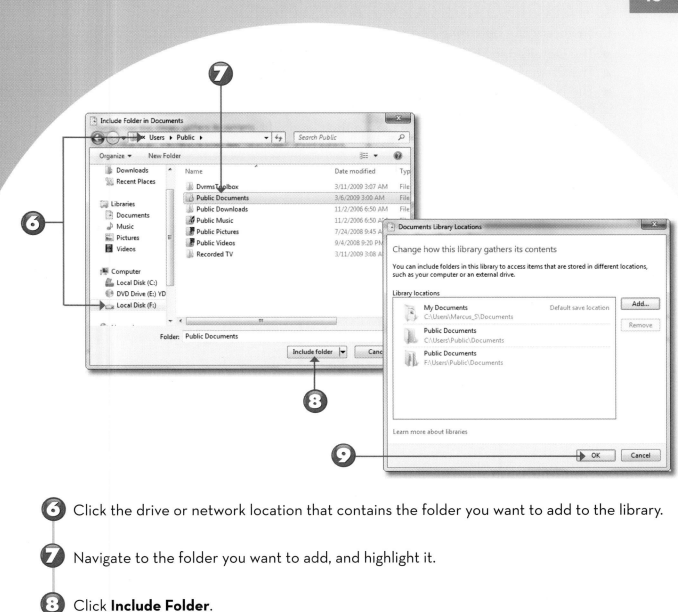

6 Click the drive or network location that contains the folder you want to add to the library.

7 Navigate to the folder you want to add, and highlight it.

8 Click **Include Folder**.

9 The folder is added to the library. Click OK to close the dialog.

End

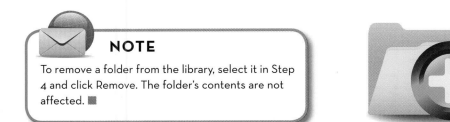

NOTE

To remove a folder from the library, select it in Step 4 and click Remove. The folder's contents are not affected. ■

CHANGING LIBRARY LAYOUTS

Each library can be configured to use the various combination of the following panes:

- The Details pane lists information about the selected document or folder.
- The Preview pane displays a preview of the selected document.
- The Navigation pane (included in the default layout) displays other locations accessible from your computer.
- The Library pane displays the files in the current library.

By selecting these options, you can customize each library to look the way you want.

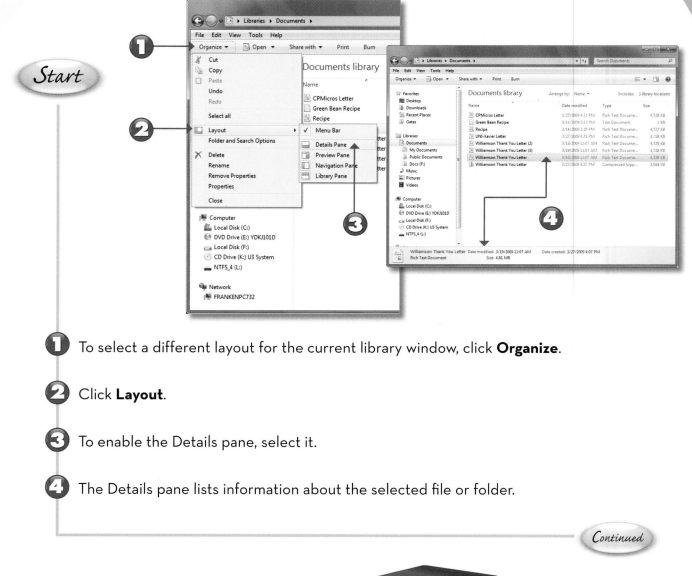

Start

1 To select a different layout for the current library window, click **Organize**.

2 Click **Layout**.

3 To enable the Details pane, select it.

4 The Details pane lists information about the selected file or folder.

Continued

NOTE

I recommend using the Details pane for any library. ■

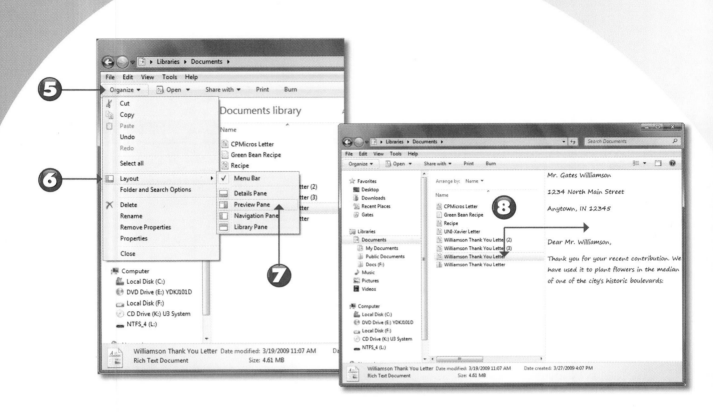

5 To enable the Preview pane, click **Organize**.

6 Click **Layout**.

7 Select **Preview Pane**.

8 The Preview pane displays a preview of the selected document or folder.

Continued

NOTE

You can use the Details and Preview panes at the same time. The Preview pane provides document previews when used in the Documents library and photo previews when used in the Pictures library. When you use it in the Music or Videos libraries, it displays a Windows Media Player window in the Preview pane. ■

9 To use the Library pane, click **Organize**.

10 Click **Layout**.

11 Select **Library Pane**.

12 The Library pane displays only the files and folders in the current pane.

End

NOTE

To learn more about working with files, see Chapter 5, "Working with Your Files." ■

USING SEND TO

The Send To option is unusual because it can be used in many ways. In addition to copying a folder to a different drive, you can also use Send To to create a compressed (ZIP-format) folder, to email or fax the contents of a folder, to place a shortcut to the folder on the desktop, or to copy the folder to another drive.

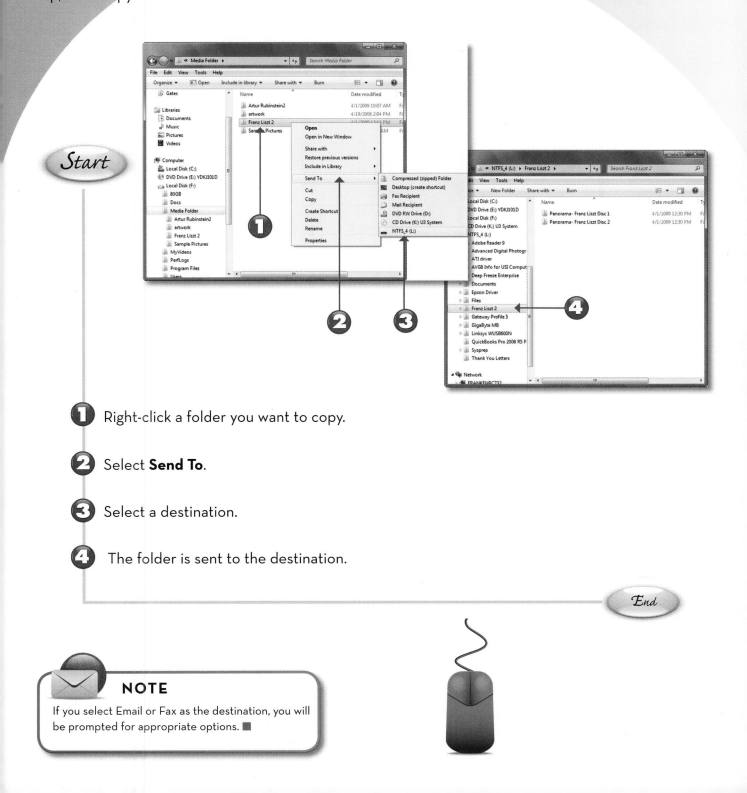

1 Right-click a folder you want to copy.

2 Select **Send To**.

3 Select a destination.

4 The folder is sent to the destination.

NOTE

If you select Email or Fax as the destination, you will be prompted for appropriate options. ■

USING DRAG AND DROP TO COPY A FOLDER

When you use Drag and Drop, you click and hold the left mouse button on the folder or file you want to copy or move, drag the folder or file to the destination, and then release the left mouse button.

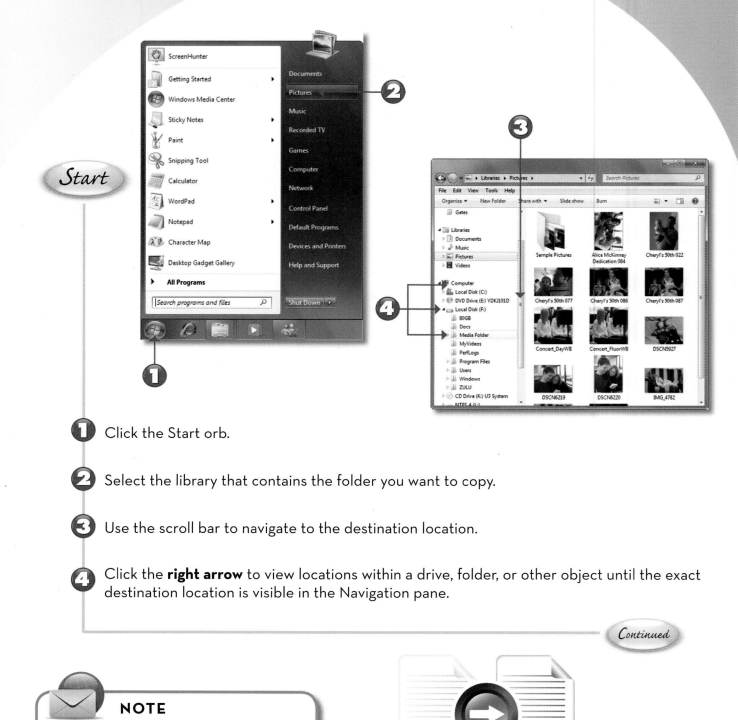

① Click the Start orb.

② Select the library that contains the folder you want to copy.

③ Use the scroll bar to navigate to the destination location.

④ Click the **right arrow** to view locations within a drive, folder, or other object until the exact destination location is visible in the Navigation pane.

Continued

NOTE

If the Navigation pane isn't visible, enable it as discussed in the previous exercise. ■

5 Select the folder to copy in the right pane.

6 Click and drag the folder to the new location.

7 Release the mouse button, and a copy of the folder appears in the new location.

End

NOTE

If you want to copy more than one folder using Drag and Drop, select the first folder, hold down either Ctrl key, and click the other folders you want to copy. ■

USING DRAG AND DROP TO MOVE A FOLDER

You can also use Drag and Drop to move a folder from one location to another. When you want to move a folder with Drag and Drop, you use either Shift key along with the mouse.

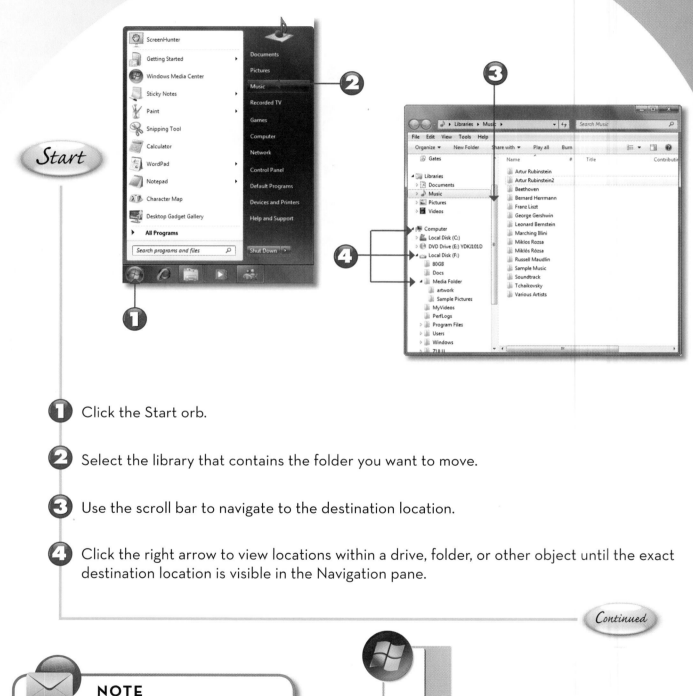

Start

① Click the Start orb.

② Select the library that contains the folder you want to move.

③ Use the scroll bar to navigate to the destination location.

④ Click the right arrow to view locations within a drive, folder, or other object until the exact destination location is visible in the Navigation pane.

Continued

NOTE

If the Navigation pane isn't visible, enable it as discussed previously. ■

5 Select the folder to move in the right pane.

6 Hold down either **Shift** key as you click and drag the folder to the new location.

7 Release the **mouse button and Shift key,** and the folder appears in the new location.

End

NOTE

If you want to move more than one folder using Drag and Drop, select the first folder, hold down either Ctrl key, and click the other folders you want to move.

USING COPY AND PASTE TO COPY A FOLDER

If you are not comfortable using Drag and Drop to copy or move a folder, you can use Copy and Paste instead. When you use Copy and Paste, the folder you copy is temporarily stored in an area of memory called the Windows Clipboard. To use Copy and Paste, you can use the menu bar or the right-click menu. In this example, we use the menu bar.

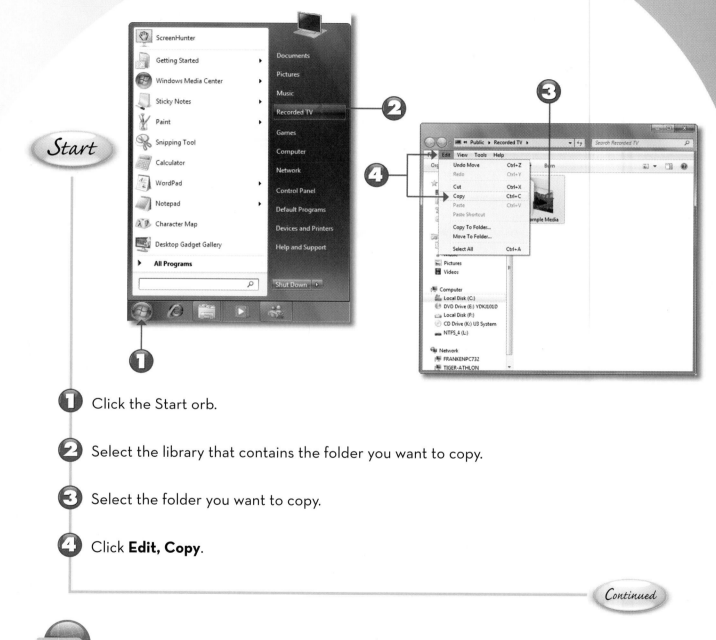

1 Click the Start orb.

2 Select the library that contains the folder you want to copy.

3 Select the folder you want to copy.

4 Click **Edit, Copy**.

Continued

NOTE

If you do not use the menu bar, right-click the folder you want to copy and select Copy from the right-click menu. ■

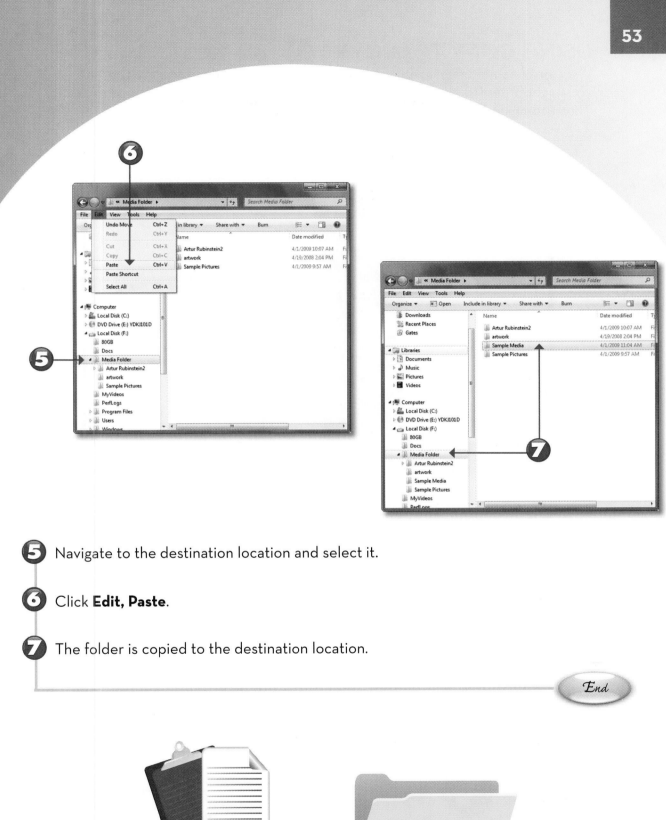

5 Navigate to the destination location and select it.

6 Click **Edit, Paste**.

7 The folder is copied to the destination location.

End

USING COPY TO/MOVE TO

If you are uncomfortable with working with the left and right panes of the Navigation pane, you might prefer to use the Copy To and Move To commands to copy or move a folder. These commands use a pop-up window to select the destination location.

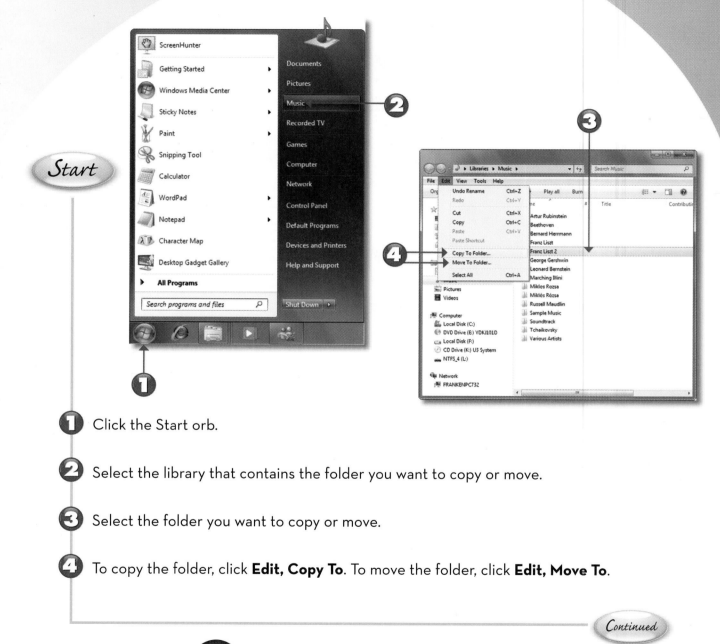

1 Click the Start orb.

2 Select the library that contains the folder you want to copy or move.

3 Select the folder you want to copy or move.

4 To copy the folder, click **Edit, Copy To**. To move the folder, click **Edit, Move To**.

Continued

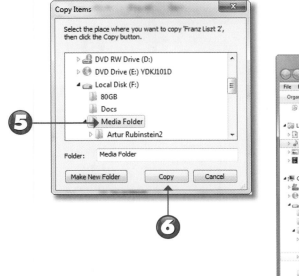

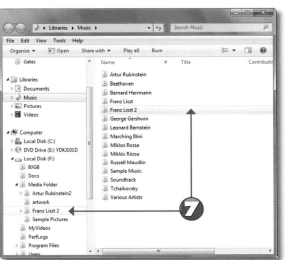

5 Navigate to the destination location and select it.

6 Click Copy or Move to copy or move the folder.

7 The folder is copied (or moved) to the destination location.

End

CREATING NEW FOLDERS

Windows 7 enables you to make a new folder with options in the File and right-click menus. This tutorial shows you how to use the File menu option.

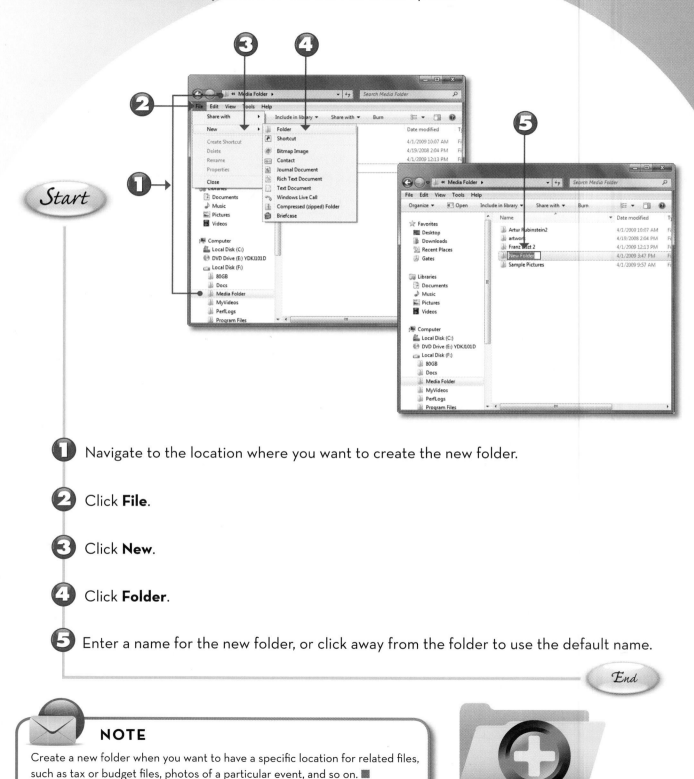

① Navigate to the location where you want to create the new folder.

② Click **File**.

③ Click **New**.

④ Click **Folder**.

⑤ Enter a name for the new folder, or click away from the folder to use the default name.

NOTE

Create a new folder when you want to have a specific location for related files, such as tax or budget files, photos of a particular event, and so on. ▪

RENAMING FOLDERS

You can rename a folder from the Organize menu or from the right-click menu. This tutorial shows you how to rename a folder using the Organize menu.

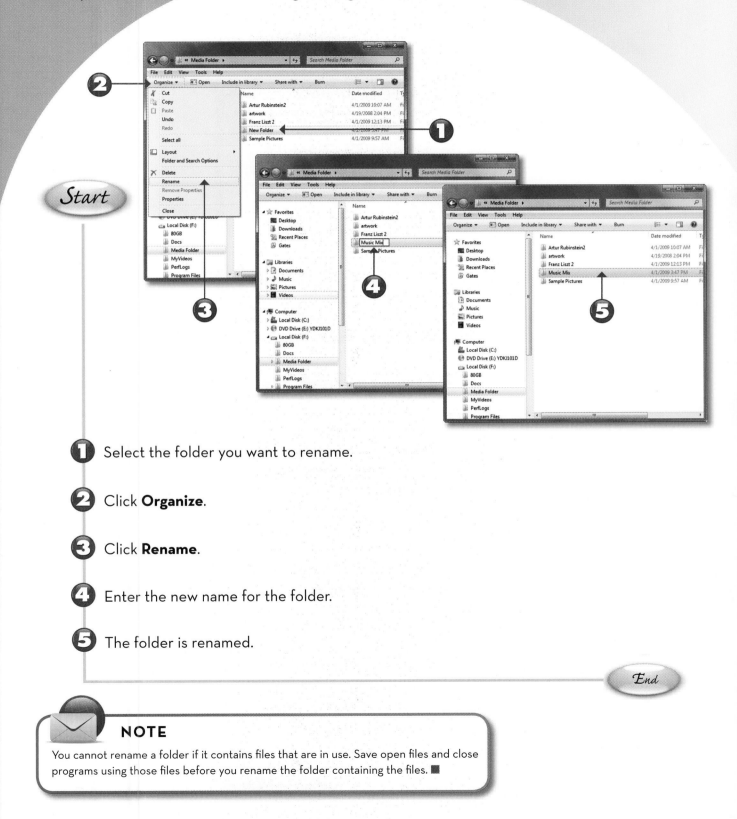

Start

1. Select the folder you want to rename.

2. Click **Organize**.

3. Click **Rename**.

4. Enter the new name for the folder.

5. The folder is renamed.

End

NOTE

You cannot rename a folder if it contains files that are in use. Save open files and close programs using those files before you rename the folder containing the files. ■

DELETING FOLDERS

You can delete folders and folders from the File or Organize menus or with the right-click menu. This tutorial uses the Organize menu.

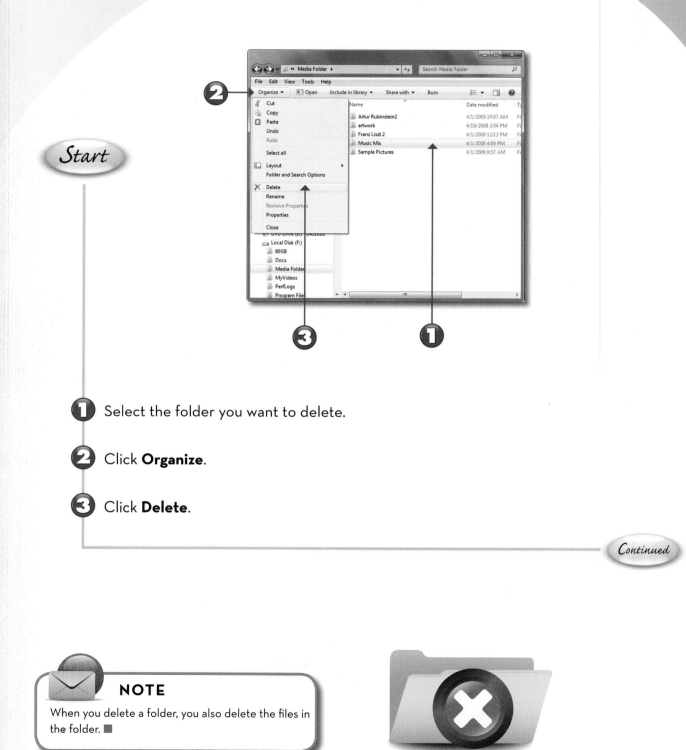

Start

1 Select the folder you want to delete.

2 Click **Organize**.

3 Click **Delete**.

Continued

NOTE

When you delete a folder, you also delete the files in the folder. ■

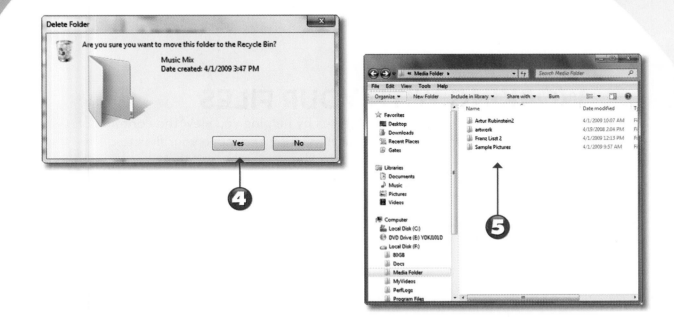

4 Click **Yes** when prompted.

5 The folder and its contents are moved to the Recycle Bin.

End

NOTE

To remove the folder completely, hold down the Shift key before selecting Delete in Step 3. ■

NOTE

To retrieve deleted files or folders from the Recycle Bin, open the Recycle Bin from Computer or the Windows desktop, right-click the files or folders to retrieve, and select Restore. ■

Chapter 5

WORKING WITH YOUR FILES

Windows 7 helps you work with your files by helping you view the contents of your files, find information about your files, copy and move your files to different locations, search for files, and delete files you no longer need.

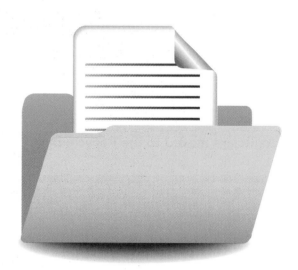

Windows 7 provides many ways to view your files, with Extra Large, Large, and Medium Icons providing thumbnails of image files

Windows 7 enables you to sort files using a wide variety of criteria

CHANGING FILE-VIEWING OPTIONS

You can select different ways to view your files in any Windows folder, including libraries (see Chapter 4, "Working with Your Folders"). This tutorial shows you how to change viewing options so you can choose the best viewing option for your needs or file types.

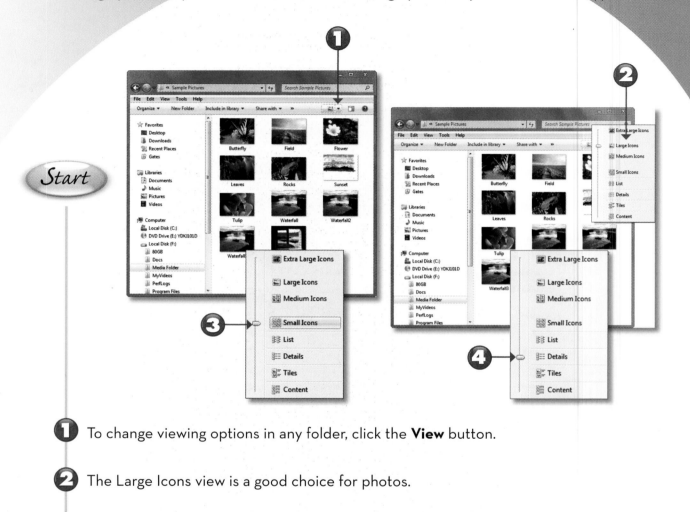

Start

1 To change viewing options in any folder, click the **View** button.

2 The Large Icons view is a good choice for photos.

3 The Small Icons view uses different icons for different file types.

4 The Details view provides size, type, and date modified information for all types of files.

End

NOTE

Extra Large Icons provides a larger thumbnail of image files than Large Icons, whereas Medium Icons provides a smaller thumbnail. List uses the same size and types of icons as Small Icons, but lists files in multiple columns. Tiles and Content display the file type and size, and Content also displays the last-modified date. ■

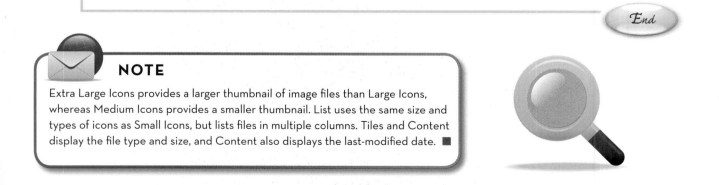

VIEWING FILE INFORMATION (PROPERTIES)

To learn more about a file, such as when it was originally created or last changed, or if you want to compress it (to save space on your hard disk), you need to open the file's properties sheet. Here's how.

1 Open the folder containing the file.

2 Right-click the file.

3 Select **Properties**.

4 The file's properties sheet opens.

End

NOTE

Although you can view basic file properties from the library view, if you want to compress a file, you need to view the file in its actual folder location. ■

COMPRESSING A FILE

If you are concerned about how much space a file takes up, you can compress the file. Compression is performed through the file properties sheet's Advanced menu. A compressed file uses less space than the uncompressed version, but you must uncompress the file before you can edit it.

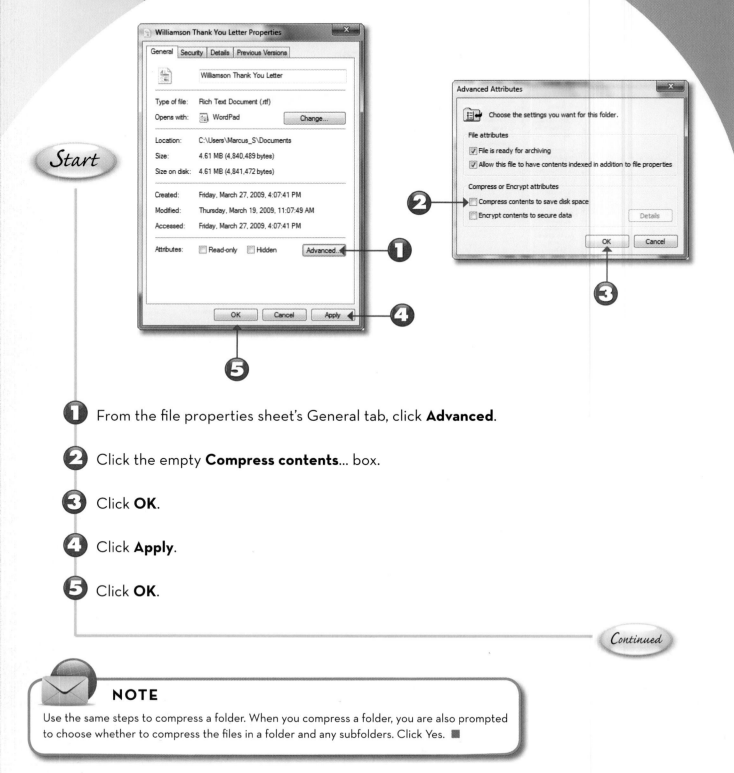

1 From the file properties sheet's General tab, click **Advanced**.

2 Click the empty **Compress contents**... box.

3 Click **OK**.

4 Click **Apply**.

5 Click **OK**.

Continued

NOTE

Use the same steps to compress a folder. When you compress a folder, you are also prompted to choose whether to compress the files in a folder and any subfolders. Click Yes. ■

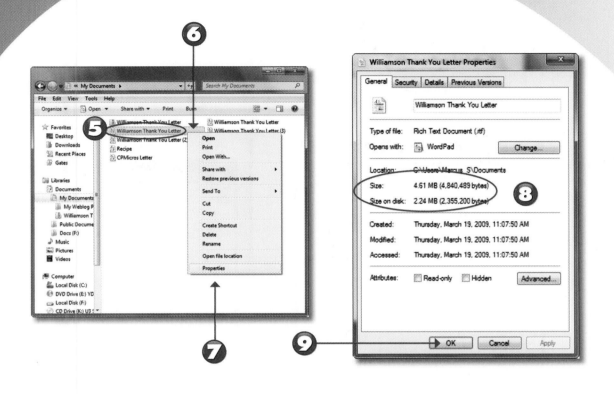

5️⃣ Compressed filenames are listed in blue text.

6️⃣ To see how much smaller the compressed file is, right-click the file.

7️⃣ Select **Properties**.

8️⃣ This file is about 50% smaller.

9️⃣ Click **OK** to close the dialog.

End

NOTE

Some Windows 7 versions also support file encryption, which protects a file from being opened by an unauthorized user. To encrypt a file, select the Encryption option in Step 2. A notification is displayed when you encrypt a file—click it to start the encryption key backup wizard. Note that you can either encrypt or compress a file. Encrypted filenames use green text, instead of the blue text used for compressed filenames. ■

RENAMING A GROUP OF FILES

You can also rename a group of files. When you rename a group of files, each file after the first file in the group has a number appended to the name, such as (2), (3), and so on.

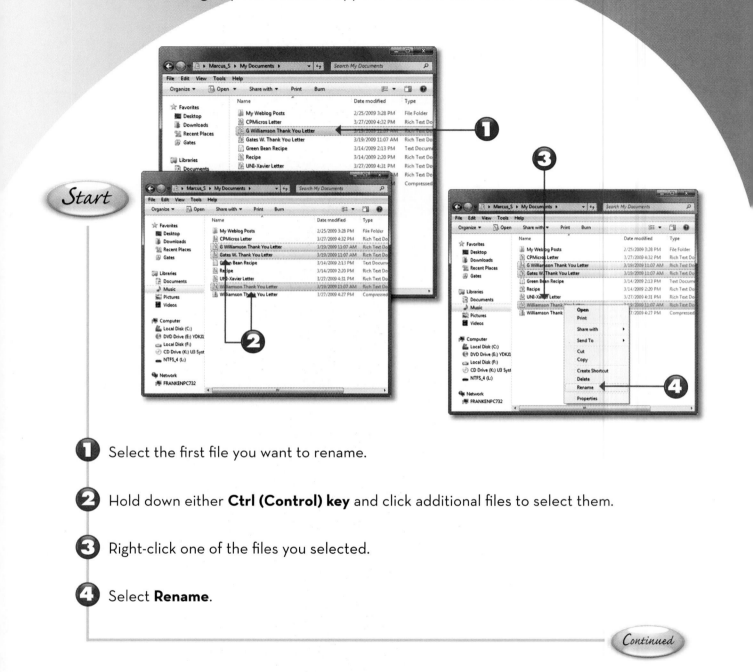

1 Select the first file you want to rename.

2 Hold down either **Ctrl (Control) key** and click additional files to select them.

3 Right-click one of the files you selected.

4 Select **Rename**.

Continued

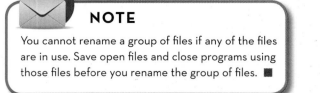

NOTE

You cannot rename a group of files if any of the files are in use. Save open files and close programs using those files before you rename the group of files. ∎

5 Enter the new name for the selected files.

6 The files are renamed.

End

NOTE

Use the same steps to rename a group of folders. ■

RENAMING A FILE

Renaming a file is performed in the same way as renaming a folder. The file-renaming process can be performed from the Organize menu, the File menu, the file's properties sheet, or, as in this example, the right-click menu.

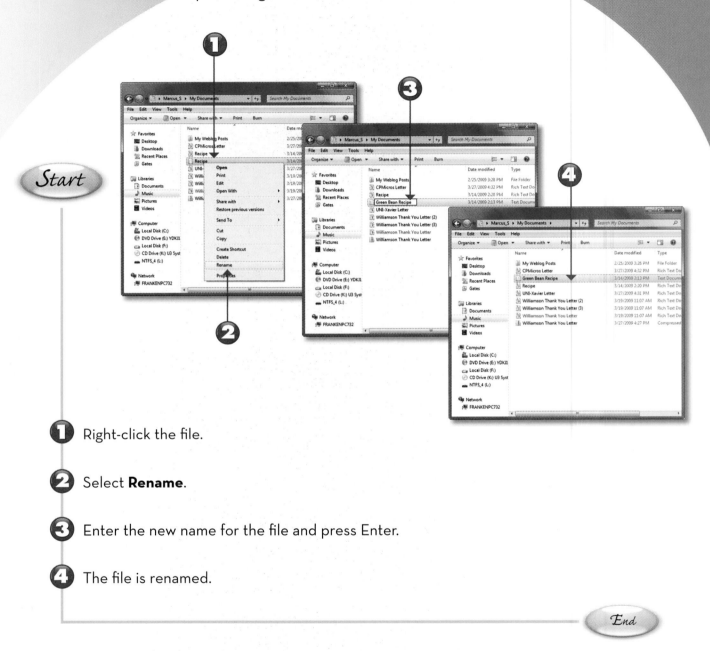

Start

1 Right-click the file.

2 Select **Rename**.

3 Enter the new name for the file and press Enter.

4 The file is renamed.

End

COPYING A FILE TO THE SAME FOLDER

The methods discussed in Chapter 4 for copying folders (Drag and Drop, Copy and Paste, Copy To/Move To, and Send To) can also be used for copying files to a different folder. When you copy a file to the same folder it came from, as you might want to do to make a backup copy or to create a duplicate file you can edit, Windows automatically renames the copy for you.

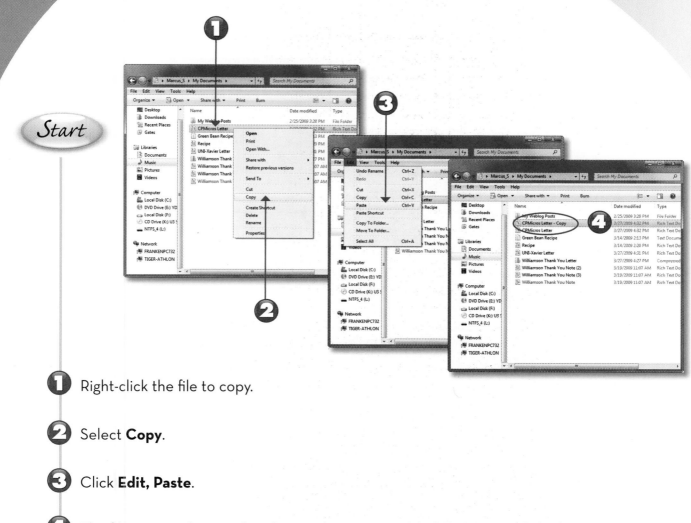

1 Right-click the file to copy.

2 Select **Copy**.

3 Click **Edit, Paste**.

4 The file is copied. Note that the word "Copy" is added to the end of the filename.

End

NOTE
You can also select the file and use Edit, Copy or Organize, Copy to copy the file. ∎

NOTE
You can also right-click an empty portion of the folder and select Paste or use Organize, Paste to paste the file. ∎

MOVING A FILE OR GROUP OF FILES

The file-moving process combines the copy/paste process and the delete original file process. You can use the Move To menu selection (see Chapter 4) to move files, or a modified version of Drag and Drop to move files, as in this exercise.

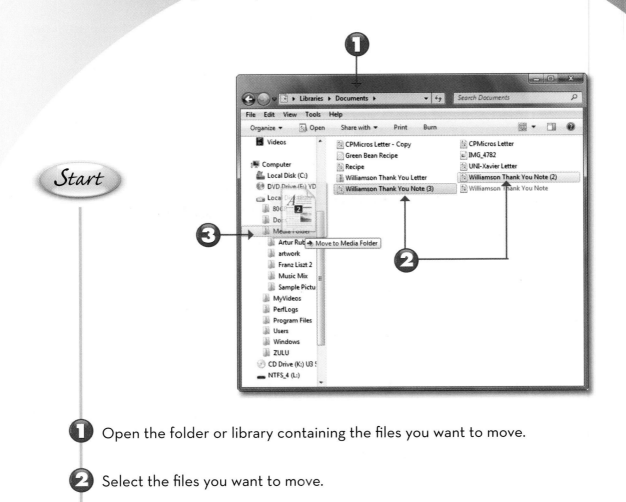

Start

① Open the folder or library containing the files you want to move.

② Select the files you want to move.

③ Drag the files to the destination folder while holding down either Shift key and drop them.

Continued

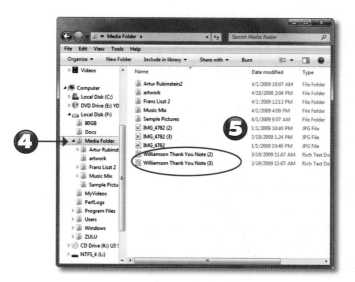

4 Open the destination folder.

5 The files have been moved to the destination folder.

End

NOTE

To select the first file, click it. Use Ctrl-click to select additional files. ■

SORTING, GROUPING, AND STACKING FILES IN A FOLDER

Windows 7 enables you to sort, group, and stack files in any folder or library so you can easily find the files you need.

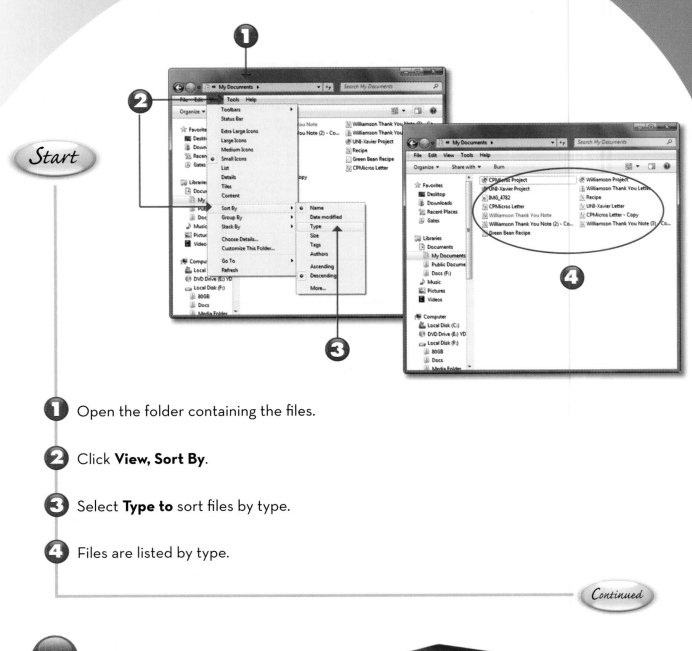

Start

1 Open the folder containing the files.

2 Click **View, Sort By**.

3 Select **Type to** sort files by type.

4 Files are listed by type.

Continued

NOTE

If you are not using the menu bar, right-click an empty part of the folder and select Sort By, Type in Steps 2 and 3. ■

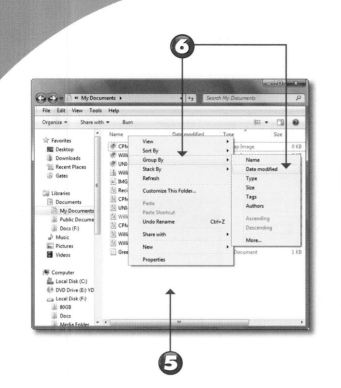

5 Right-click an empty part of the folder.

6 Select **Group By, Date Modified**.

7 Files are grouped by date.

Continued

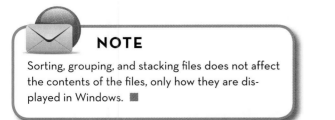

NOTE

Sorting, grouping, and stacking files does not affect the contents of the files, only how they are displayed in Windows.

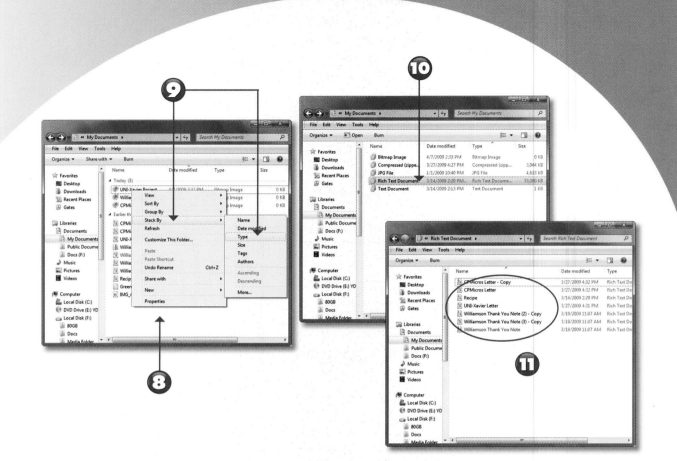

8 Right-click an empty part of the folder.

9 Select **Stack By, Type**.

10 Double-click a stack.

11 The files in the stack are displayed.

Continued

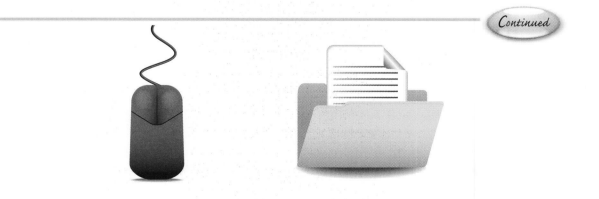

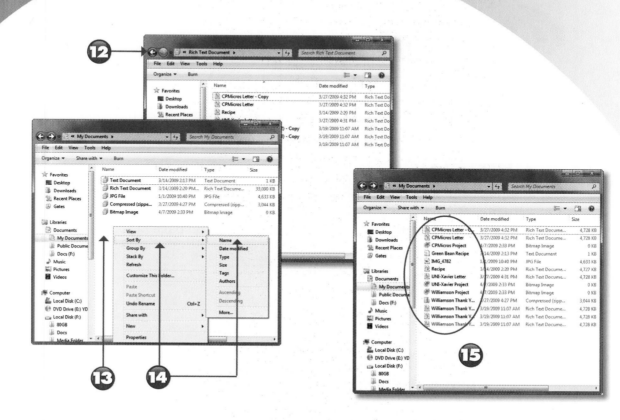

12 Click the back arrow.

13 Right-click an empty part of the folder.

14 Select **Sort By, Name**.

15 Files are again listed in order by name.

End

NOTE

To change sort order, select Descending from the Sort By menu. ■

Chapter 6

PRINTING

Printing continues to be one of the most important ways to share information with others. Windows 7 includes many new features to help you work with printers, including the Device Stage dialog shown on page 80.

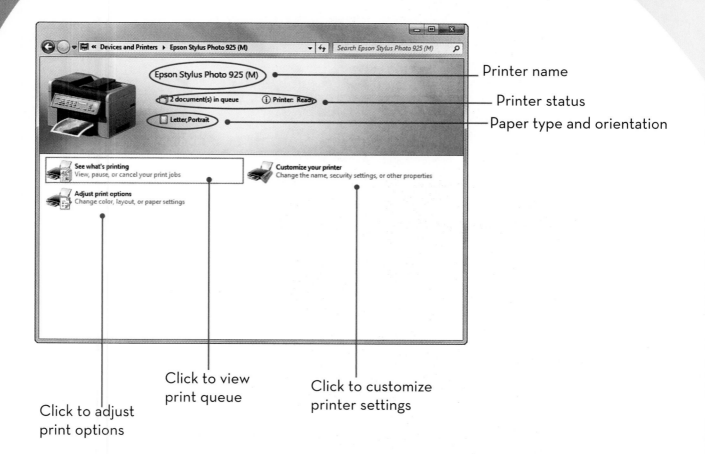

Printer name

Printer status

Paper type and orientation

Click to view
print queue

Click to customize
printer settings

Click to adjust
print options

VIEWING AVAILABLE PRINTERS

The Devices and Printers folder, a new feature of Windows 7, displays devices and printers on your system.

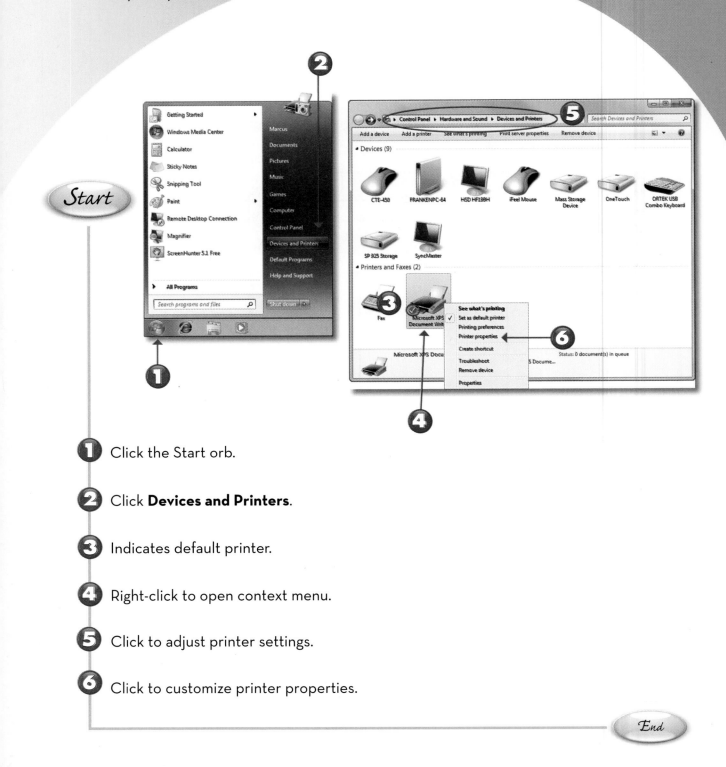

1 Click the Start orb.

2 Click **Devices and Printers**.

3 Indicates default printer.

4 Right-click to open context menu.

5 Click to adjust printer settings.

6 Click to customize printer properties.

End

INSTALLING A NEW PRINTER

When you connect a USB printer to your computer and turn it on, the printer is installed automatically. Here's what you see if you perform this task while Devices and Printers is open.

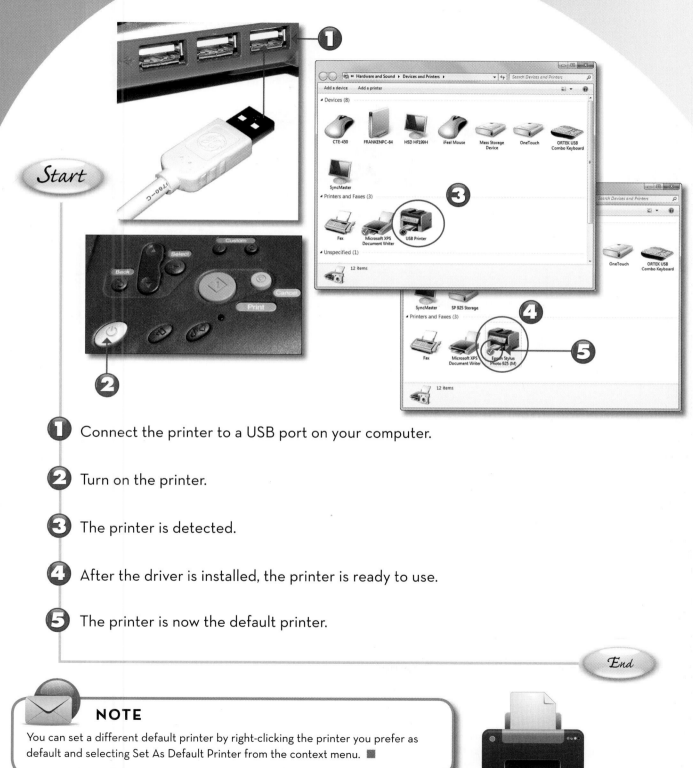

1 Connect the printer to a USB port on your computer.

2 Turn on the printer.

3 The printer is detected.

4 After the driver is installed, the printer is ready to use.

5 The printer is now the default printer.

NOTE

You can set a different default printer by right-clicking the printer you prefer as default and selecting Set As Default Printer from the context menu. ■

USING DEVICE STAGE TO VIEW AND CHANGE PRINTER PROPERTIES

Device Stage is a new feature in Windows 7. It enables you to access all management functions for printers or other devices from a single interface. In this example, you see how to use Device Stage to change print options.

Start

1 Double-click the printer in Devices and Printers.

2 Double-click to adjust print options.

3 Adjust print preferences as desired.

4 Click **OK** to close the preferences menu.

End

NOTE

Printers with drivers made especially for Windows 7 offer additional options in the Device Stage menu. These options could include ordering ink or updating drivers. ■

NOTE

Printing preferences menus vary a great deal from printer model to printer model. To clean printheads on an inkjet printer, for example, you might find the option in various locations, such as on a Maintenance tab or elsewhere. See the printer's documentation for details. ■

PRINTING A TEST PAGE TO A LOCAL PRINTER

As you learned in a previous section, Windows 7 does not prompt you to print a test page when you install a USB printer. However, it's easy to print a test page for any local or network printer whenever you want. Here's how.

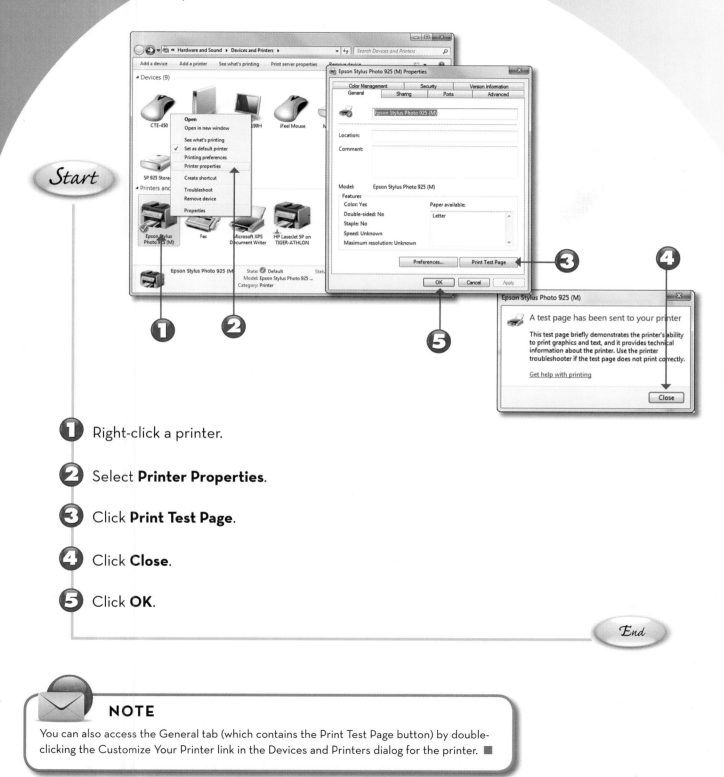

1 Right-click a printer.

2 Select **Printer Properties**.

3 Click **Print Test Page**.

4 Click **Close**.

5 Click **OK**.

NOTE

You can also access the General tab (which contains the Print Test Page button) by double-clicking the Customize Your Printer link in the Devices and Printers dialog for the printer. ■

INSTALLING A NETWORK PRINTER

If you have a home network with a shared printer, you can connect to that printer and use it in Windows 7. Here's how.

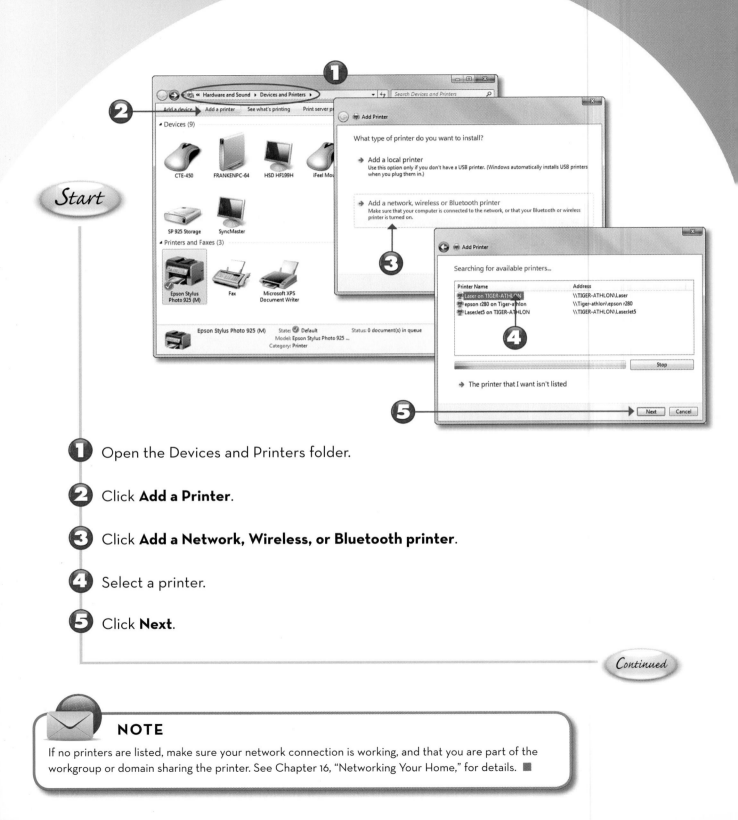

Start

1. Open the Devices and Printers folder.

2. Click **Add a Printer**.

3. Click **Add a Network, Wireless, or Bluetooth printer**.

4. Select a printer.

5. Click **Next**.

Continued

NOTE

If no printers are listed, make sure your network connection is working, and that you are part of the workgroup or domain sharing the printer. See Chapter 16, "Networking Your Home," for details. ◼

Add Printer

You've successfully added HP LaserJet 5P on TIGER-ATHLON

Printer name: HP LaserJet 5P on TIGER-ATHLON

This printer has been installed with the HP LaserJet 5P driver.

6

Next   Cancel

Start

Add Printer

You've successfully added HP LaserJet 5P on TIGER-ATHLON

7

☑ Set as the default printer

10

To check if your printer is working properly, or to see troubleshooting information for the printer, print a test page.

8 Print a test page

Finish   Cancel

HP LaserJet 5P on TIGER-ATHLON

A test page has been sent to your printer

This test page briefly demonstrates the printer's ability to print graphics and text, and it provides technical information about the printer. Use the printer troubleshooter if the test page does not print correctly.

Get help with printing

Close

9

6 Click **Next**.

7 If you don't want the printer to be the active printer, click to clear the checkbox.

8 Click to print a test page.

9 Click **Close**.

10 Click **Finish**.

End

NOTE

If you are installing an all-in-one device that connects directly to the network (rather than to a specific computer), you might be prompted to share the printer and to select multiple default printers for different locations. ■

SHARING A PRINTER

Windows 7 uses a multi-tabbed interface for printer properties. In this tutorial, you learn how to use the Sharing tab to share a printer on the network.

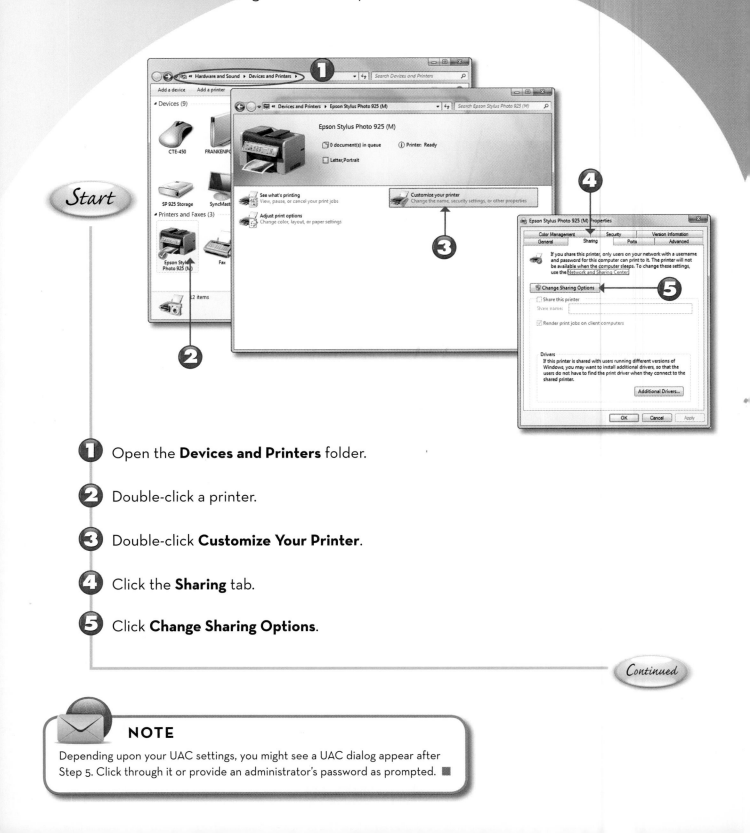

Start

1. Open the **Devices and Printers** folder.

2. Double-click a printer.

3. Double-click **Customize Your Printer**.

4. Click the **Sharing** tab.

5. Click **Change Sharing Options**.

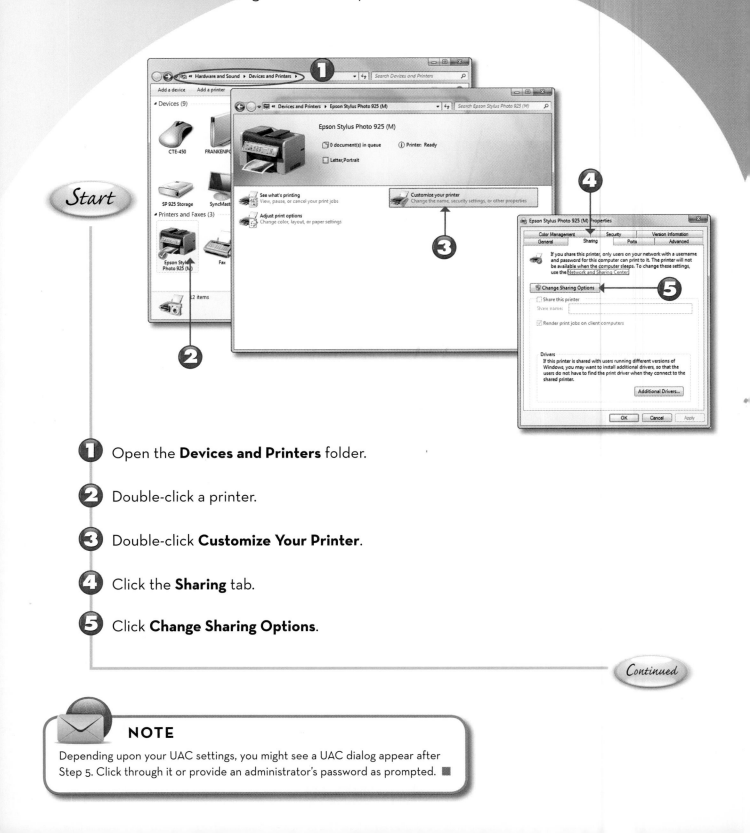

Continued

NOTE

Depending upon your UAC settings, you might see a UAC dialog appear after Step 5. Click through it or provide an administrator's password as prompted. ▪

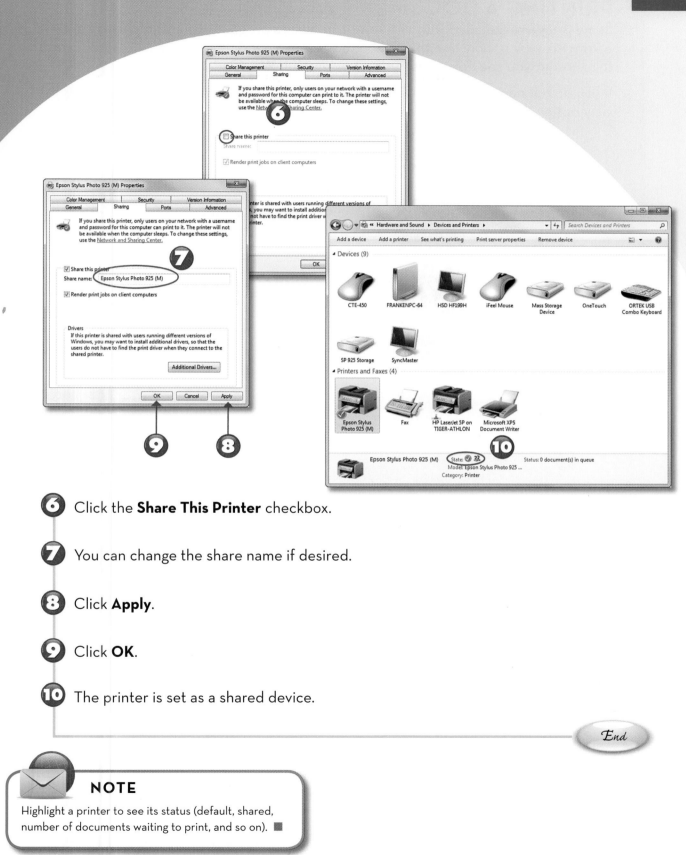

6 Click the **Share This Printer** checkbox.

7 You can change the share name if desired.

8 Click **Apply**.

9 Click **OK**.

10 The printer is set as a shared device.

End

NOTE

Highlight a printer to see its status (default, shared, number of documents waiting to print, and so on). ■

PRINTING A DOCUMENT WITH PRINT PREVIEW

Some programs included with Windows 7, as well as programs you might install later, include a Print Preview option. Use this option to see how your document will look when printed. In this tutorial, you see how to use Print Preview with WordPad.

If you do not need to use Print Preview, select the Print option rather than the Print Preview option.

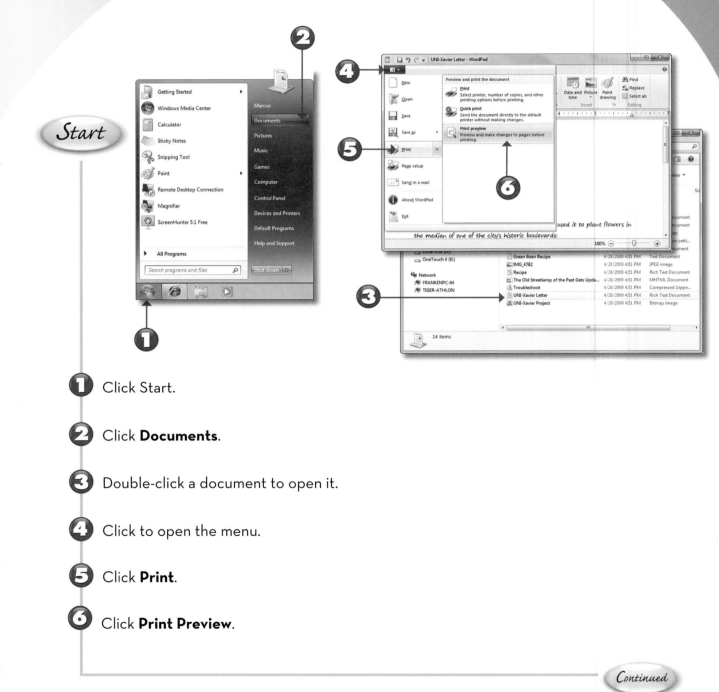

1 Click Start.

2 Click **Documents**.

3 Double-click a document to open it.

4 Click to open the menu.

5 Click **Print**.

6 Click **Print Preview**.

Continued

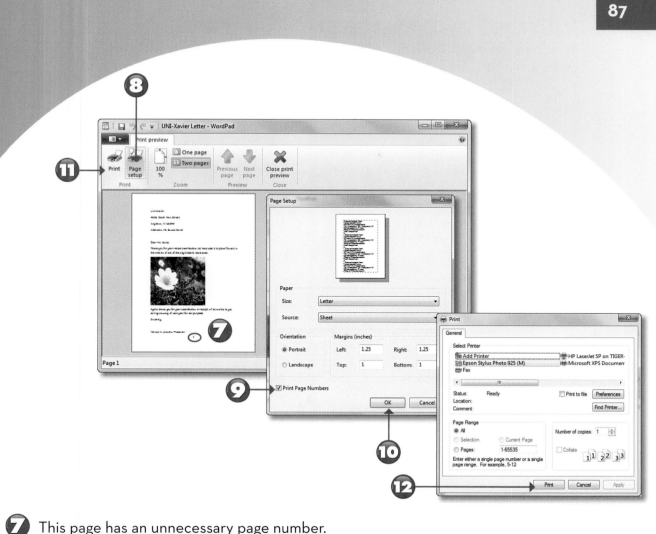

7 This page has an unnecessary page number.

8 Click **Page Setup**.

9 Clear the **Print Page Numbers** checkbox.

10 Click **OK**.

11 Click **Print**.

12 Click the **Print** button.

End

VIEWING AND MANAGING THE PRINT QUEUE

Windows saves print jobs as temporary files managed by the print queue. In this exercise, you learn how to view the print queue and delete a print job.

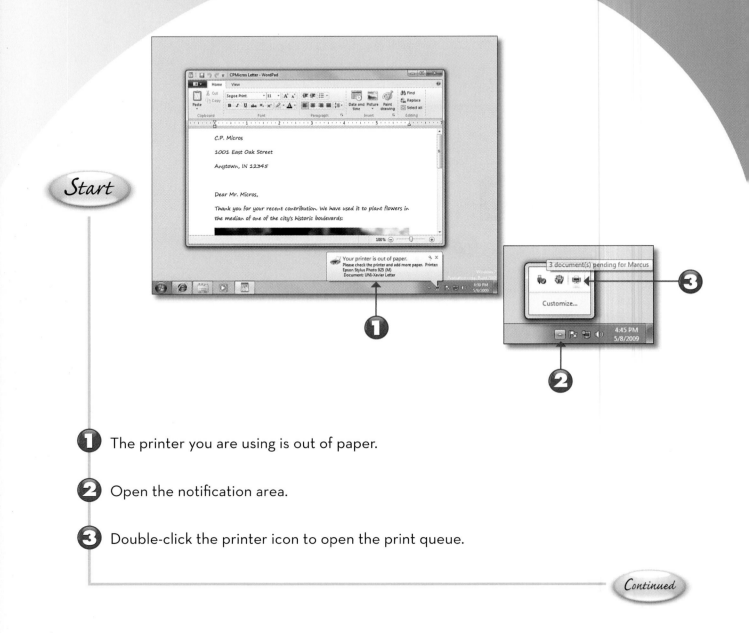

Start

1 The printer you are using is out of paper.

2 Open the notification area.

3 Double-click the printer icon to open the print queue.

Continued

NOTE

To see the number of documents waiting to print (Step 3), hover the mouse over the printer icon before double-clicking the icon. ∎

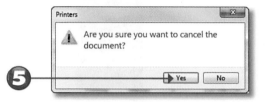

4 Right-click a document and select Cancel.

5 Click **Yes**.

6 The document is removed from the queue. Click **X** to close the window.

End

NOTE

You can also view print jobs by clicking See What's Printing in the Devices and Printers listing for the printer. ■

VIEWING FONTS

Using different fonts in printed documents and labels for photos can make them more interesting. Windows 7 includes a brand-new font manager that makes it easier than ever before to preview and organize fonts. Here's how to use it to preview a particular font family.

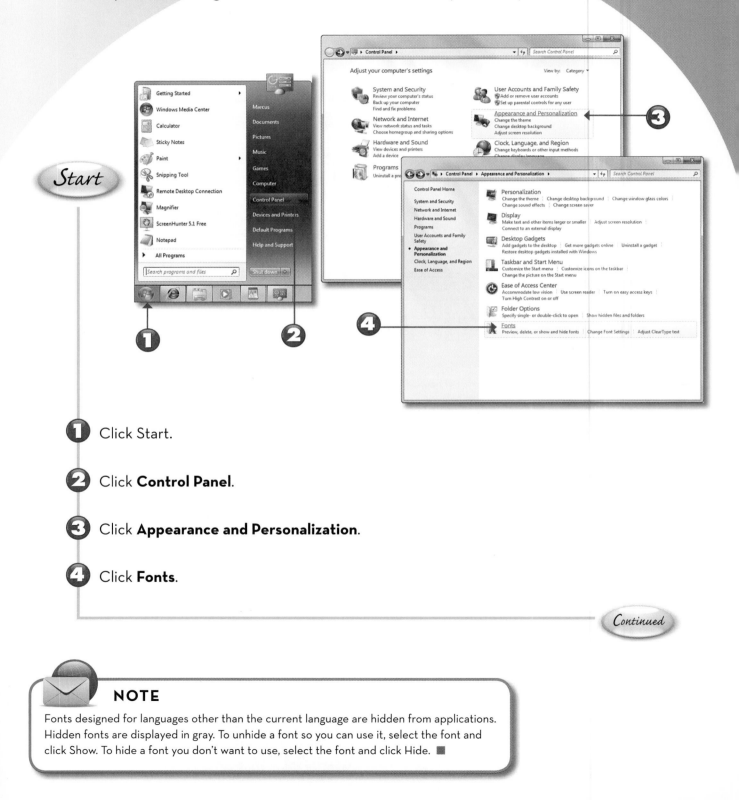

1 Click Start.

2 Click **Control Panel**.

3 Click **Appearance and Personalization**.

4 Click **Fonts**.

Continued

NOTE

Fonts designed for languages other than the current language are hidden from applications. Hidden fonts are displayed in gray. To unhide a font so you can use it, select the font and click Show. To hide a font you don't want to use, select the font and click Hide. ■

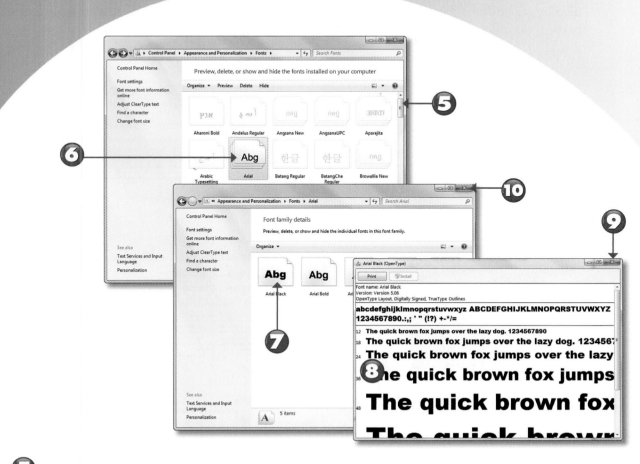

5 Scroll until the font family you want to preview is visible.

6 Double-click the font family.

7 Double-click a specific font.

8 The font is displayed in different sizes.

9 Click to close the preview.

10 Click to close the Fonts folder.

End

NOTE

When you install a new application that includes fonts, the fonts are automatically installed to the Fonts folder. However, if you download fonts, make sure you place them in the Fonts folder. ■

USING THE CLEARTYPE WIZARD

Most computers are used with LCD flat panel displays; portable computers also use LCD displays. Windows 7 includes the ClearType wizard to help you fine-tune the appearance of text on your screen.

Do not use ClearType if you use a CRT or other type of non-LCD display.

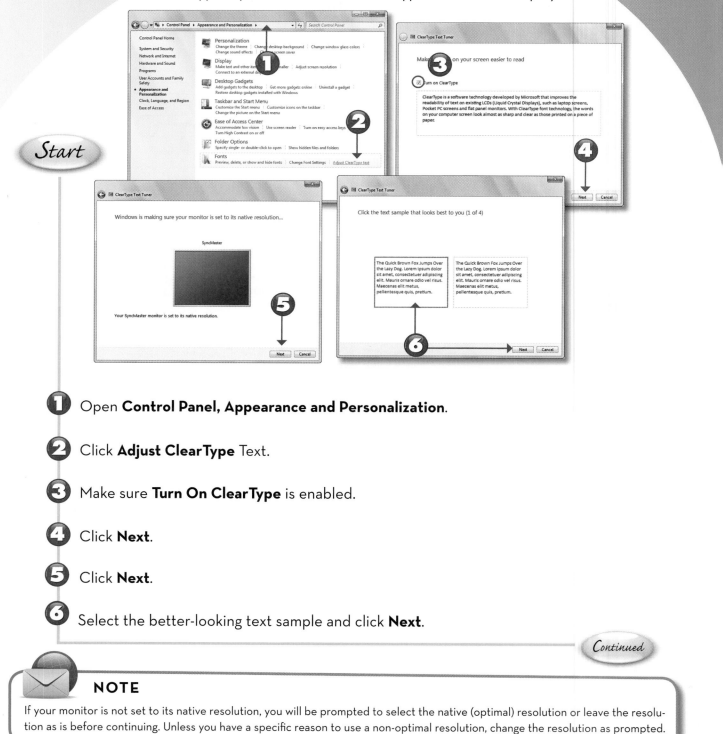

Start

1 Open **Control Panel, Appearance and Personalization**.

2 Click **Adjust ClearType** Text.

3 Make sure **Turn On ClearType** is enabled.

4 Click **Next**.

5 Click **Next**.

6 Select the better-looking text sample and click **Next**.

Continued

NOTE

If your monitor is not set to its native resolution, you will be prompted to select the native (optimal) resolution or leave the resolution as is before continuing. Unless you have a specific reason to use a non-optimal resolution, change the resolution as prompted.

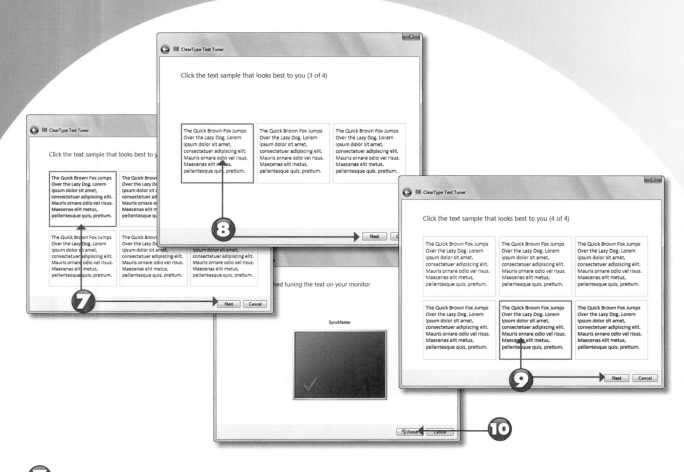

7 Select the best-looking text sample and click **Next**.

8 Select the best-looking text sample and click **Next**.

9 Select the best-looking text sample and click **Next**.

10 Click **Finish**.

End

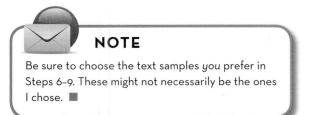

NOTE

Be sure to choose the text samples *you* prefer in Steps 6–9. These might not necessarily be the ones I chose.

Chapter 7

WORKING WITH WINDOWS MEDIA PLAYER

Windows Media Player enables you to play and create digital music tracks from CDs, watch video clips, watch DVDs, and share media with other WMP users.

NOTE

For more information about sharing media on your network, see Chapter 16, "Networking Your Home." ∎

Use Windows Media Player to convert all or
selected tracks from your favorite CDs into
digital music files

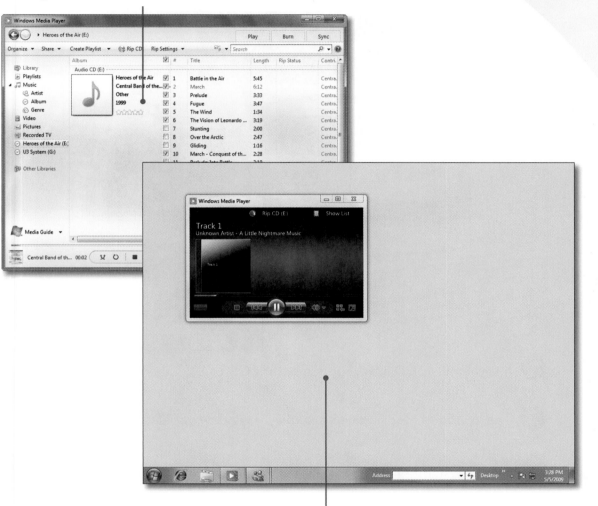

You can also run Windows Media Player in a resizable window
on your desktop to enjoy music, videos, and DVD movies

PLAYING AN AUDIO CD FROM THE WINDOWS DESKTOP

Playing an audio CD with Windows Media Player is as easy as inserting the CD into your computer's CD or DVD drive. You don't even need to have WMP open to use it to play a CD from your music library. Here's how.

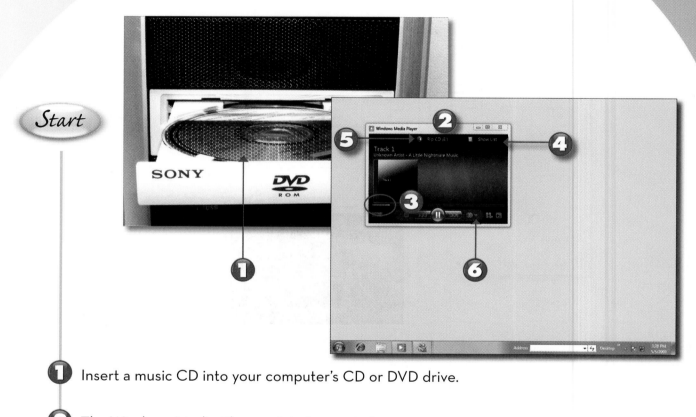

Start

1 Insert a music CD into your computer's CD or DVD drive.

2 The Windows Media Player mini-player window appears.

3 Album begins to play.

4 Click to show music list.

5 Click to rip CD to hard disk.

6 Open to adjust volume.

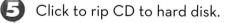

Continued

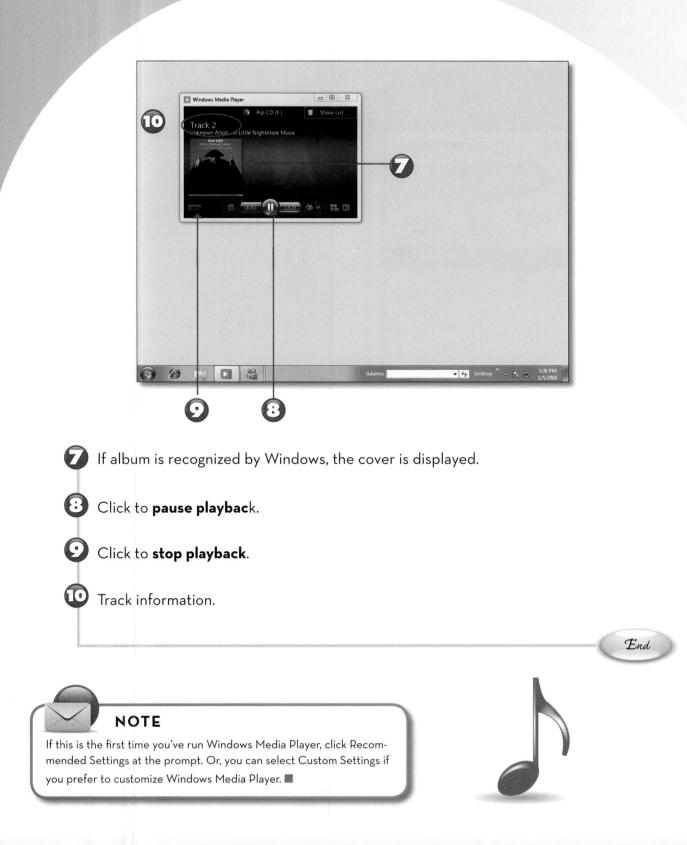

7 If album is recognized by Windows, the cover is displayed.

8 Click to **pause playbac**k.

9 Click to **stop playback**.

10 Track information.

End

NOTE

If this is the first time you've run Windows Media Player, click Recommended Settings at the prompt. Or, you can select Custom Settings if you prefer to customize Windows Media Player. ■

PLAYING AN AUDIO CD FROM WINDOWS MEDIA CENTER

If you insert an audio CD while Windows Media Center is running, this tutorial describes how you play it.

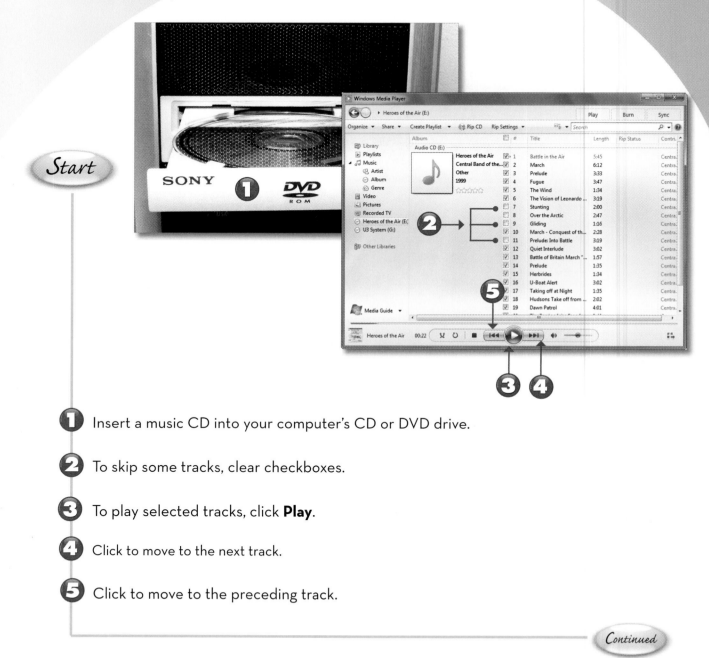

Start

1. Insert a music CD into your computer's CD or DVD drive.

2. To skip some tracks, clear checkboxes.

3. To play selected tracks, click **Play**.

4. Click to move to the next track.

5. Click to move to the preceding track.

Continued

NOTE

By default, all tracks from a music CD are selected. ■

6 Click to pause playback.

7 Click and drag to adjust volume.

8 Click to shuffle tracks.

9 Click to repeat selected tracks.

10 Click to stop playback.

End

RIPPING (COPYING) AN AUDIO CD

When you insert an audio CD into your computer, you can use Windows Media Player to make a digital copy of all or selected audio tracks. This process is called "ripping," and you can specify not only which tracks to rip, but the format and bit rate as well.

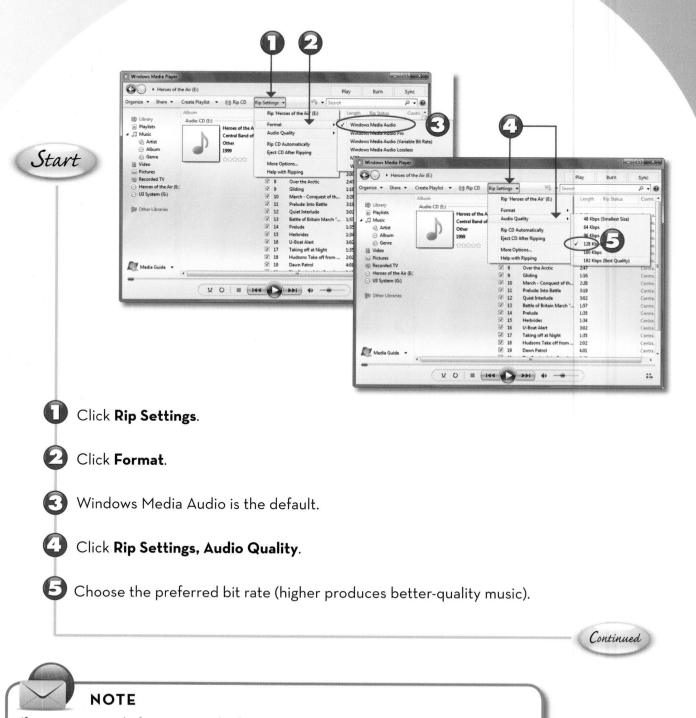

Start

1. Click **Rip Settings**.

2. Click **Format**.

3. Windows Media Audio is the default.

4. Click **Rip Settings, Audio Quality**.

5. Choose the preferred bit rate (higher produces better-quality music).

Continued

NOTE

If you are ripping audio for use on a media player that does not work with WMA, such as an Apple iPod, choose MP3. See the documentation for your media player for recommended audio formats. ■

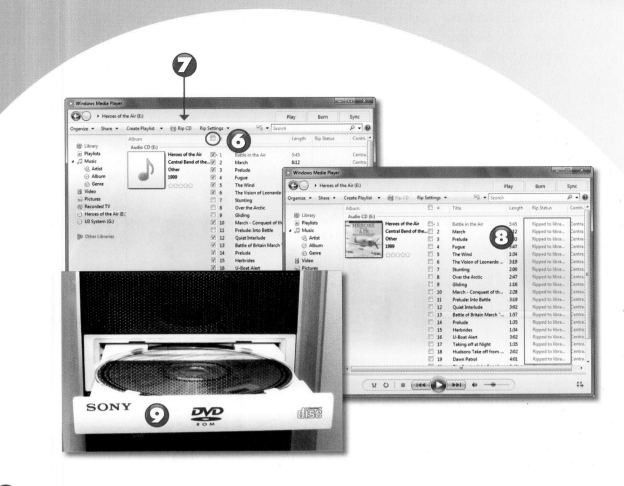

6 If some tracks are not selected, click the empty checkbox to select all tracks.

7 Click **Rip CD**.

8 Each track is ripped to the library.

9 When all tracks have been ripped, remove the CD.

End

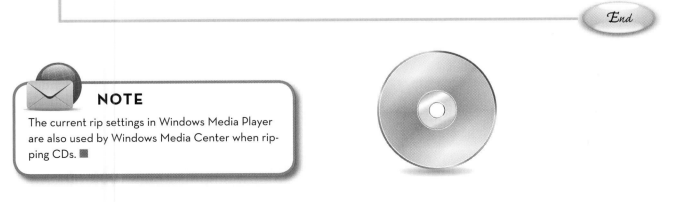

NOTE

The current rip settings in Windows Media Player are also used by Windows Media Center when ripping CDs. ▪

PLAYING ALBUMS

Whether you have ripped your own CDs into digital music or purchased digital music from online stores, you can play individual music tracks or entire albums. Here's how to play an album.

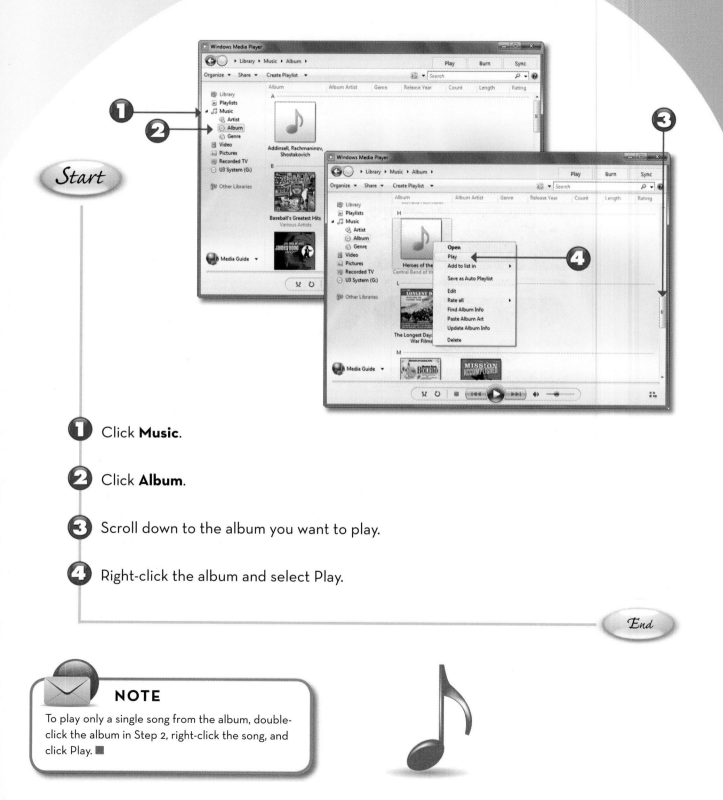

1 Click **Music**.

2 Click **Album**.

3 Scroll down to the album you want to play.

4 Right-click the album and select Play.

NOTE

To play only a single song from the album, double-click the album in Step 2, right-click the song, and click Play. ■

PLAYING INDIVIDUAL TRACKS

You can play individual tracks from the Artist, Album, or Genre views of Music in Windows Media Player. In this example, we'll use the Artist view.

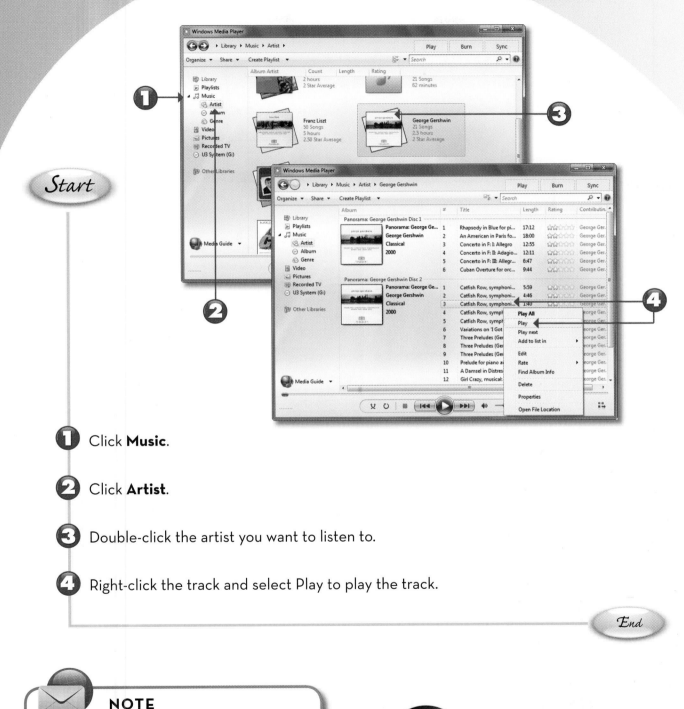

Start

1 Click **Music**.

2 Click **Artist**.

3 Double-click the artist you want to listen to.

4 Right-click the track and select Play to play the track.

End

NOTE

To play multiple tracks, click the first track, hold down either Ctrl key and click additional tracks, right-click the first track selected, and select Play. ■

SETTING UP PLAYLISTS

Playlists enable you to play custom mixes of your favorite music or other media with the click of a button. You can create playlists by selecting your favorite tracks, or automatically. This tutorial covers the manual process.

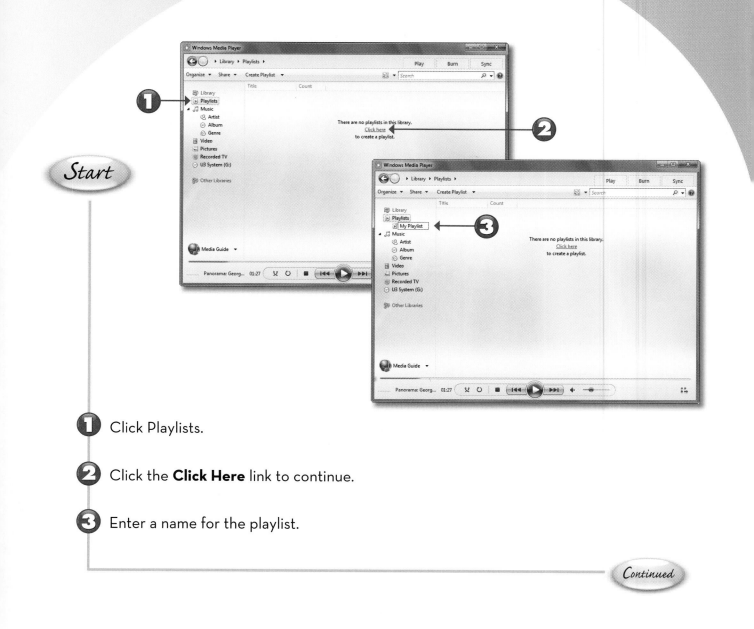

Start

1 Click Playlists.

2 Click the **Click Here** link to continue.

3 Enter a name for the playlist.

Continued

NOTE

The playlists you create in Windows Media Player are also used by Windows Media Center. ■

4 To add a track to the playlist, drag it to the playlist.

5 Click the **playlist** to display its contents.

6 Click **Play** to play the tracks in the playlist.

End

NOTE

Repeat Step 4 until the playlist is complete. Note that you can also add other types of media—such as videos, photos, TV shows, or videos—to a playlist. ■

NOTE

To create an auto playlist, click Create Playlist, Create Auto Playlist, and specify types of media and other criteria. ■

BURNING (CREATING) A MUSIC CD

Whether you have created a playlist or not, you can select music and burn it to a CD that will play in most CD players. In this example, we'll burn the contents of a playlist to a CD.

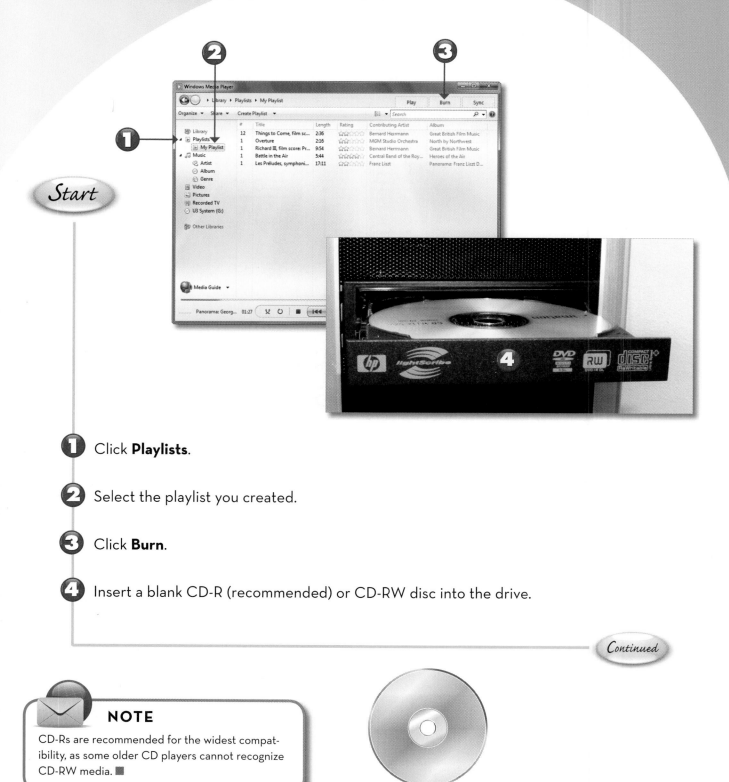

Start

1 Click **Playlists**.

2 Select the playlist you created.

3 Click **Burn**.

4 Insert a blank CD-R (recommended) or CD-RW disc into the drive.

Continued

NOTE

CD-Rs are recommended for the widest compatibility, as some older CD players cannot recognize CD-RW media. ■

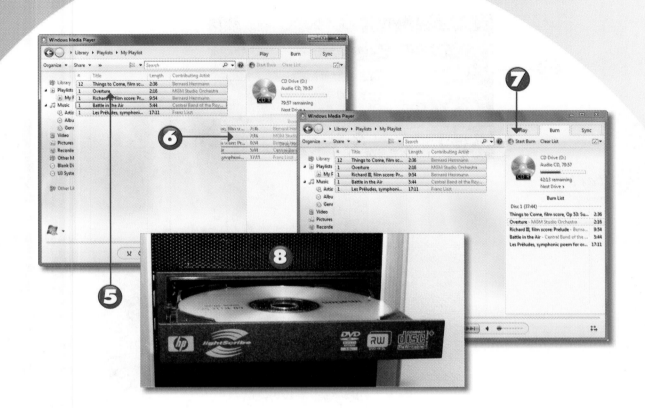

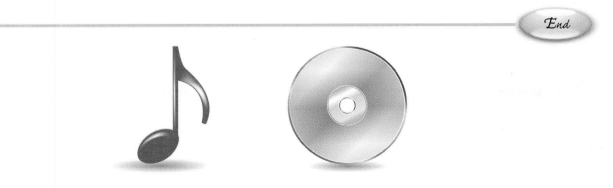

5 Select the songs in the playlist.

6 Drag them to the burn list.

7 Click Start **Burn**.

8 At the end of the burn process, the CD is ejected.

End

VIEWING DVDS WITH WINDOWS MEDIA PLAYER

You can also use Windows Media Player to view most commercial DVD movies in full-screen or in a window.

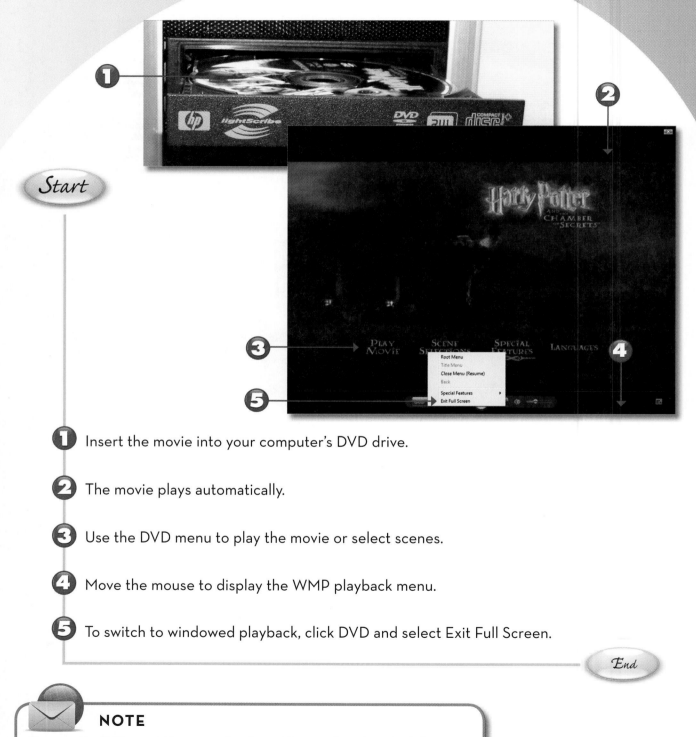

Start

Root Menu
Title Menu
Close Menu (Resume)
Back
Special Features
Exit Full Screen

1. Insert the movie into your computer's DVD drive.

2. The movie plays automatically.

3. Use the DVD menu to play the movie or select scenes.

4. Move the mouse to display the WMP playback menu.

5. To switch to windowed playback, click DVD and select Exit Full Screen.

End

NOTE

To access the DVD's special features, select Special Features from the right-click menu in Step 5, or click Special Features on the DVD menu shown in the playback window. ■

VIEWING VIDEO CLIPS WITH WINDOWS MEDIA PLAYER

You can use Windows Media Player to view video clips from your DV camcorder or downloaded videos. Here's how.

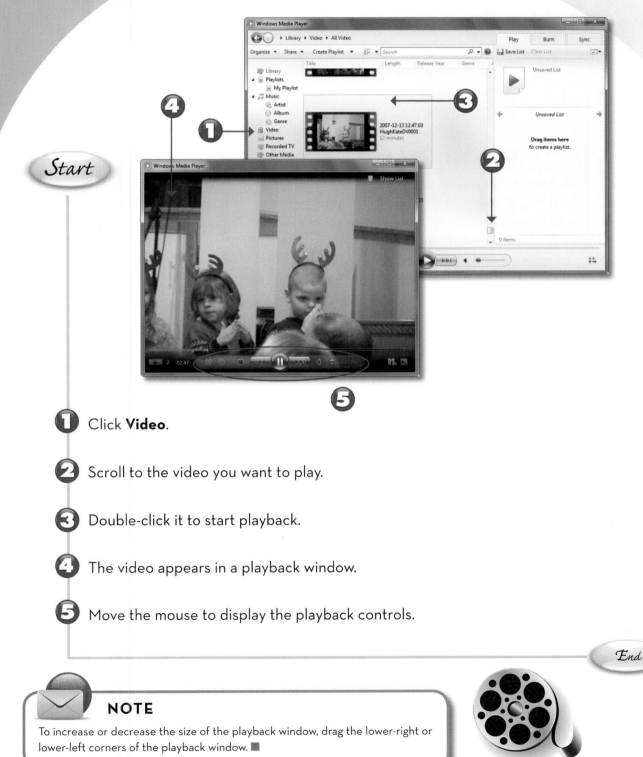

Start

1. Click **Video**.

2. Scroll to the video you want to play.

3. Double-click it to start playback.

4. The video appears in a playback window.

5. Move the mouse to display the playback controls.

End

NOTE

To increase or decrease the size of the playback window, drag the lower-right or lower-left corners of the playback window. ■

Chapter 8

WINDOWS MEDIA CENTER

Windows Media Center, an integral part of Windows 7 Home Premium and higher editions, turns your Windows 7 PC into a multimedia powerhouse that's HDTV and home theater friendly. Whether you use WMC on your desktop PC or as the hub of your home entertainment system, Windows Media Center makes TV viewing and recording, music playback, video playback, and photo viewing more enjoyable than ever before.

Windows Media Center uses a so-called "10-foot UI" to make it compatible with computer displays, standard TVs, and HDTVs. By using a wireless keyboard and mouse or Windows Media Center-compatible remote control, you can enjoy your media through Windows Media Center from a comfortable easy chair or couch.

You can also view WMC in a small window by using the Windows Media Center desktop gadget. See Chapter 3, "Using the Windows 7 Desktop," for details.

Watch live on recorded TV

Play or rip your favorite CDs

history

PGA Tour Golf: Nationwide: South Georgia
Classic, First Round - "Nationwide: South..."

Sort by Date

Sort by Status

Sort by Title

Clear History

THURSDAY, APRIL 23

PGA Tour Golf: Zurich Classic o   Recorded

PGA Tour Golf: Nationwide: So   Recorded

Spice Up My Kitchen   Canceled

Spice Up My Kitchen: Out of

Deadliest Catch: Friends and

NASCAR Racing

SATURDAY, APRIL 11

FOX News Watch

album   actions   ‹ ›

Heroes of the Air
Central Band of the Royal Air Force
21 tracks 1:02:24 1999

+ add to now playing

▶ play album

Battle in the Air   5:43
March   6:11
Prelude   3:32
Fugue   3:46
The Wind   1:34
The Vision of Leonardo Da Vinci   3:18
Stunting   1:59
Over the Arctic   2:46

OPENING AND CONFIGURING WINDOWS MEDIA CENTER

The first time you start Windows Media Center, you need to configure it to use the hardware in your PC. This section assumes that you have installed a TV tuner connected to either cable or broadcast TV.

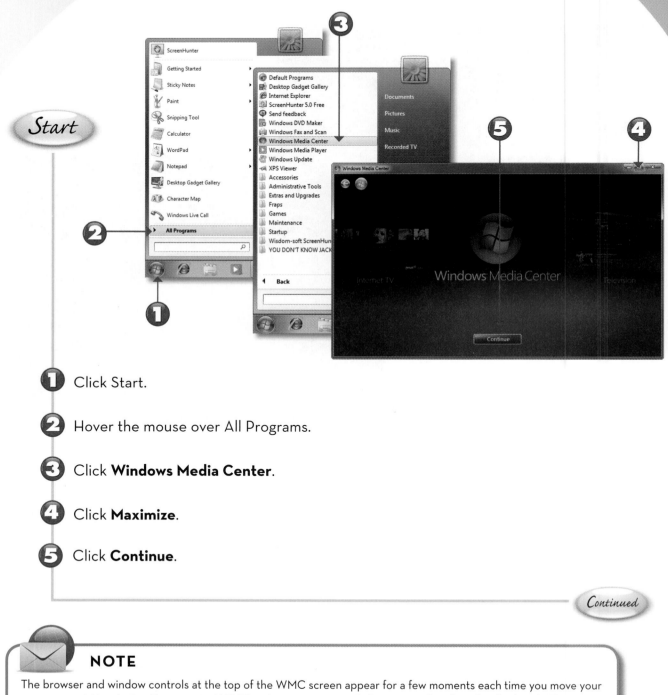

1 Click Start.

2 Hover the mouse over All Programs.

3 Click **Windows Media Center**.

4 Click **Maximize**.

5 Click **Continue**.

Continued

NOTE

The browser and window controls at the top of the WMC screen appear for a few moments each time you move your mouse or pointing device. If you control WMC with a remote control, these controls will not be displayed. ■

6 Click **Express**.

7 WMC downloads information and then displays the WMC desktop.

End

NOTE

Express Setup is recommended if you want to start using WMC right away but don't have a TV tuner or don't want to use it immediately. Custom Setup is recommended if you are not sure that you have your speakers or display configured correctly for WMC. You can perform Custom Setup at any time through the Tasks menu. ▪

CONFIGURING THE TV SIGNAL

If you have a TV tuner card or USB device, you can use WMC to watch, pause, and record live TV. In other words, WMC and a TV tuner enable your computer to function like a DVR. To enable WMC to display TV signals after you install a TV tuner card or USB device, you must set up your TV source. In this section, you learn how to set up WMC for use with cable TV.

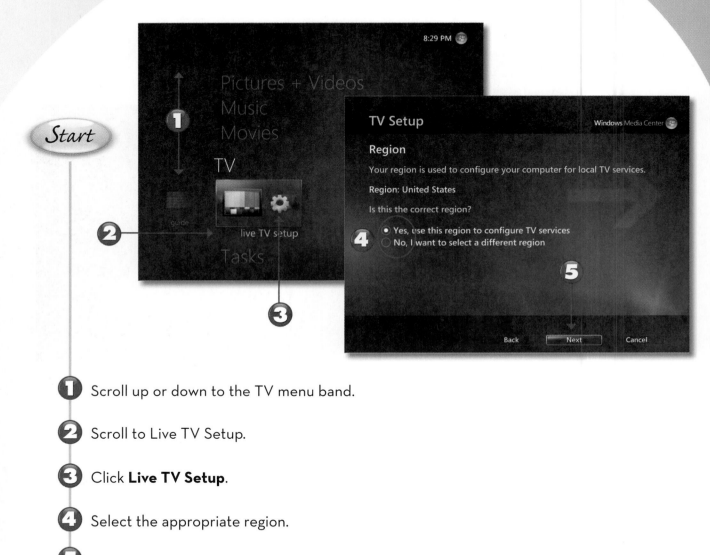

1 Scroll up or down to the TV menu band.

2 Scroll to Live TV Setup.

3 Click **Live TV Setup**.

4 Select the appropriate region.

5 Click **Next**.

Continued

NOTE

This tutorial assumes that the answer selected in step 4 was "yes." If WMC incorrectly identifies your region, you will be prompted to identify it before you can continue. ■

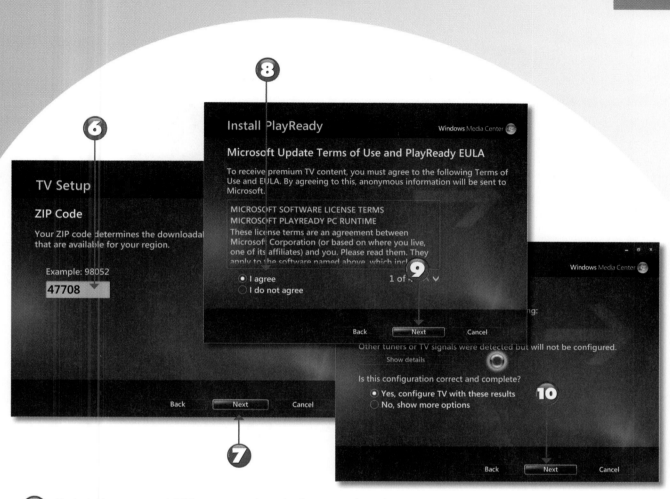

6 Enter the correct ZIP or postal code for your locality.

7 Click **Next**.

8 Select **I Agree**.

9 Click **Next**.

10 After WMC checks for TV signals, it displays the results. Click **Next** to continue.

Continued

NOTE

PlayReady is a new Microsoft technology for protecting digital media content from illegal copying. ■

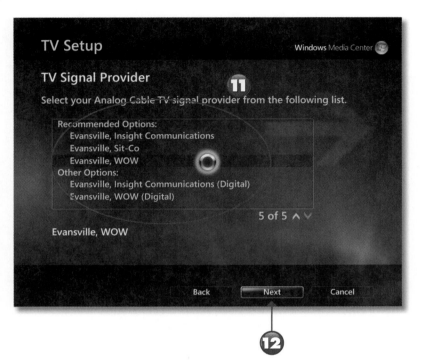

 Select your TV signal provider.

 Click **Next**.

Continued

NOTE

If you select digital cable TV in Step 11, you might need to edit the channel listings. Go to the main WMC menu and choose Tasks, Settings, TV, Guide to access these options. ■

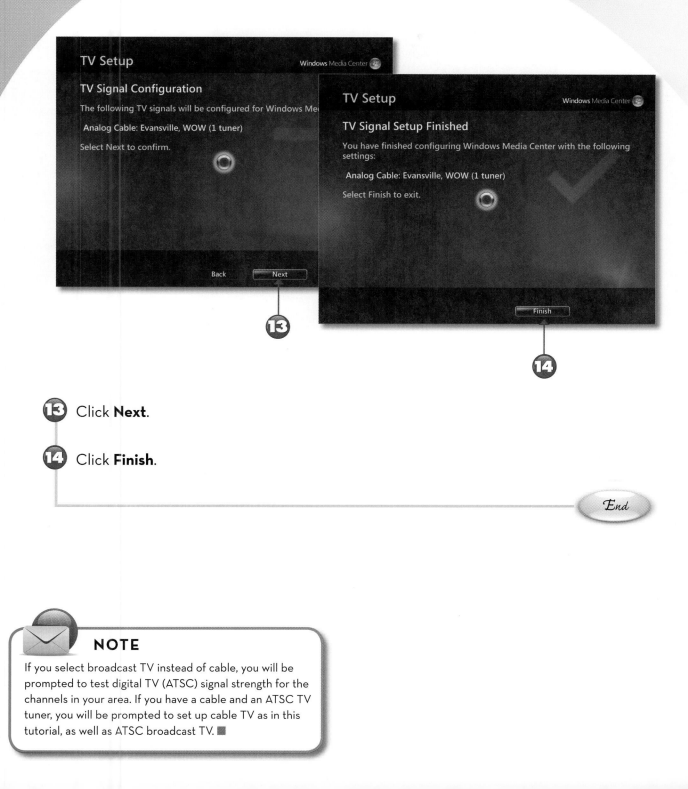

13 Click **Next**.

14 Click **Finish**.

End

NOTE

If you select broadcast TV instead of cable, you will be prompted to test digital TV (ATSC) signal strength for the channels in your area. If you have a cable and an ATSC TV tuner, you will be prompted to set up cable TV as in this tutorial, as well as ATSC broadcast TV.

VIEWING THE PROGRAM GUIDE

The Program Guide displays up to fourteen days of programming for the channels you can receive. Use it to plan your live TV and movie watching and recording.
In Windows 7, Windows Media Center's Program Guide also includes Internet TV programs.

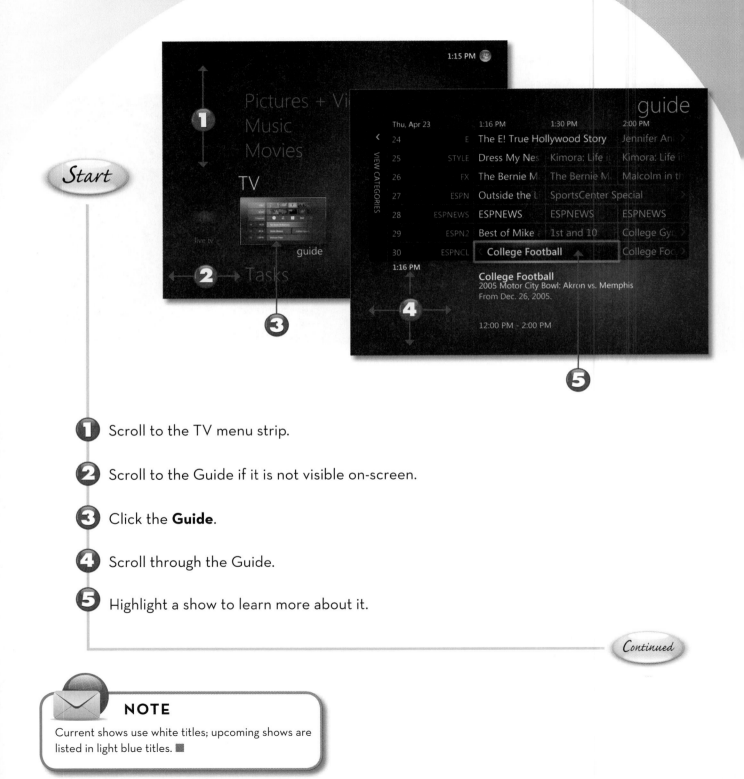

1 Scroll to the TV menu strip.

2 Scroll to the Guide if it is not visible on-screen.

3 Click the **Guide**.

4 Scroll through the Guide.

5 Highlight a show to learn more about it.

Continued

NOTE

Current shows use white titles; upcoming shows are listed in light blue titles. ■

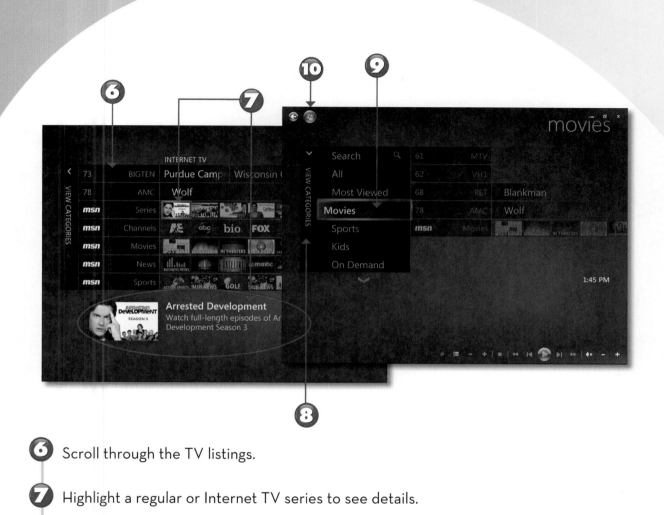

6 Scroll through the TV listings.

7 Highlight a regular or Internet TV series to see details.

8 Click **View Categories**.

9 Select a category to view matching channels and Internet TV results.

10 Click the **WMC button** on the screen or on your WMC remote to return to the WMC desktop.

End

TIP

To find specific programs, actors, or directors, use the Search feature. ■

WATCHING TV

The Guide makes it easy to watch live TV on either standard or widescreen displays.

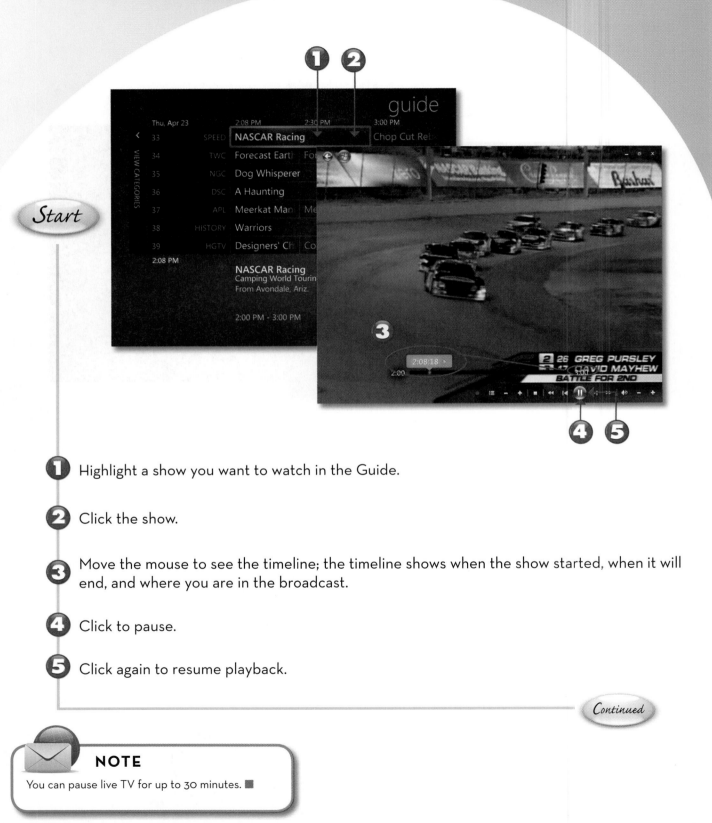

Start

① Highlight a show you want to watch in the Guide.

② Click the show.

③ Move the mouse to see the timeline; the timeline shows when the show started, when it will end, and where you are in the broadcast.

④ Click to pause.

⑤ Click again to resume playback.

Continued

NOTE

You can pause live TV for up to 30 minutes. ■

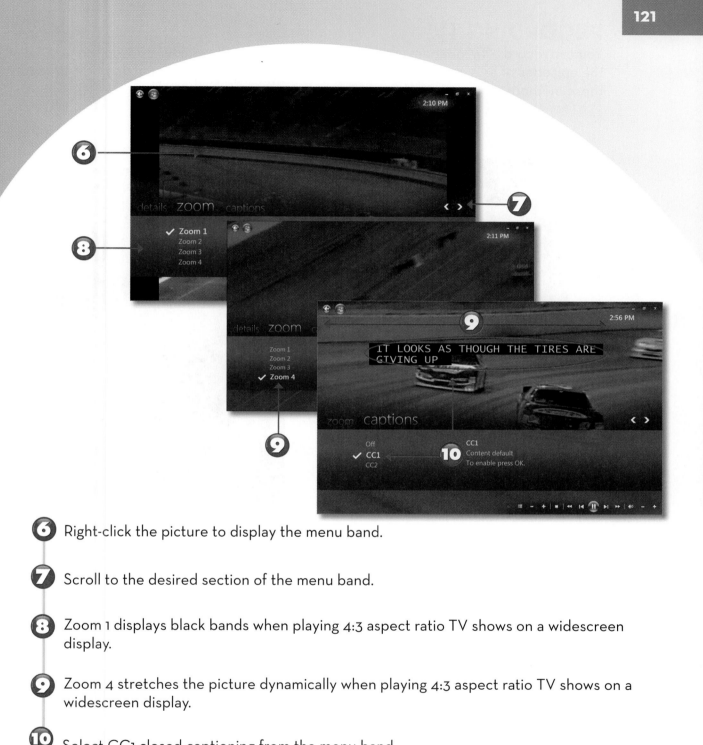

6 Right-click the picture to display the menu band.

7 Scroll to the desired section of the menu band.

8 Zoom 1 displays black bands when playing 4:3 aspect ratio TV shows on a widescreen display.

9 Zoom 4 stretches the picture dynamically when playing 4:3 aspect ratio TV shows on a widescreen display.

10 Select CC1 closed captioning from the menu band.

End

NOTE

Zoom settings are available only if you are using a widescreen display in widescreen mode. ■

RECORDING TV

You can record a TV program while you watch it or from the Guide, and you can also set all the episodes of a TV series to be recorded as they appear. This tutorial demonstrates all these methods.

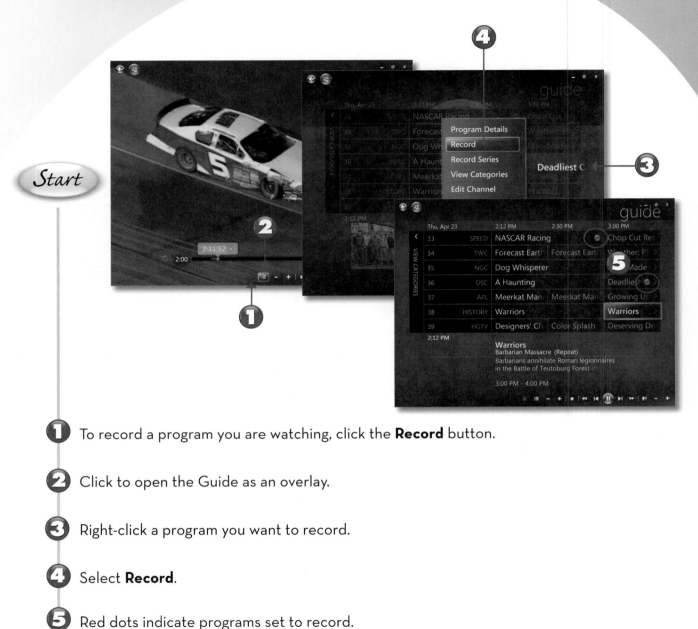

Start

1. To record a program you are watching, click the **Record** button.

2. Click to open the Guide as an overlay.

3. Right-click a program you want to record.

4. Select **Record**.

5. Red dots indicate programs set to record.

Continued

6 Right-click a program you want to record as a series.

7 Select **Record Series**.

8 Overlapping red dots indicate that the program is being recorded as part of a series.

End

NOTE

To discontinue recording a program or a series, right-click the listing, select Program Details, and select the appropriate option from the menu. ■

SEARCHING FOR TV SHOWS AND MOVIES

The Search tool in the TV menu enables you to find TV shows and movies by title, actor/ actress, director, keyword, or categories. In this example, you'll see how to search by title.

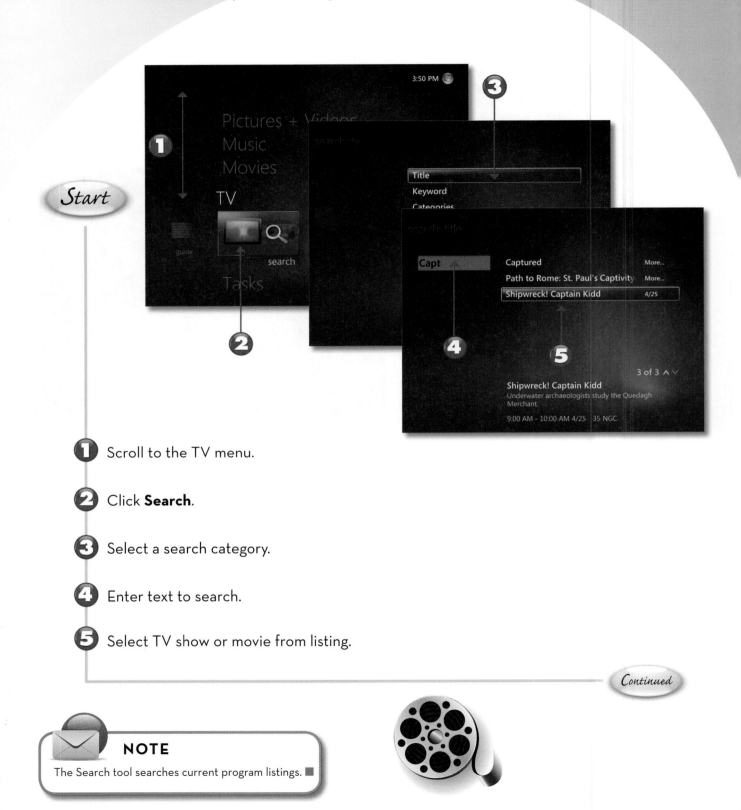

Start

1. Scroll to the TV menu.

2. Click **Search**.

3. Select a search category.

4. Enter text to search.

5. Select TV show or movie from listing.

Continued

NOTE

The Search tool searches current program listings. ■

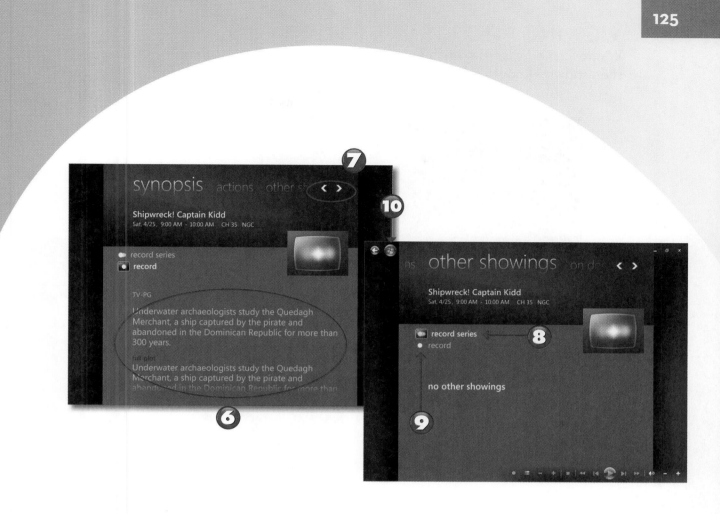

6 Review synopsis and full plot.

7 Scroll to see other showings, or other information.

8 Click to record series.

9 Click to record listed episode.

10 Click to return to WMC desktop.

End

NOTE

The Search tool searches current program listings. ▪

NOTE

To specify how long to keep a recording, what recording quality to use, and other settings, open the Advanced Recording section of this dialog. ▪

VIEWING PHOTOS IN A SLIDE SHOW

Windows Media Center enables you to browse your photos in a variety of ways and play slide shows without additional software.

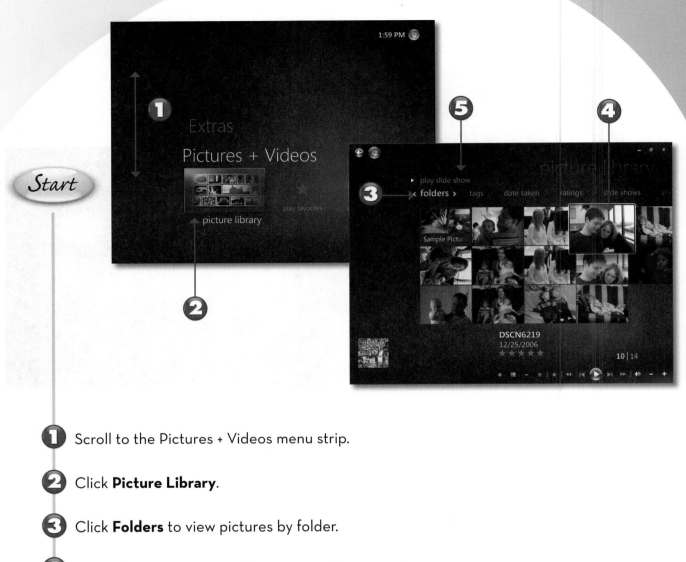

Start

1 Scroll to the Pictures + Videos menu strip.

2 Click **Picture Library**.

3 Click **Folders** to view pictures by folder.

4 Hover the mouse over a photo to see a larger version.

5 Click to view the photos in a slide show.

Continued

NOTE

By default, Windows Media Center displays photos in the current user's Pictures folder and photos in the Public\Pictures folder. You can have WMC watch additional folders for photos through the Tasks menu. ▪

6 Displays previous photo.

7 Displays next photo.

8 Pause/continue show.

9 Volume control.

10 Stops slide show.

End

VIEWING PHOTOS BY TAGS AND DATES

Windows Media Center provides several ways to view your photos. In addition to the default Folders view, you can also view photos by tags, date taken, and ratings. In this tutorial, you will see how to view photos by tags and dates.

Tags can be applied through the Details tab of the properties sheet for a photo, or through the Tags view in Windows Live Photo Gallery (see Chapter 17, "Using Windows Live Essentials," for details).

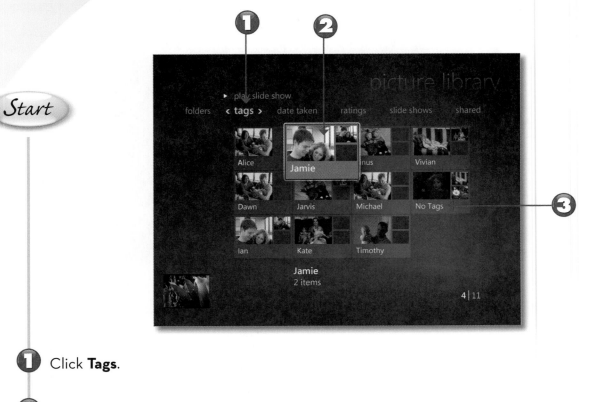

Start

1 Click **Tags**.

2 Photos identified with the same tag are grouped together.

3 Photos with no tags are grouped together.

Continued

NOTE

If a photo has more than one tag, it will be displayed in each tag group. ∎

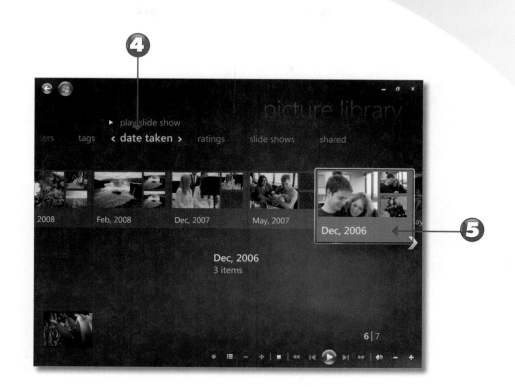

4 Click **Date Taken**.

5 Photos are grouped by month and year taken.

End

NOTE
To see individual photos, double-click the grouping. ■

CHANGING SLIDE SHOW SETTINGS

Windows Media Center can now use your photos as a screen saver. Use this tutorial to see and change slide show settings as desired.

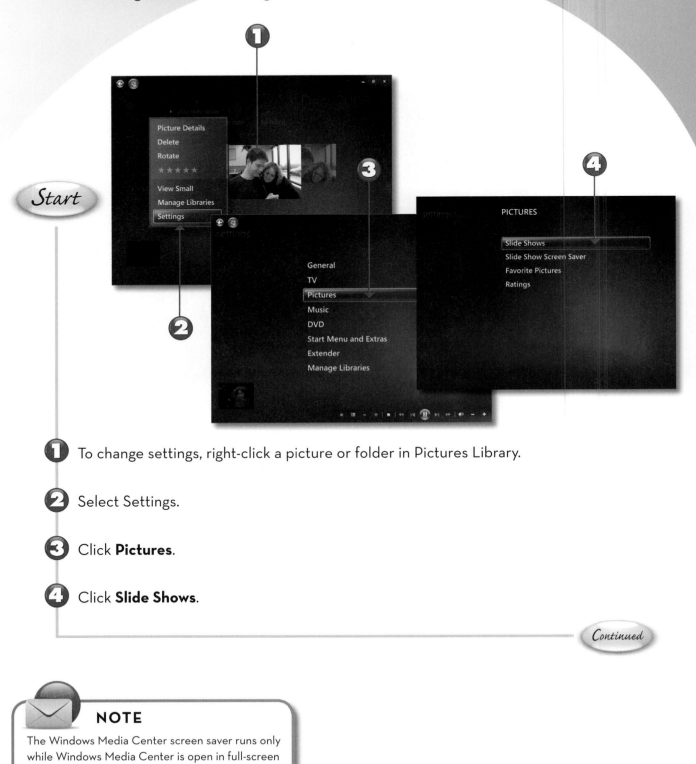

1 To change settings, right-click a picture or folder in Pictures Library.

2 Select Settings.

3 Click **Pictures**.

4 Click **Slide Shows**.

Continued

NOTE

The Windows Media Center screen saver runs only while Windows Media Center is open in full-screen mode and is idle. ■

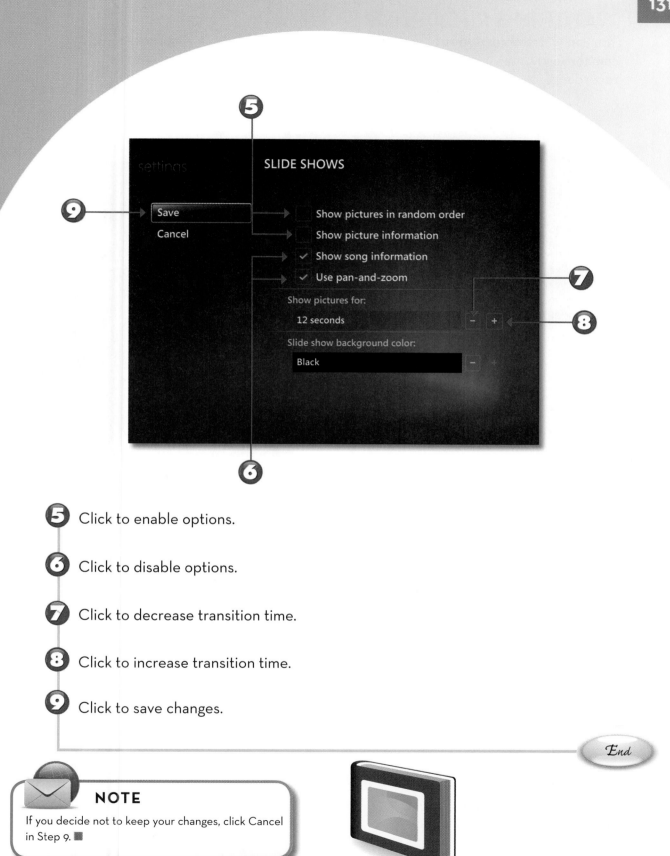

5 Click to enable options.

6 Click to disable options.

7 Click to decrease transition time.

8 Click to increase transition time.

9 Click to save changes.

End

NOTE

If you decide not to keep your changes, click Cancel in Step 9. ∎

WATCHING RECORDED TV

You can watch three types of videos with Windows Media Center: recorded TV, DV camcorder/home video, and Internet video. This tutorial shows you how to watch TV recordings.

Start

① Scroll to the TV menu strip.

② Click **Recorded TV**.

③ Select an option for listing recordings.

④ Click a recording.

⑤ Click Play.

End

NOTE

You can also restart the recording from the beginning or delete the recording from disk. ■

DELETING A TV RECORDING

You can manually delete TV recordings you no longer need.

1 In the Recorded TV menu, right-click a recording.

2 Select **Delete** to erase it from your system.

3 Click **Yes**.

4 The recording is deleted from your system.

NOTE

Make sure you no longer need the recording before you delete it. Windows Media Center bypasses the Recycle Bin. ■

MANAGING RECORDINGS

In addition to viewing and deleting recordings, you can also see what recordings you have scheduled and what has happened with shows you previously scheduled for recording.

1. In the Recorded TV menu, click View Scheduled.

2. Scroll through the listing.

3. Select a listing for more information.

4. Click **History**.

Continued

NOTE

To cancel a scheduled recording, right-click the list-ing and select Do Not Record. ■

5 Scroll to see information for each recording.

6 Click to return to the previous menu.

End

NOTE

If you clear the history, only recordings made after the history is cleared will be listed. ■

WATCHING VIDEOS

Windows Media Center delivers videos from your DV camcorder to your desktop or easy chair. Here's how to enjoy all of that digital goodness.

Start

1 Scroll to the Pictures + Videos menu.

2 Click **Video Library**.

3 Double-click the video you want to play.

4 The video plays.

End

NOTE

If you need to restart a video or delete it from the system, right-click the video, select Video Details, and choose the appropriate option. ∎

PLAYING MUSIC

Combine Windows Media Center with your home theater system, and you also have a great platform for enjoying your favorite digital music. Here's how it works.

Start

1 Scroll to Music.

2 Click **Music Library**.

3 Double-click an album.

4 Click **Play Album**.

End

NOTE

You can also view your music collection by artist, genres, songs, playlists (created in Windows Media Player), and composer. Click the links above the album titles (Step 3). ■

NOTE

Use the playback controls in Step 4 or your WMC remote to pause/continue playback, adjust volume, change tracks, or stop playback. ■

PLAYING AND RIPPING A CD

You can also play and rip CDs within Windows Media Center. Here's how.

Start

1 Insert a music CD. The CD begins to play.

2 To add the CD to your digital music collection, click **Rip CD**.

3 Click **Do Not Add Copy Protection to My Music**.

4 Click **Next**.

Continued

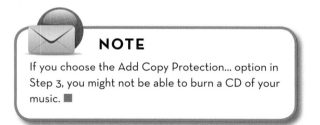

NOTE

If you choose the Add Copy Protection... option in Step 3, you might not be able to burn a CD of your music. ■

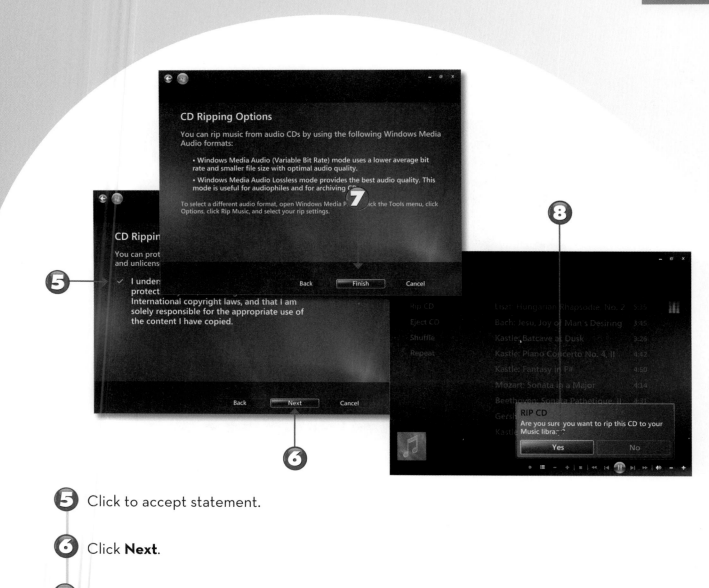

5 Click to accept statement.

6 Click **Next**.

7 Click **Finish**.

8 Click **Yes**.

Continued

NOTE

To change CD ripping settings, open Windows Media Player and select the format and bit rate preferred. See Chapter 7 for details. ■

now playing

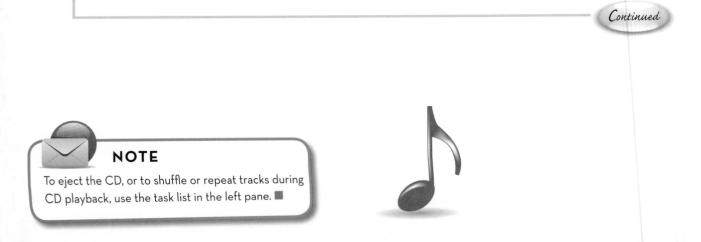

Rip CD	Liszt: Hungarian Rhapsodie, No. 2	5:35
Eject CD	Bach: Jesu, Joy of Man's Desiring	50%
Shuffle	Kastle: Batcave at Dusk	3:26
Repeat	Kastle: Piano Concerto No. 4, II	4:42
	Kastle: Fantasy in F#	4:50
	Mozart: Sonata in a Major	4:14
	Beethoven: Sonata Pathetique, II	4:31
	Gershwin: Rhapsody in Blue	6:53
	Kastle: Atlantis	6:37

9 Completed track.

10 Track being played.

11 Track being ripped.

Continued

NOTE

To eject the CD, or to shuffle or repeat tracks during CD playback, use the task list in the left pane. ■

12 Ripped album.

13 Album in CD/DVD drive.

End

NOTE

Some older albums might not display cover art when they are ripped. ■

STARTING A GAME FROM WINDOWS MEDIA CENTER

Windows 7 includes several casual games that are perfect for playback on TVs as well as computer screens. You can start these games from within Windows 7. Here's how to play one of those games, Chess Titans.

Start

End

1. Scroll to Extras.

2. Click **Extras Library**.

3. Double-click **Chess Titans**.

4. Select a game option to start.

5. Click to quit the game.

NOTE

When you exit, you have the option to save the game. When you start the game again, you can continue a saved game or start a new game. ■

QUITTING WMC

In Windows 7, the WMC Shutdown task has been enhanced with new options.

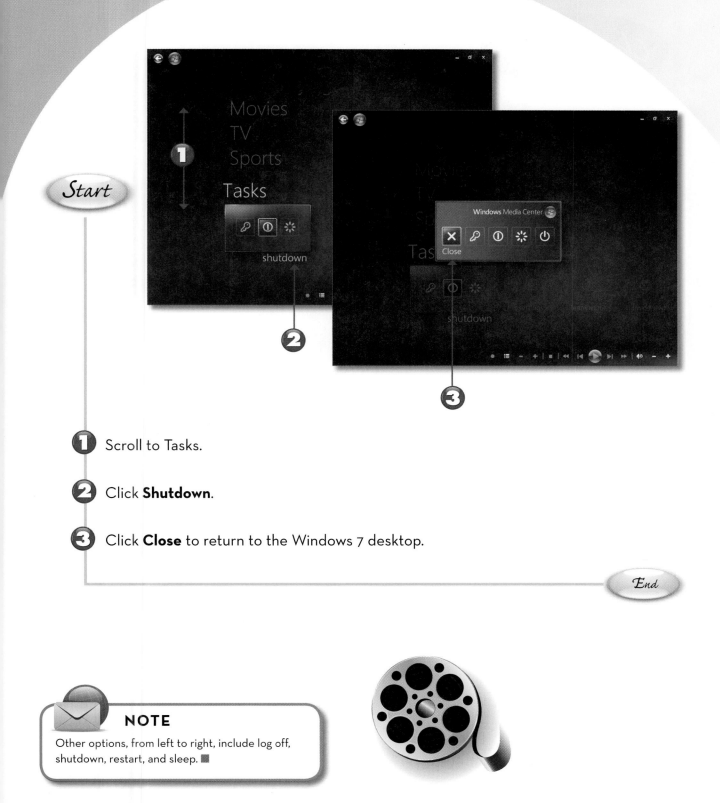

Start

1 Scroll to Tasks.

2 Click **Shutdown**.

3 Click **Close** to return to the Windows 7 desktop.

End

NOTE

Other options, from left to right, include log off, shutdown, restart, and sleep. ◼

Chapter 9

GAMING

Windows 7 makes it easy to organize your games. Games Explorer provides one-click access to games made for Windows, helps you find out how powerful your computer needs to be to run games, and makes it easy to restart saved games. If you have games that don't automatically install into Games Explorer, you can easily add shortcuts, and use Games Explorer to help you solve problems with games that aren't running. Let the games begin!

Games Explorer stores
game play statistics

Select a game to see
its CSRD rating

Play games in window or full-screen modes

USING THE GAMES EXPLORER

The Games Explorer library provides access to all preinstalled games on Windows 7. Games that are specially designed for Windows Vista and Windows 7 will also be installed to Games Explorer. Some older games might not be installed to Games Explorer.

1. Click the Start orb.

2. Click **Games**.

3. The **Games Explorer** window.

4. Your system's performance information.

NOTE

The first time you open the Games Explorer, a Set Up Game Updates and Options dialog appears. Click OK to continue. To learn more about this dialog, see "Setting Up Game Updates and Options," this chapter, p. 152. ■

LEARNING MORE ABOUT A GAME

Before you start a game, you can display its rating, the Performance Rating (Windows Experience Index) recommended for the game, and other information, such as the publisher. Note that not all games provide this information.

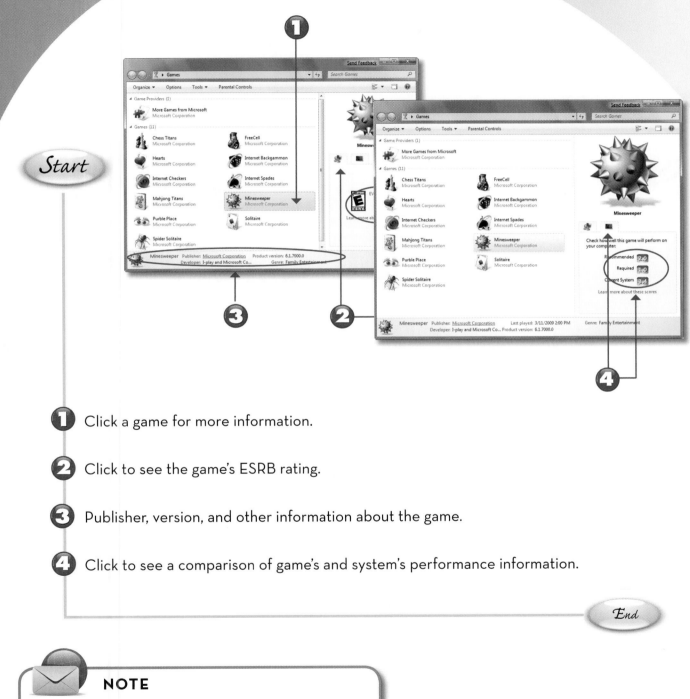

Start

1 Click a game for more information.

2 Click to see the game's ESRB rating.

3 Publisher, version, and other information about the game.

4 Click to see a comparison of game's and system's performance information.

End

NOTE

If you try to play a game that requires or recommends a higher Performance Rating than your system has, the game might not run or might run very slowly. ■

PLAYING, SAVING, AND CONTINUING A GAME

Preinstalled games in Games Explorer are sometimes referred to as "casual games," and one of the features of most of these games is the ability to start a game, save it, and continue it later.

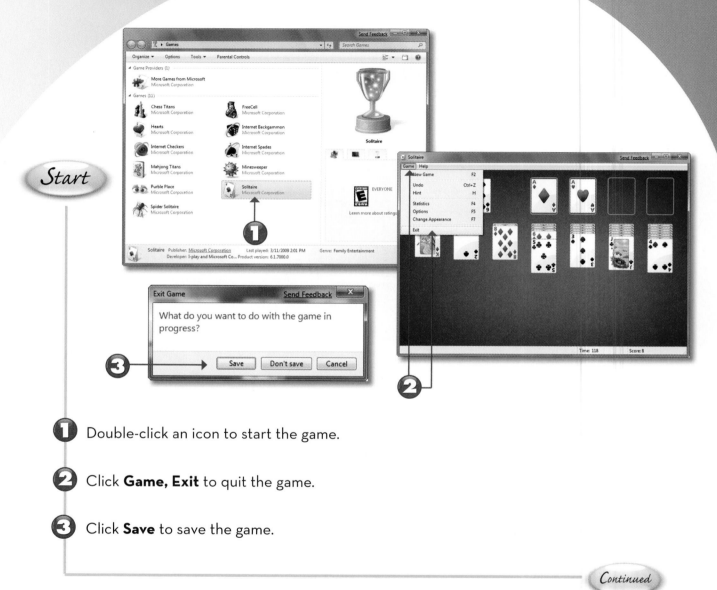

1 Double-click an icon to start the game.

2 Click **Game, Exit** to quit the game.

3 Click **Save** to save the game.

Continued

NOTE

With some games, you might see a prompt to select a gameplay level before the game window opens. ■

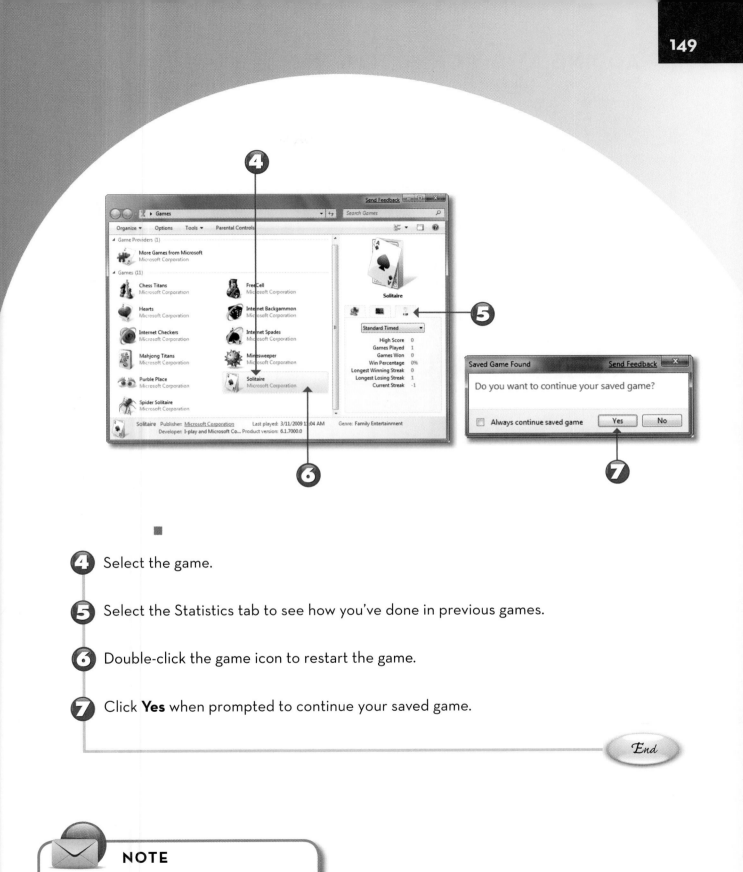

4 Select the game.

5 Select the Statistics tab to see how you've done in previous games.

6 Double-click the game icon to restart the game.

7 Click **Yes** when prompted to continue your saved game.

End

NOTE

If you answer No in Step 7, a new game begins. ■

ADDING A NEW GAME TO GAMES EXPLORER

Some games install themselves automatically to Games Explorer. However, if you install a game that does not install itself into Games Explorer, you can add it manually.

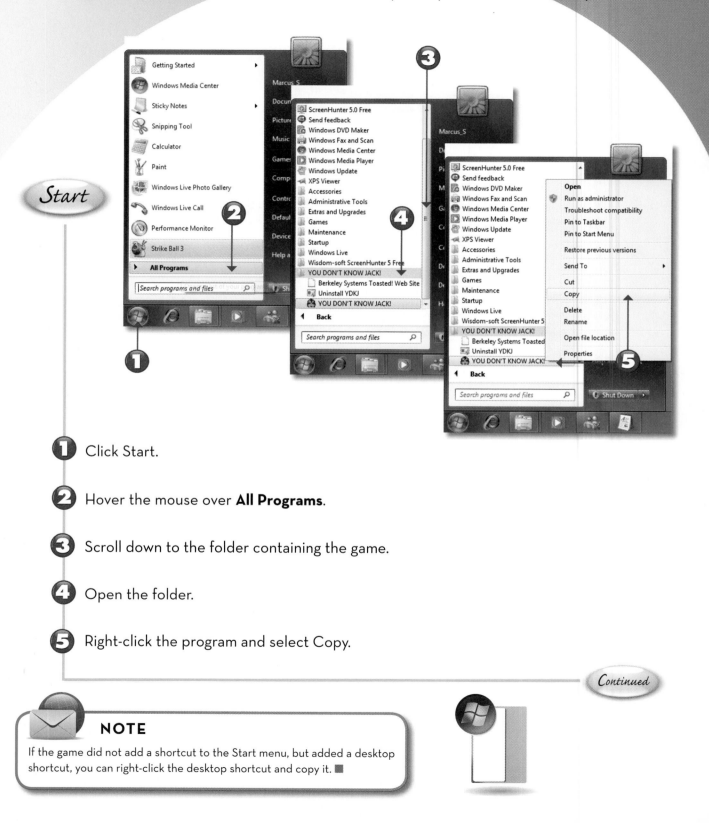

1 Click Start.

2 Hover the mouse over **All Programs**.

3 Scroll down to the folder containing the game.

4 Open the folder.

5 Right-click the program and select Copy.

Continued

NOTE

If the game did not add a shortcut to the Start menu, but added a desktop shortcut, you can right-click the desktop shortcut and copy it. ■

6 Open the Games Explorer.

7 Click **Organize, Paste**.

8 The game appears at the bottom of the Games Explorer.

End

NOTE

Games you add manually to Games Explorer generally will not have performance ratings or publisher information, and might not list ESRB ratings. ■

SETTING UP GAME UPDATES AND OPTIONS

To control how Games Explorer works, use the Set Up Game Updates and Options menu. This menu is used to specify options for automatically updating game updates, game news, and games folders settings.

Start

1 Click **Options**.

Continued

NOTE

To solve problems with hardware, your video card or monitor, input devices (controllers, mice, keyboards), audio, Windows Firewall, or programs and features, open the Tools menu and select the appropriate option. ■

TIP

You can control access to games by some users by setting up different accounts, installing parental control software, and using the Parental Controls dialog in Games Explorer. See Chapter 11, "User Accounts and System Security," for details. ■

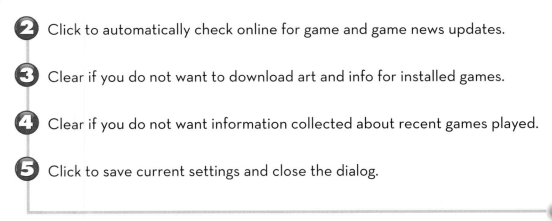

2 Click to automatically check online for game and game news updates.

3 Clear if you do not want to download art and info for installed games.

4 Clear if you do not want information collected about recent games played.

5 Click to save current settings and close the dialog.

End

Chapter 10

BROWSING THE INTERNET

Windows 7 includes Internet Explorer 8, the latest version of Microsoft's web browser. Internet Explorer 8 adds many new features to the browsing experience, including better protection against fraudulent websites and better integration with search, mapping, and other online tools. This chapter shows you how to use IE8's most important features.

InPrivate browsing

Live Search mapping web accelerator

Instant search in address bar

The Favorites menu

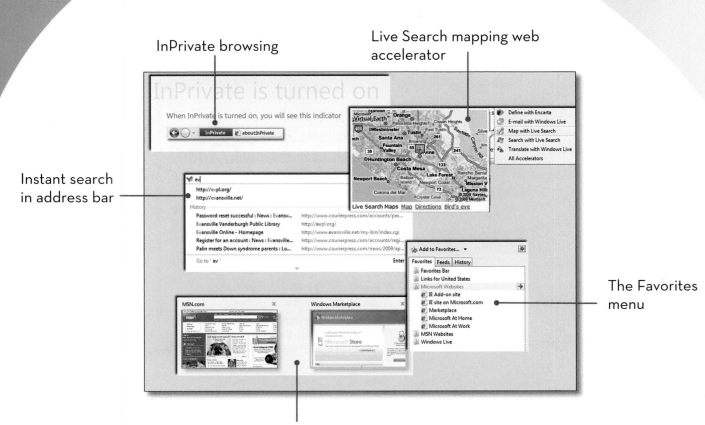

Thumbnail view of open web pages

THE INTERNET EXPLORER 8 INTERFACE

You can start Internet Explorer 8 from the taskbar or from the Start menu. Windows 7 includes a shortcut to IE8 on the taskbar, so you'll probably start it from that location most of the time.

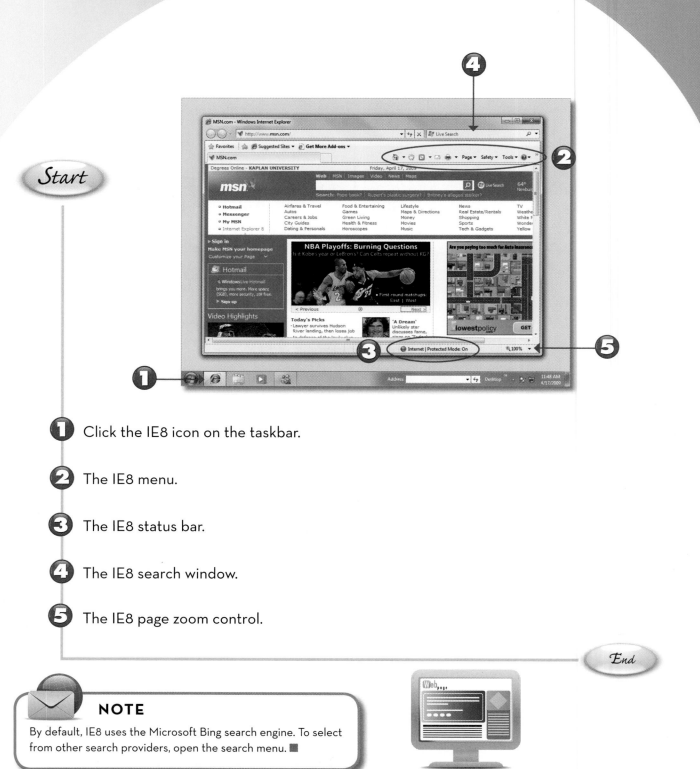

Start

1 Click the IE8 icon on the taskbar.

2 The IE8 menu.

3 The IE8 status bar.

4 The IE8 search window.

5 The IE8 page zoom control.

End

NOTE

By default, IE8 uses the Microsoft Bing search engine. To select from other search providers, open the search menu. ■

ENTERING A WEBSITE ADDRESS (URL)

Internet Explorer 8 now displays more information about website addresses you've previously visited when you enter an address (URL). It's now easier to go back to an address you've previously visited, even if you have visited several pages in the same domain.

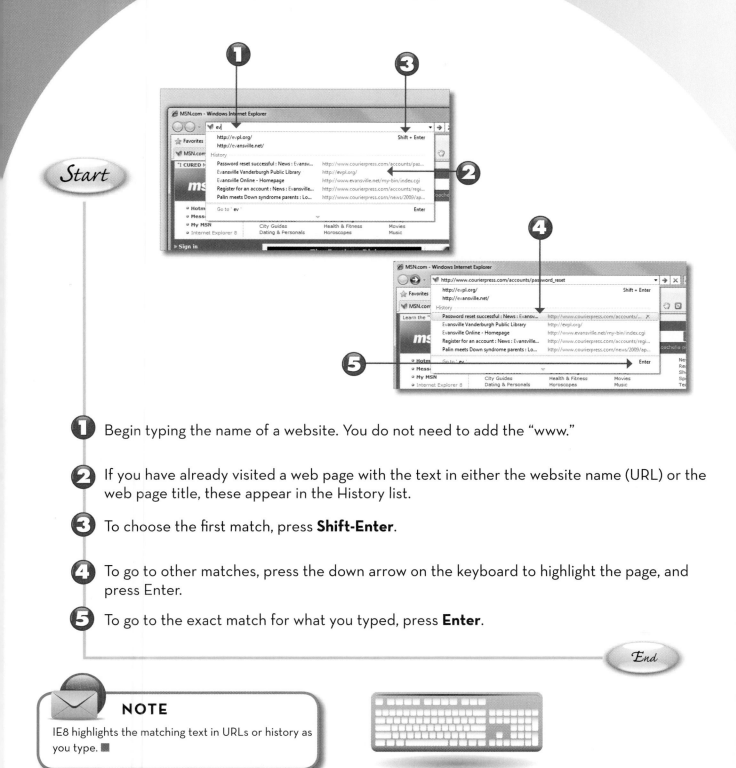

Start

1. Begin typing the name of a website. You do not need to add the "www."

2. If you have already visited a web page with the text in either the website name (URL) or the web page title, these appear in the History list.

3. To choose the first match, press **Shift-Enter**.

4. To go to other matches, press the down arrow on the keyboard to highlight the page, and press Enter.

5. To go to the exact match for what you typed, press **Enter**.

End

NOTE

IE8 highlights the matching text in URLs or history as you type. ■

SETTING YOUR HOME PAGE

You can reset your home page whenever you'd like with IE8, and you can also use a tab group as a home page. Here's how to do it.

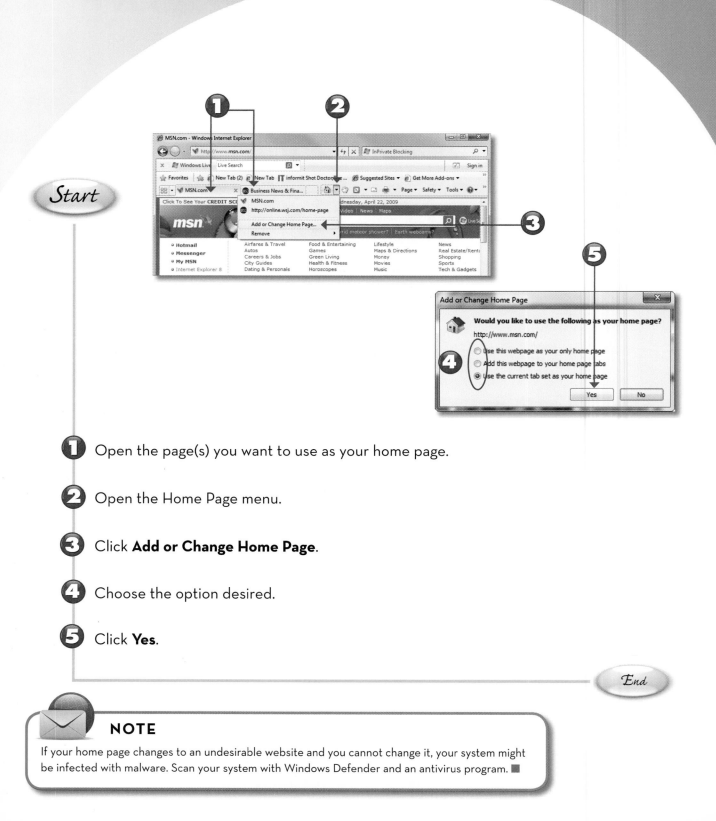

Start

1. Open the page(s) you want to use as your home page.

2. Open the Home Page menu.

3. Click **Add or Change Home Page**.

4. Choose the option desired.

5. Click **Yes**.

End

NOTE

If your home page changes to an undesirable website and you cannot change it, your system might be infected with malware. Scan your system with Windows Defender and an antivirus program. ■

WORKING WITH TABS

Internet Explorer 8 includes tabbed browsing, and gives you more options than ever before when you open a new tab. In this tutorial, you will learn how to open a new tab and how to use it.

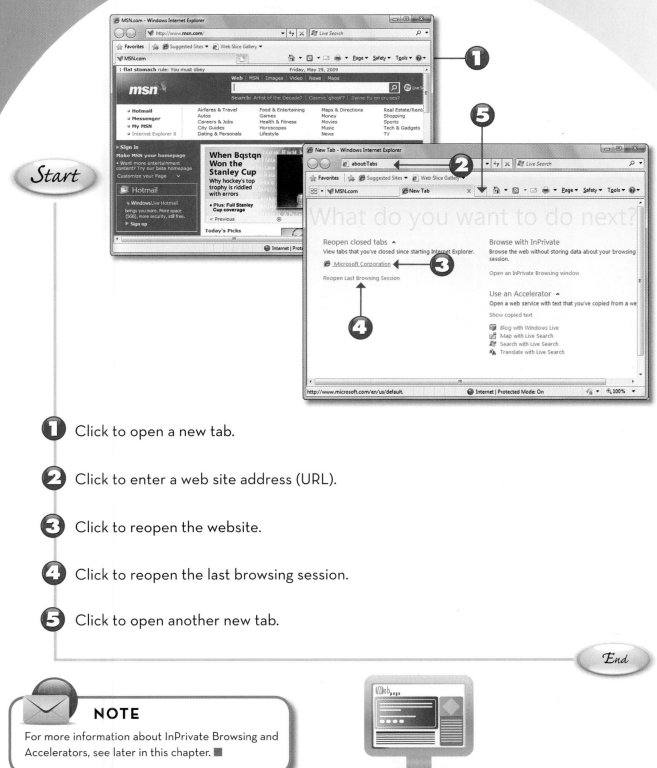

Start

1. Click to open a new tab.

2. Click to enter a web site address (URL).

3. Click to reopen the website.

4. Click to reopen the last browsing session.

5. Click to open another new tab.

End

NOTE

For more information about InPrivate Browsing and Accelerators, see later in this chapter. ■

OPENING A LINK

Because IE8 supports tabbed browsing, you can open a link to another website in three ways: as a replacement for the current page, as a new tab in the same window, or in a new window. When you click on a link, the link might open in the same window, or in a new window. To control how the link opens, use the method shown in this tutorial.

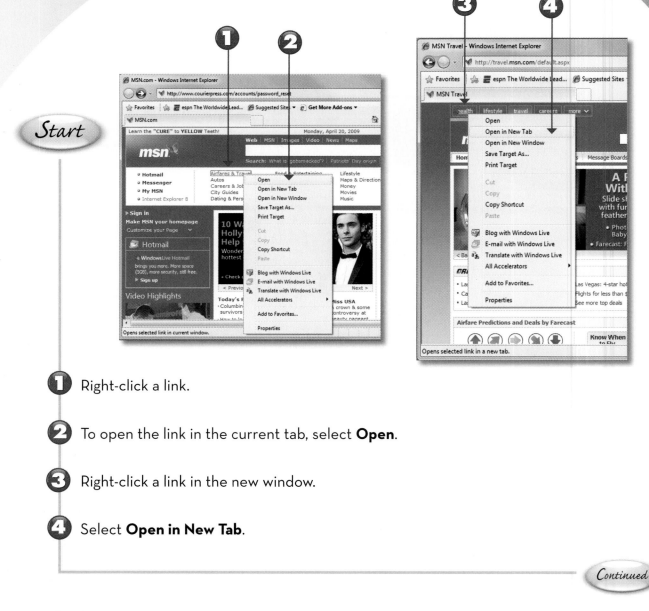

Start

1 Right-click a link.

2 To open the link in the current tab, select **Open**.

3 Right-click a link in the new window.

4 Select **Open in New Tab**.

Continued

NOTE

If you don't use the right-click menu to select how a link opens, the settings for the link determine how it opens. ■

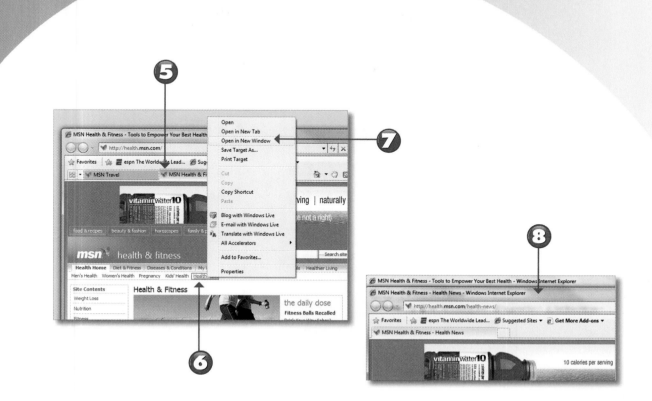

5 To view the contents of the new tab, click it.

6 Right-click a link on the new tab.

7 Select **Open in New Window**.

8 A new window opens to display the link.

End

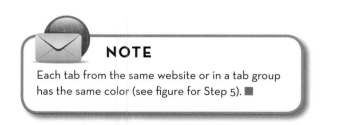

NOTE

Each tab from the same website or in a tab group
has the same color (see figure for Step 5). ■

USING THE FAVORITES BAR

The Favorites Bar enables you to access your favorite websites and sites similar to those you like. Here's how to use it.

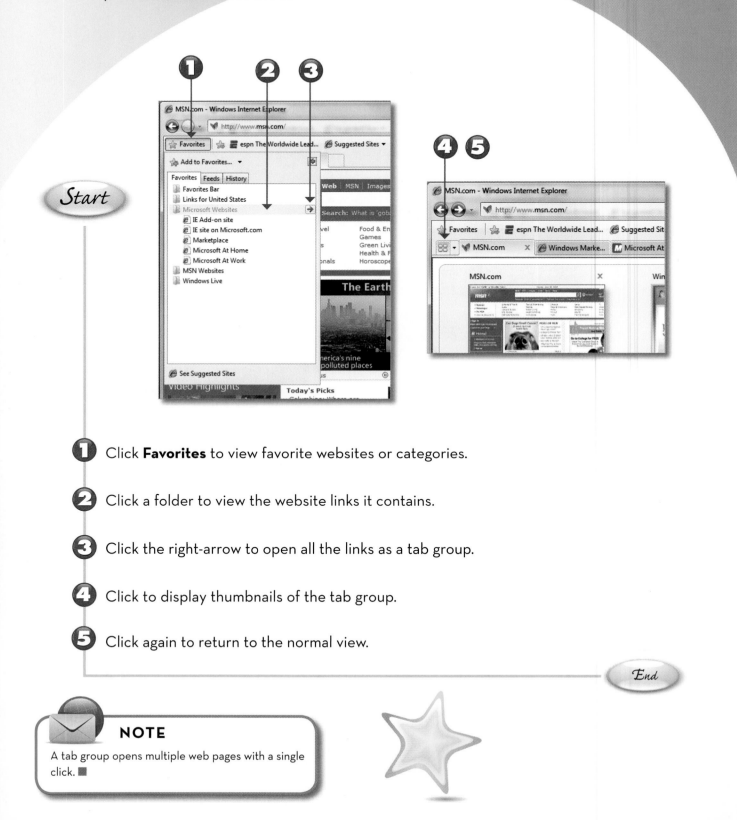

Start

1 Click **Favorites** to view favorite websites or categories.

2 Click a folder to view the website links it contains.

3 Click the right-arrow to open all the links as a tab group.

4 Click to display thumbnails of the tab group.

5 Click again to return to the normal view.

End

NOTE

A tab group opens multiple web pages with a single click. ▪

ADDING FAVORITES TO THE FAVORITES BAR

Internet Explorer 8 makes it even easier to get to your favorite websites by introducing the Favorites Bar. The Favorites Bar sits just below the address bar, providing one-click access to the sites you use most often. Here's how to add sites to the Favorites Bar.

Start

1. Navigate to a website you want to add to the Favorites Bar.

2. Click the **Add to Favorites Bar** button.

3. The website is added to the Favorites Bar.

End

NOTE

Use the Favorites Bar only for websites you want to visit very frequently, as it can get very crowded in a hurry. See the next section to learn how to add favorites to the Favorites menu. ■

ADDING FAVORITES TO THE FAVORITES MENU

For websites you want to revisit, but don't need one-click access to, you can still add them to the Favorites menu.

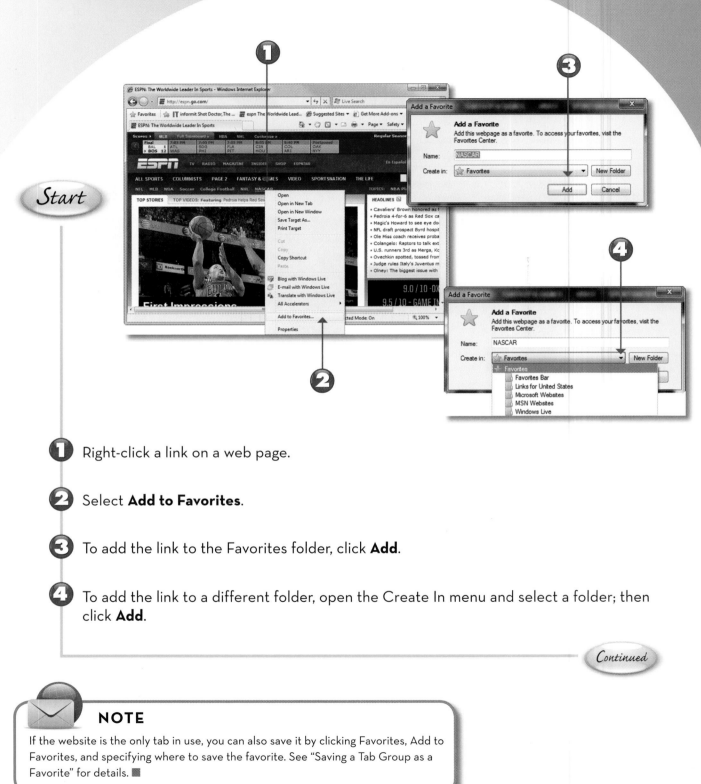

1 Right-click a link on a web page.

2 Select **Add to Favorites**.

3 To add the link to the Favorites folder, click **Add**.

4 To add the link to a different folder, open the Create In menu and select a folder; then click **Add**.

Continued

NOTE

If the website is the only tab in use, you can also save it by clicking Favorites, Add to Favorites, and specifying where to save the favorite. See "Saving a Tab Group as a Favorite" for details. ■

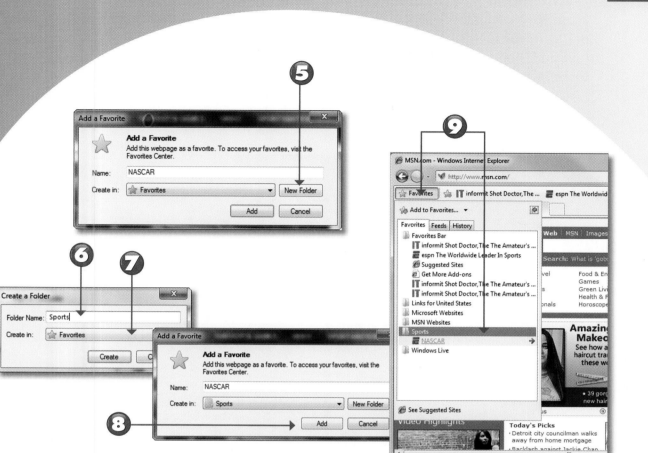

5 To add the link to a new folder, click **New Folder**.

6 Enter the name of the new folder.

7 Click **Create In**.

8 Click **Add**.

9 To see the new favorite, click **Favorites** and expand the category you used.

End

NOTE

By creating and using folders to organize favorites, you make them easier to find when you want to revisit them. ■

SAVING A TAB GROUP AS A FAVORITE

If you have several websites you rely on throughout the day, such as a web-based email client, news, or sports sites, you can save yourself time and clicks by opening them in separate tabs and then saving the tab group as a favorite. In this tutorial, you learn how to set up three tabs and save them as a tab group.

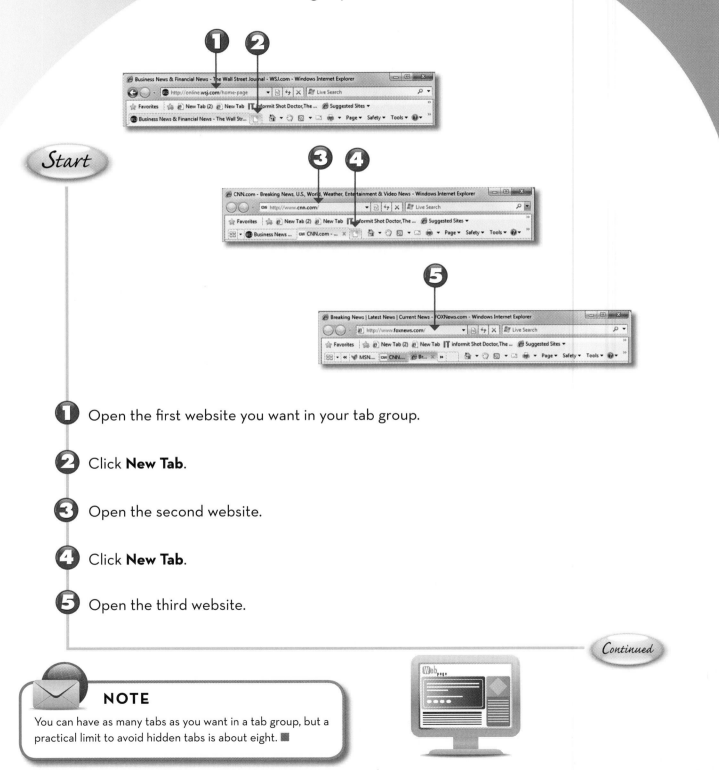

Start

1. Open the first website you want in your tab group.

2. Click **New Tab**.

3. Open the second website.

4. Click **New Tab**.

5. Open the third website.

Continued

NOTE

You can have as many tabs as you want in a tab group, but a practical limit to avoid hidden tabs is about eight. ■

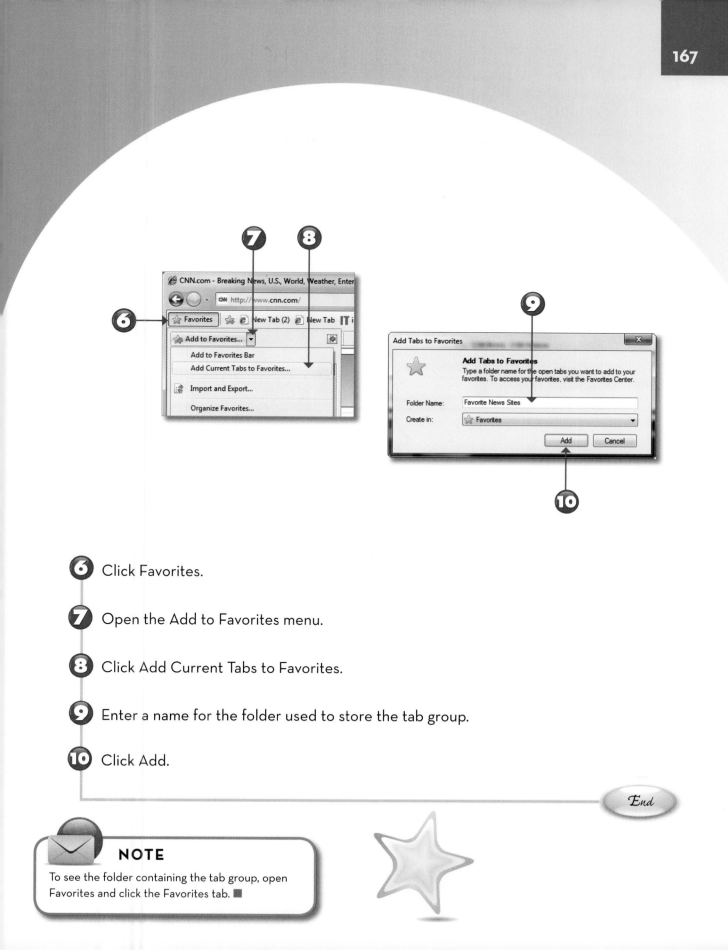

6 Click Favorites.

7 Open the Add to Favorites menu.

8 Click Add Current Tabs to Favorites.

9 Enter a name for the folder used to store the tab group.

10 Click Add.

End

NOTE

To see the folder containing the tab group, open Favorites and click the Favorites tab. ■

USING SUGGESTED SITES

Suggested sites, a new feature in Internet Explorer 8, helps you find new websites of interest by displaying links to sites that are similar to sites you've already visited. You can view suggestions for all visited sites, or only for the current website.

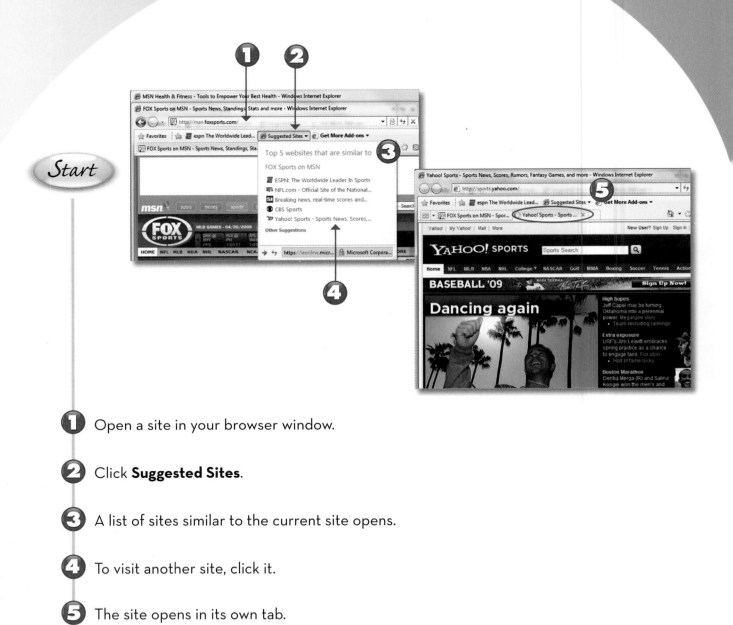

Start

1. Open a site in your browser window.

2. Click **Suggested Sites**.

3. A list of sites similar to the current site opens.

4. To visit another site, click it.

5. The site opens in its own tab.

Continued

NOTE

To see additional similar sites, click the Other Suggestions link visible in Step 4. ■

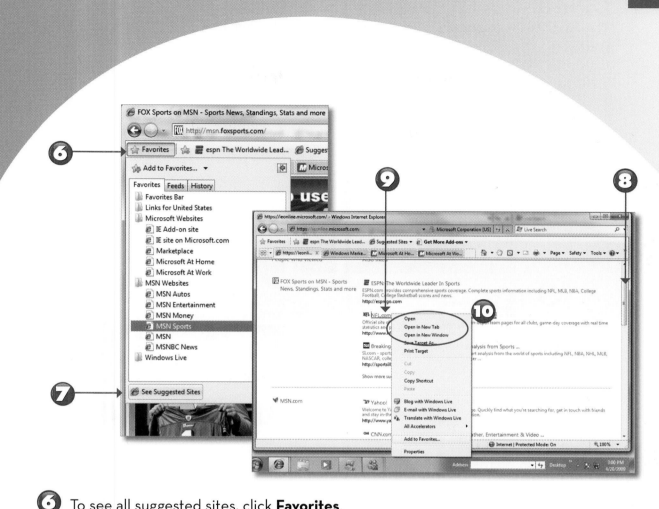

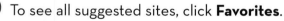

6 To see all suggested sites, click **Favorites**.

7 Click **See Suggested Sites**.

8 Scroll as needed to see suggestions.

9 Right-click a link.

10 Select how you want to open it.

End

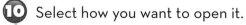

NOTE

The right-click menu in Step 10 also enables you to add the website to your favorites list. ■

OPENING A FAVORITE WEBSITE OR TAB GROUP

The Favorites menu enables you to open either individual favorites or tab groups whenever you want.

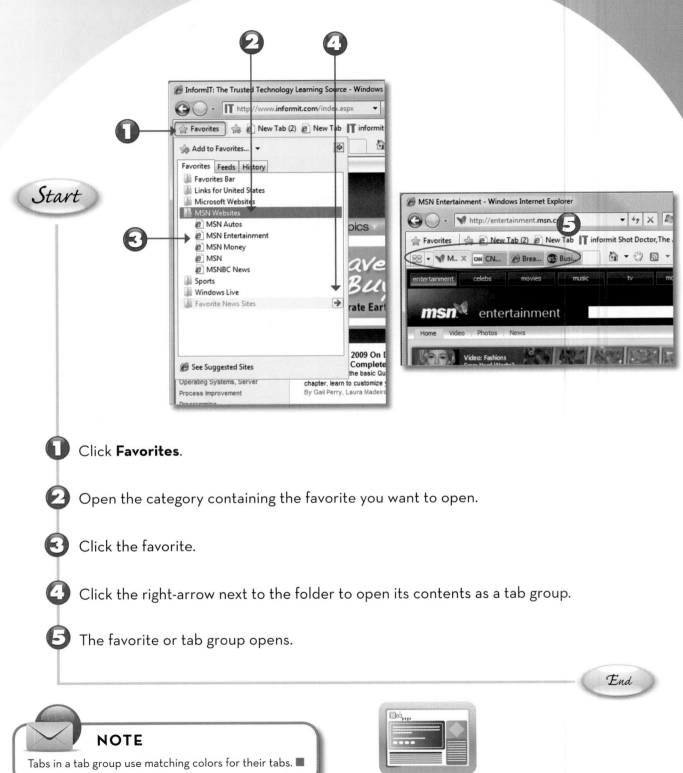

Start

1. Click **Favorites**.

2. Open the category containing the favorite you want to open.

3. Click the favorite.

4. Click the right-arrow next to the folder to open its contents as a tab group.

5. The favorite or tab group opens.

End

NOTE

Tabs in a tab group use matching colors for their tabs.

USING COMPATIBILITY VIEW

Internet Explorer 8 is designed to follow web standards far more closely than previous versions of Internet Explorer. However, many sites were designed for previous versions of IE and will not display pages properly in IE8. To enable IE8 to display problem websites properly, use the Compatibility View feature.

1 This website is incorrectly displaying tabbed content.

2 Click **Page**.

3 Click **Compatibility View**.

4 A confirmation message appears.

5 The page is now properly rendered.

NOTE

IE8 remembers the websites where you selected Compatibility View and automatically uses that setting on future visits to the same site. You can disable Compatibility View through the Page menu. ■

VIEWING RSS FEEDS

If you want information from your favorite websites as quickly as possible, you want to use RSS feeds. Internet Explorer's Favorites menu also includes a Feeds tab to make viewing and adding RSS feeds from your favorite websites easy.

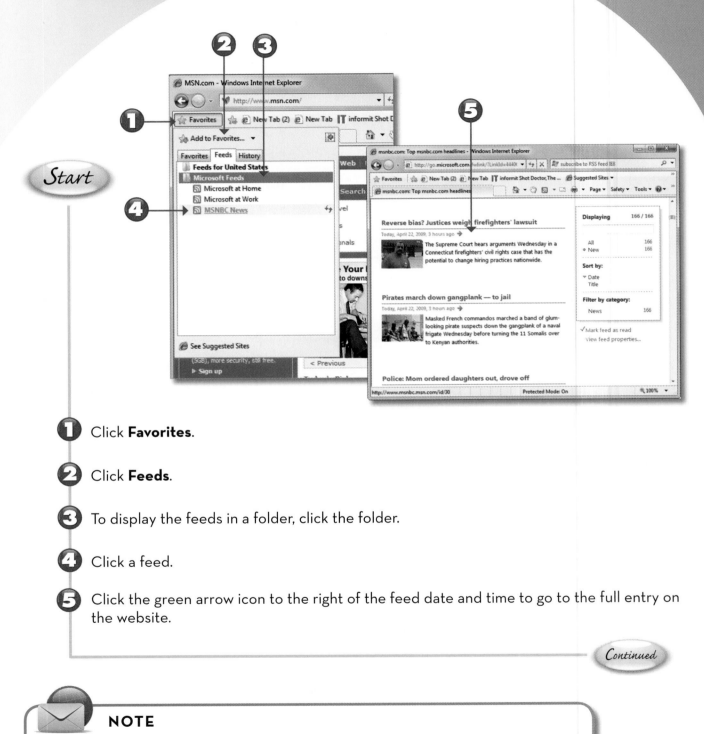

1 Click **Favorites**.

2 Click **Feeds**.

3 To display the feeds in a folder, click the folder.

4 Click a feed.

5 Click the green arrow icon to the right of the feed date and time to go to the full entry on the website.

Continued

NOTE

Click the double-arrow icon to the right of the feed listing to refresh the feed with the latest information. ■

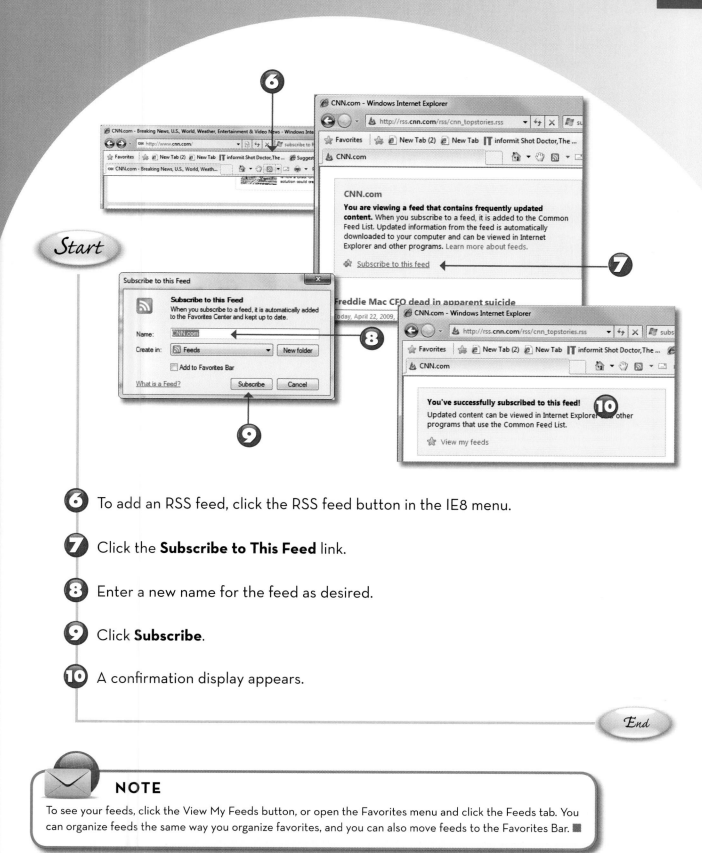

6 To add an RSS feed, click the RSS feed button in the IE8 menu.

7 Click the **Subscribe to This Feed** link.

8 Enter a new name for the feed as desired.

9 Click **Subscribe**.

10 A confirmation display appears.

End

NOTE

To see your feeds, click the View My Feeds button, or open the Favorites menu and click the Feeds tab. You can organize feeds the same way you organize favorites, and you can also move feeds to the Favorites Bar. ■

USING PAGE ZOOM

Page Zoom enables you to increase or decrease the size of text and graphics on a web page. By increasing the size, you make pages easier to read, and by reducing the size, you enable page viewing without horizontal scrolling.

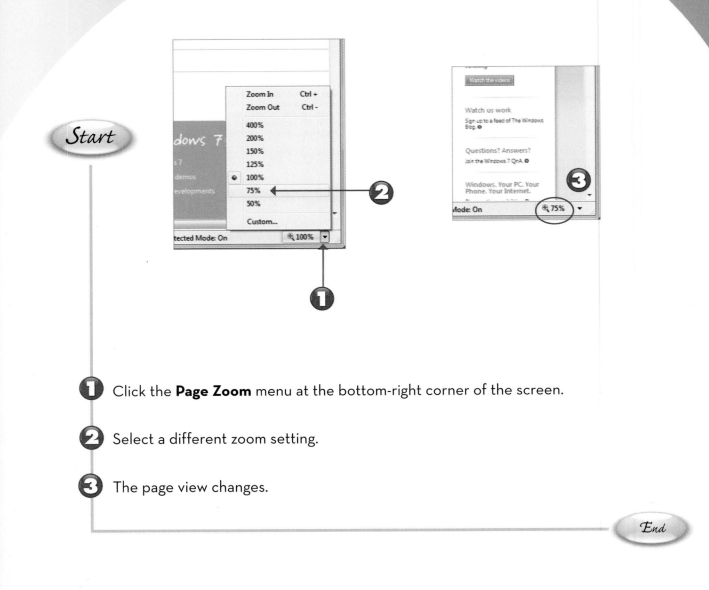

1 Click the **Page Zoom** menu at the bottom-right corner of the screen.

2 Select a different zoom setting.

3 The page view changes.

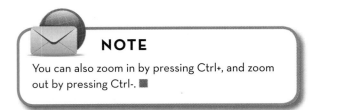

NOTE

You can also zoom in by pressing Ctrl+, and zoom out by pressing Ctrl-. ■

USING ACCELERATORS

Internet Explorer 8 makes it easier than ever to research names, places, or other information in any web page with its new Accelerators feature. Here's how to use the accelerators built into IE8.

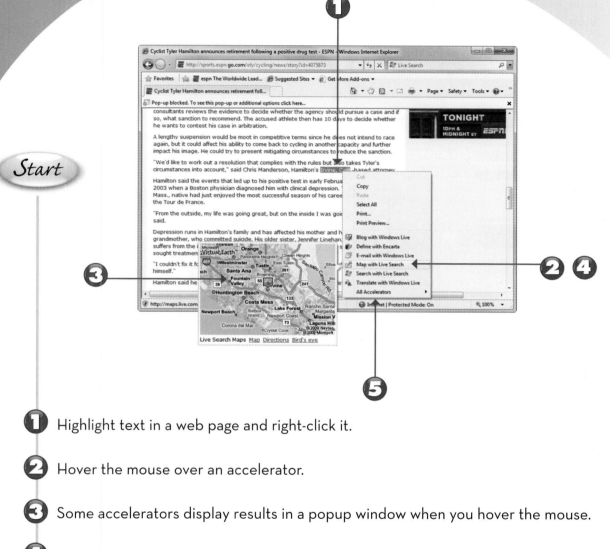

Start

1. Highlight text in a web page and right-click it.

2. Hover the mouse over an accelerator.

3. Some accelerators display results in a popup window when you hover the mouse.

4. To open the results of the accelerator in a new page, click the accelerator link.

5. Click to see more accelerators.

End

NOTE

To get more accelerators, open the All Accelerators menu and click Find More Accelerators. ∎

USING INPRIVATE BROWSING

Worried about leaving traces of where you've been online on a public computer, such as in a library or Internet cafe? Internet Explorer 8's new InPrivate Browsing feature covers your tracks. When InPrivate Browsing is enabled, browsing history, temporary Internet files, form data, cookies, and usernames and passwords are not retained. What happens in the InPrivate Browser window is forgotten as soon as you close it.

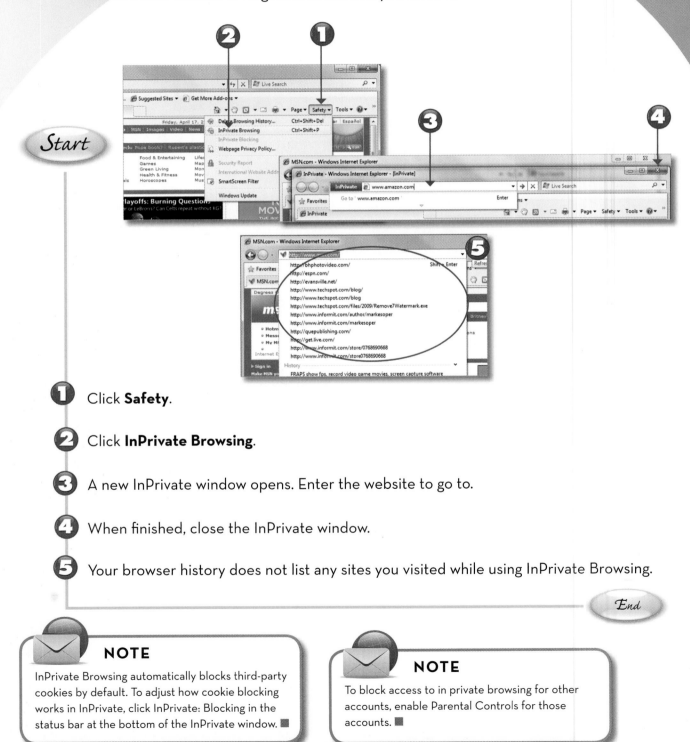

Start

1 Click **Safety**.

2 Click **InPrivate Browsing**.

3 A new InPrivate window opens. Enter the website to go to.

4 When finished, close the InPrivate window.

5 Your browser history does not list any sites you visited while using InPrivate Browsing.

End

NOTE

InPrivate Browsing automatically blocks third-party cookies by default. To adjust how cookie blocking works in InPrivate, click InPrivate: Blocking in the status bar at the bottom of the InPrivate window. ■

NOTE

To block access to in private browsing for other accounts, enable Parental Controls for those accounts. ■

DISABLING AN ADD-ON

Internet Explorer 8 includes a number of add-ons of various types, including accelerators, web slices (these display content from one website as you view another), and others. Here's how to disable an add-on.

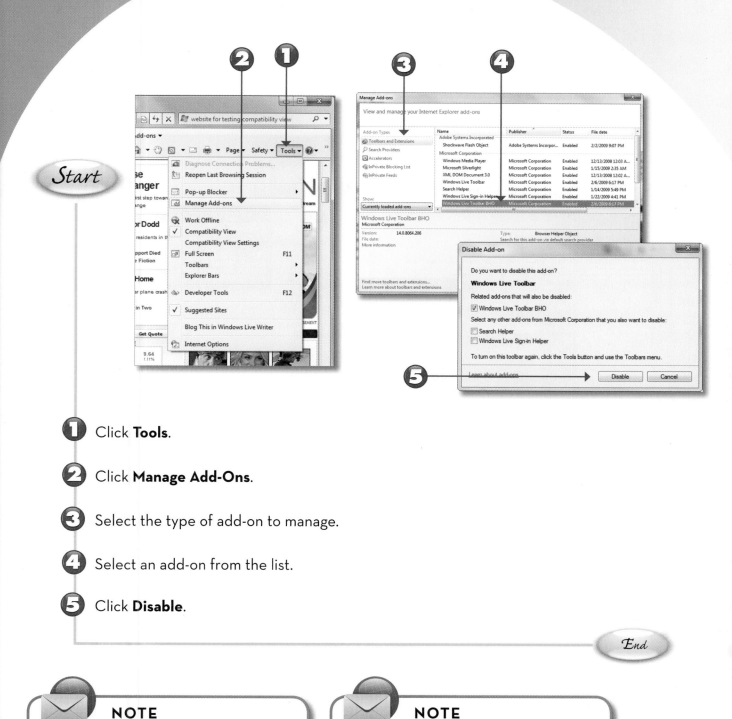

Start

1 Click **Tools**.

2 Click **Manage Add-Ons**.

3 Select the type of add-on to manage.

4 Select an add-on from the list.

5 Click **Disable**.

End

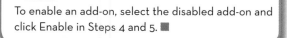

NOTE

To enable an add-on, select the disabled add-on and click Enable in Steps 4 and 5. ■

NOTE

Click Close when you are finished working with add-ons. ■

MANAGING POPUPS

By default, Internet Explorer 8 blocks popups. However, if you need to use a site that relies on popups, you can disable the blocker temporarily, turn it off for the site, or disable popup blocking entirely. The Popuptest.com website provides a convenient way to try these methods.

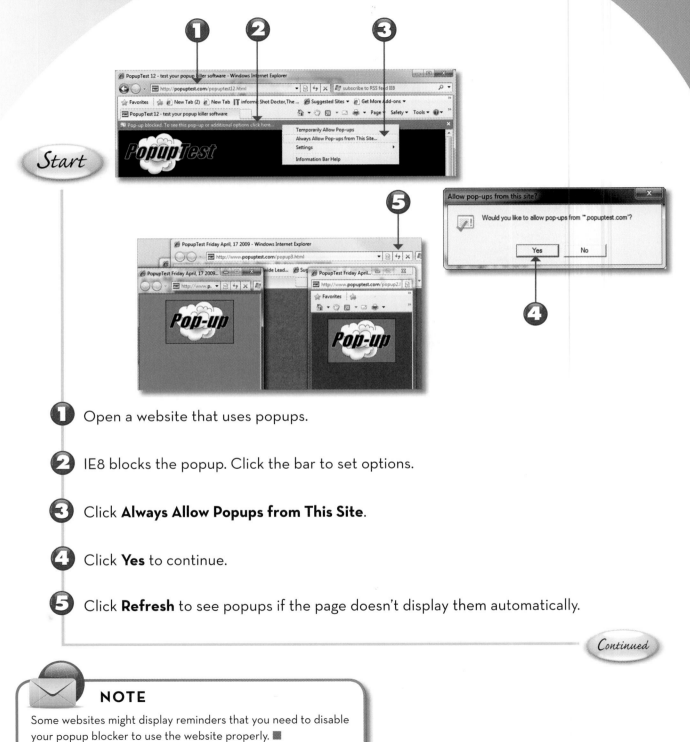

1 Open a website that uses popups.

2 IE8 blocks the popup. Click the bar to set options.

3 Click **Always Allow Popups from This Site**.

4 Click **Yes** to continue.

5 Click **Refresh** to see popups if the page doesn't display them automatically.

Continued

NOTE

Some websites might display reminders that you need to disable your popup blocker to use the website properly. ■

6 To view allowed sites or adjust settings, click **Tools**.

7 Click **Pop-Up Blocker**.

8 Click **Pop-Up Blocker Settings**.

9 Sites on the allowed list.

10 Click to close dialog.

End

NOTE

You can manually enter websites to the allowed list, remove some or all listed websites from the allowed list, or adjust other settings with the Pop-Up Blocker Settings dialog. ■

SETTING INTERNET PRIVACY FEATURES

The Internet Options setting in Tools is used to configure many features of Internet Explorer 8, including privacy features. Here's how to protect your privacy.

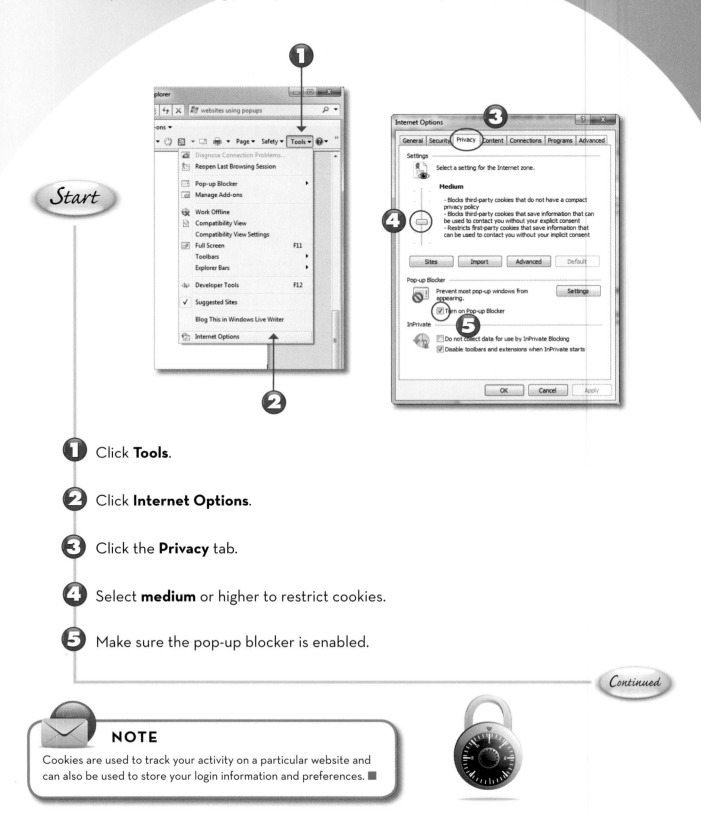

Start

1 Click **Tools**.

2 Click **Internet Options**.

3 Click the **Privacy** tab.

4 Select **medium** or higher to restrict cookies.

5 Make sure the pop-up blocker is enabled.

Continued

NOTE

Cookies are used to track your activity on a particular website and can also be used to store your login information and preferences. ■

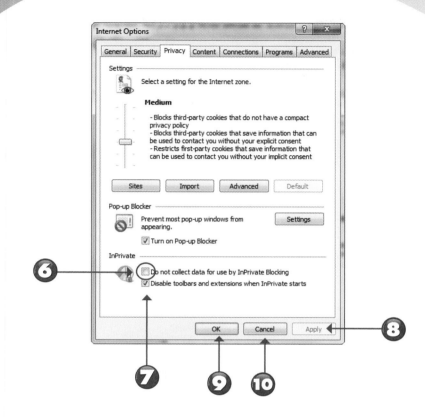

6 Make sure the "**Do Not Collect Data**" box is not checked.

7 Make sure the "**Disable Toolbars**" box is checked.

8 If you need to make changes, click here.

9 Click to close the dialog after making changes.

10 Click to cancel changes.

End

NOTE

If you are unsure of the setting to use for Privacy, read the description next to the Privacy slider for each setting. ∎

DELETING SELECTED ITEMS FROM YOUR HISTORY LIST

Internet Explorer 8 enables you to delete specified listings on your website history. Here's how.

1 Open the History menu on your address bar.

2 Select an entry you want to remove.

3 Click the **X**.

4 The entry is removed.

End

NOTE

To delete additional items from the history list, repeat Steps 1-3. ■

DELETING ALL ITEMS FROM YOUR HISTORY LIST

Internet Explorer 8 also enables you to clear all items from your History list, as well as other files created during web surfing.

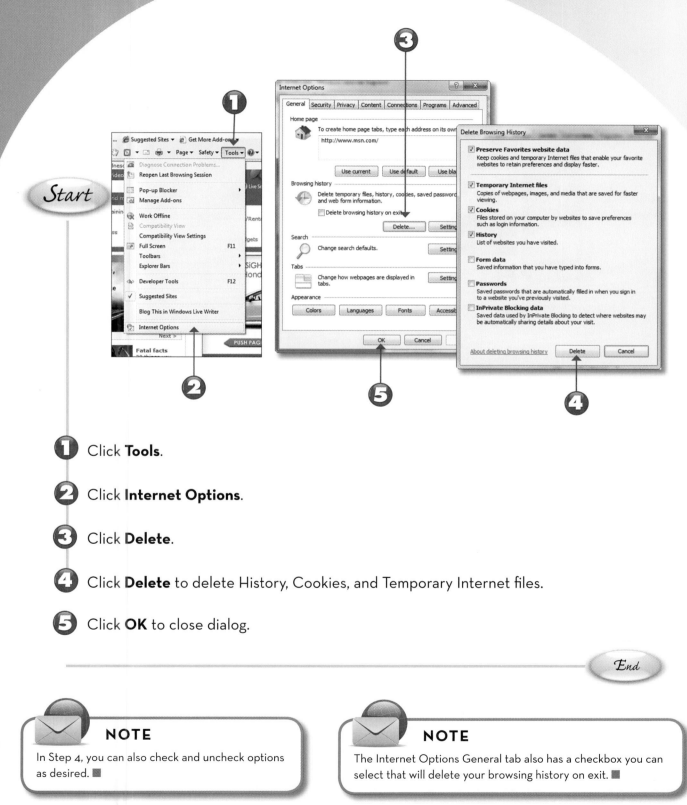

1. Click **Tools**.

2. Click **Internet Options**.

3. Click **Delete**.

4. Click **Delete** to delete History, Cookies, and Temporary Internet files.

5. Click **OK** to close dialog.

NOTE

In Step 4, you can also check and uncheck options as desired. ■

NOTE

The Internet Options General tab also has a checkbox you can select that will delete your browsing history on exit. ■

EMAILING LINKS

You can email links to your favorite web pages using IE8's right-click menu. In this example, we'll use Windows Live Email, part of the optional Windows Live Essentials package (see Chapter 17 for more information).

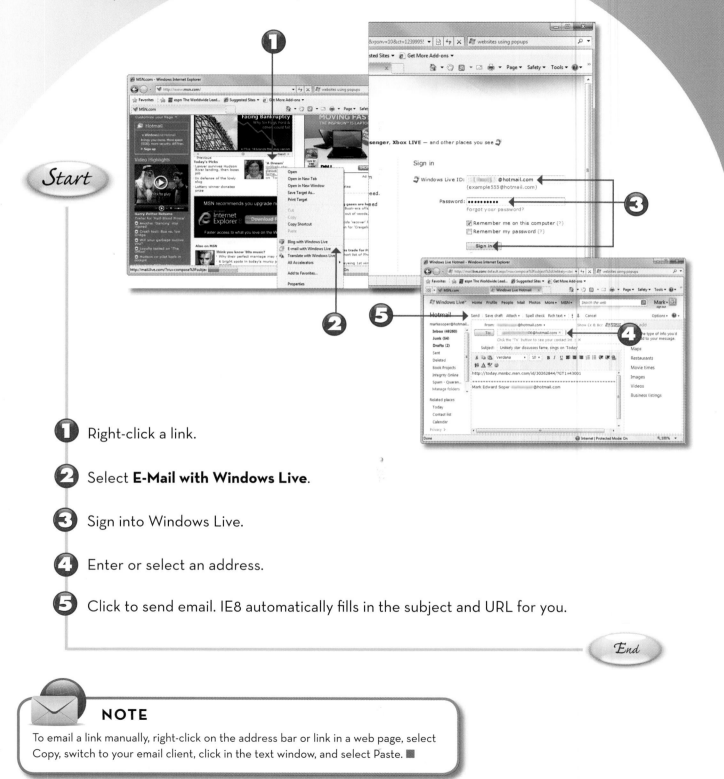

1 Right-click a link.

2 Select **E-Mail with Windows Live**.

3 Sign into Windows Live.

4 Enter or select an address.

5 Click to send email. IE8 automatically fills in the subject and URL for you.

NOTE

To email a link manually, right-click on the address bar or link in a web page, select Copy, switch to your email client, click in the text window, and select Paste. ▪

PRINTING A WEB PAGE

Internet Explorer 8, like IE7, enables you to print web pages intelligently. Whether you want to save paper or make full-size page printouts, IE8 does the job the way you want it.

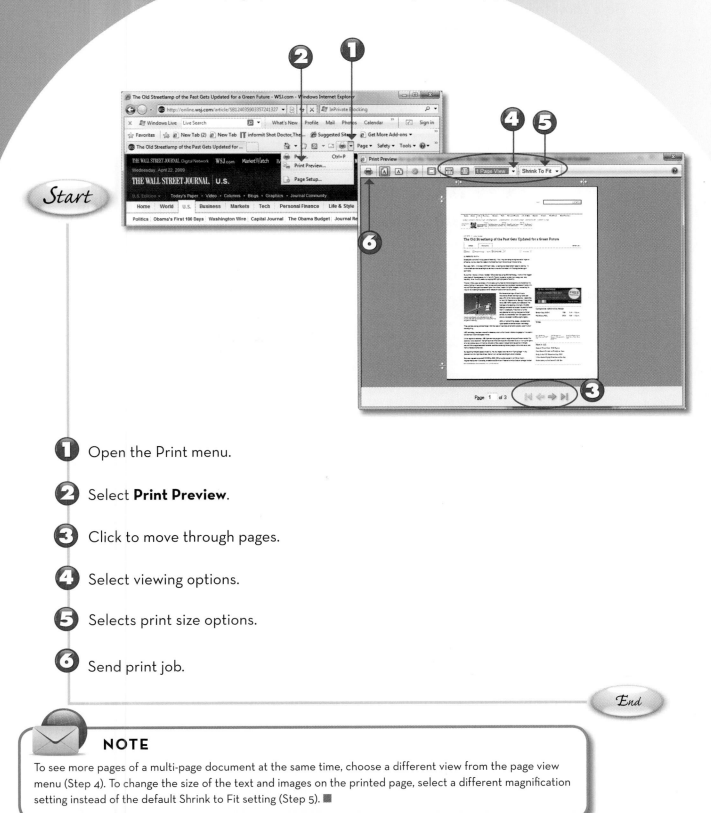

Start

1 Open the Print menu.

2 Select **Print Preview**.

3 Click to move through pages.

4 Select viewing options.

5 Selects print size options.

6 Send print job.

End

NOTE

To see more pages of a multi-page document at the same time, choose a different view from the page view menu (Step 4). To change the size of the text and images on the printed page, select a different magnification setting instead of the default Shrink to Fit setting (Step 5). ■

SAVING A WEB PAGE

Internet Explorer 8 can save web pages as a single MHTML (also known as web archive) file for easy retrieval or emailing to other users. You can also save pages in other formats. Here's how to build a library of web pages.

1 Open the Page menu.

2 Select **Save As**.

Continued

NOTE

You can save your web pages to any folder. ■

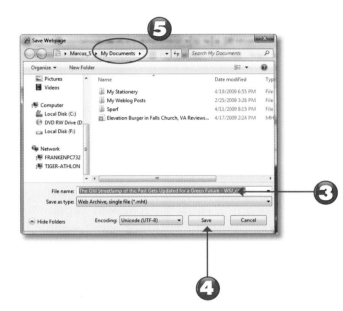

5

3 Enter a different name if desired.

4 Click **Save**.

5 The page is saved in your My Documents folder by default.

End

NOTE

To choose a different file format than the default web archive, open the Save As Type menu. Other options include Web Page, Complete (saves images and other components to a folder below the target folder); Web Page, HTML (saves HTML only); or Text (plain text only). ■

Chapter 11

USER ACCOUNTS AND SYSTEM SECURITY

Windows 7 is designed to be the most secure version of Windows ever developed. However, part of keeping you and your family as secure as possible depends on you. In this chapter, you'll learn how to set up multiple users on a PC, select the right account type for different users, enable Parental Controls, use Windows Defender to protect your system from spyware, and use Action Center to find out how secure and well-maintained your system is.

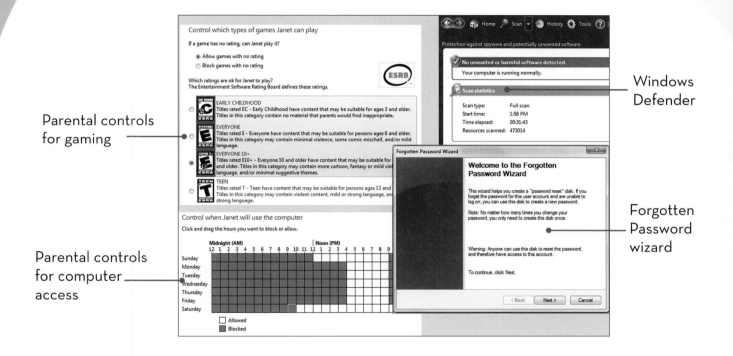

Parental controls for gaming

Parental controls for computer access

Windows Defender

Forgotten Password wizard

SETTING UP WINDOWS 7 FOR MULTIPLE USERS

If you share your PC with other users, whether they're adults, teenagers, or children, you should set up different accounts for each user. Here's how to use Control Panel to create a standard account.

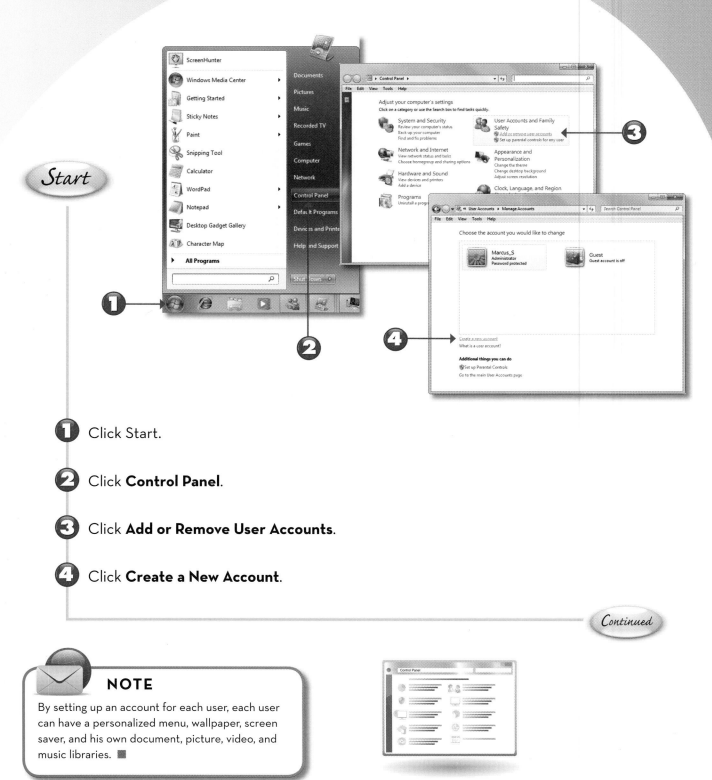

Start

1. Click Start.

2. Click **Control Panel**.

3. Click **Add or Remove User Accounts**.

4. Click **Create a New Account**.

Continued

NOTE

By setting up an account for each user, each user can have a personalized menu, wallpaper, screen saver, and his own document, picture, video, and music libraries. ■

5 Enter a name for the new user.

6 Select **Standard User**.

7 Click **Create Account**.

8 The user account is created.

End

NOTE

Most systems need only one administrator. An administrator can perform all management tasks without providing a password. Other users of the same system should be set up as standard users. Standard users can perform tasks that are not marked with the Windows security shield, but if they try to perform a shield-marked task, they will usually need to provide the password for the system's administrator. This function is configured by User Account Control (UAC). ■

CHANGING ACCOUNT SETTINGS

When you set up a new account, you're not prompted to select a photo, set up a password, or select other options. Here's how to access the menu to make those changes. In this example, we'll change the picture for a user's account.

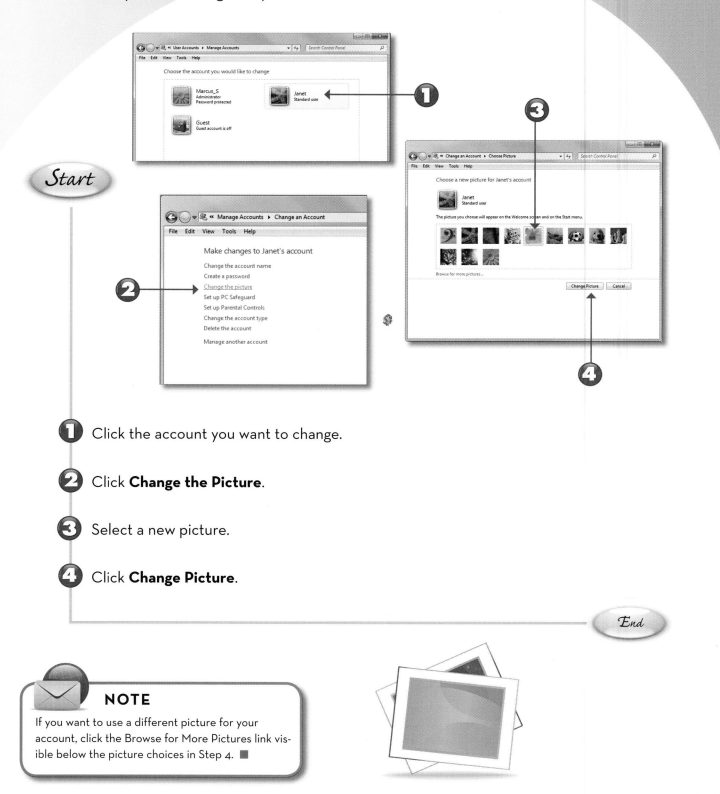

1 Click the account you want to change.

2 Click **Change the Picture**.

3 Select a new picture.

4 Click **Change Picture**.

NOTE

If you want to use a different picture for your account, click the Browse for More Pictures link visible below the picture choices in Step 4. ■

ADDING/CHANGING A PASSWORD

When you create a new user account, you are not required to set up a password for that account. However, it's usually a good idea to set up a password as soon as you set up a new user. Adding a password helps prevent unauthorized users from using the computer. Here's how to do it.

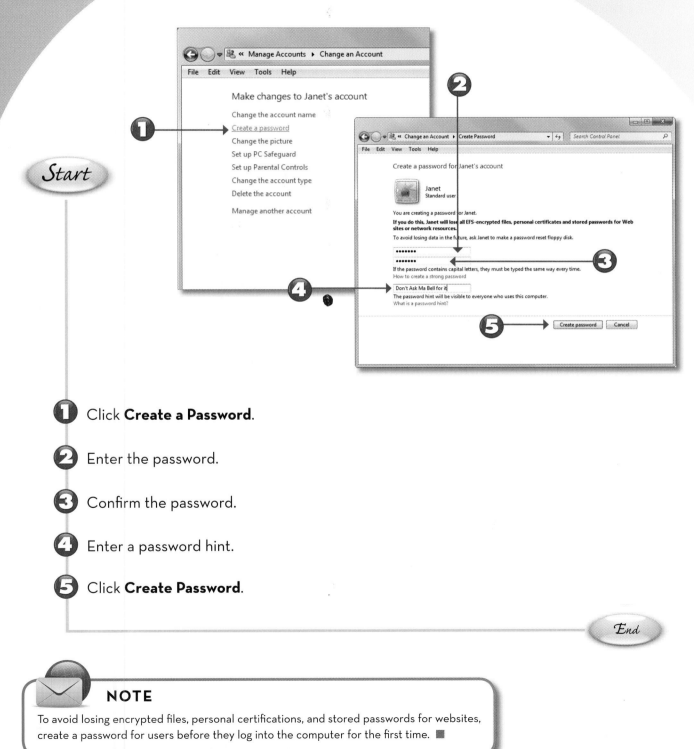

1 Click **Create a Password**.

2 Enter the password.

3 Confirm the password.

4 Enter a password hint.

5 Click **Create Password**.

NOTE

To avoid losing encrypted files, personal certifications, and stored passwords for websites, create a password for users before they log into the computer for the first time. ■

CREATING A PASSWORD RESET DISK

If a password is lost, a user is "locked out" of their files. If the administrator loses the password, there's no way for anyone to access their files (an administrator can access files belonging to users). To prevent this kind of disaster, create a password reset disk. Even if the user doesn't use a password, making a password reset disk is important, because the user will still be able to access files, even if someone else adds a password to the account. In this example, you'll learn how to make a password reset disk for the current user's account.

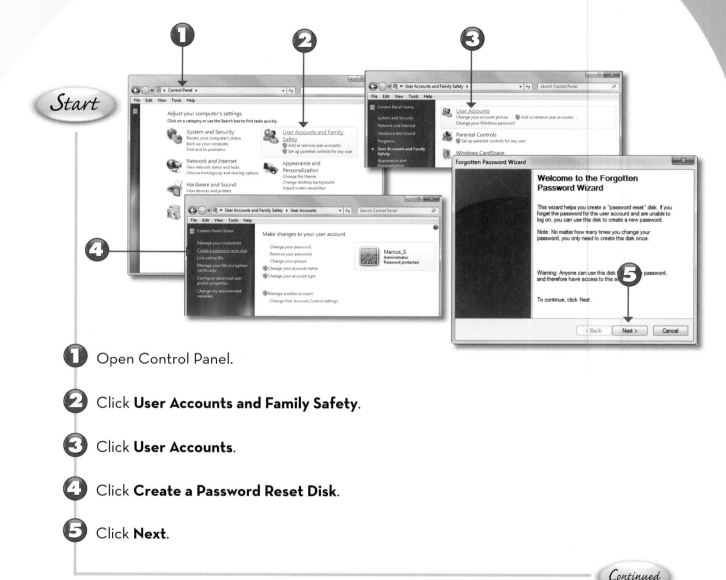

1 Open Control Panel.

2 Click **User Accounts and Family Safety**.

3 Click **User Accounts**.

4 Click **Create a Password Reset Disk**.

5 Click **Next**.

Continued

NOTE

Each user must make his own password reset disk. The password information uses very little space, so you can use virtually any flash drive or flash memory card. When the process is complete, mark the disk or flash drive "Password Reset" and put it in a safe place. ■

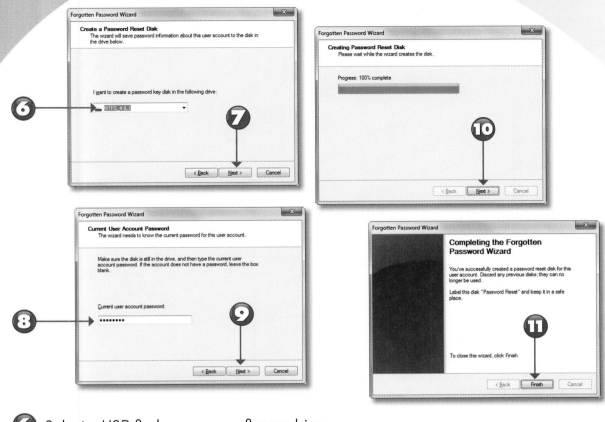

6 Select a USB flash memory or floppy drive.

7 Click **Next**.

8 Enter the current password.

9 Click **Next**.

10 Click **Next**.

11 Click **Finish**.

End

ENABLING PARENTAL CONTROLS

Windows 7 includes several features designed to protect underage computer users, including time limits, game access limits, and program access limits. These features are collectively known as Parental Controls. This section shows you how an administrator enables and configures Parental Controls for a standard user. In this tutorial, you learn how to set up time limits and game rating limits.

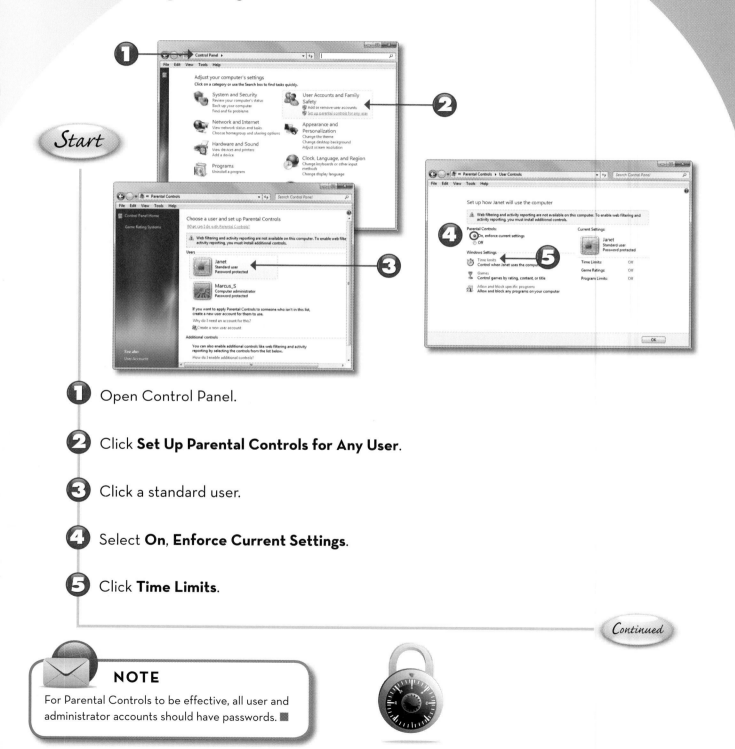

Start

1 Open Control Panel.

2 Click **Set Up Parental Controls for Any User**.

3 Click a standard user.

4 Select **On, Enforce Current Settings**.

5 Click **Time Limits**.

Continued

NOTE

For Parental Controls to be effective, all user and administrator accounts should have passwords. ▬

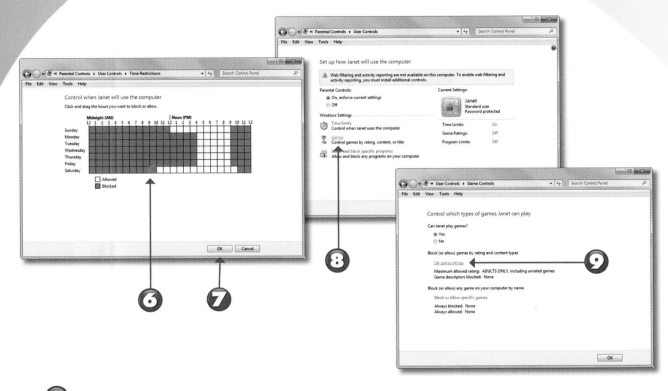

6 Click and drag the mouse across the hours when you want to prevent computer access.

7 Click **OK**.

8 Click **Games**.

9 Click **Set Game Ratings**.

Continued

NOTE

You can also block specific programs with the dialog shown in Step 8. ■

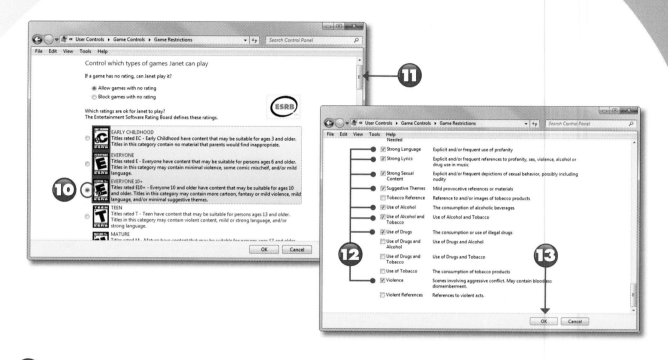

10 Select the maximum allowed rating.

11 Scroll down to select game descriptors.

12 Check the descriptors you want to use to block unsuitable games.

13 Click **OK**.

Continued

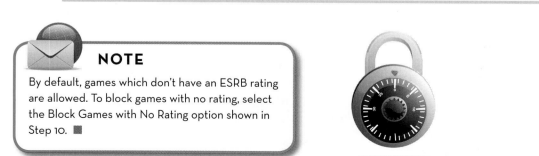

NOTE

By default, games which don't have an ESRB rating are allowed. To block games with no rating, select the Block Games with No Rating option shown in Step 10. ∎

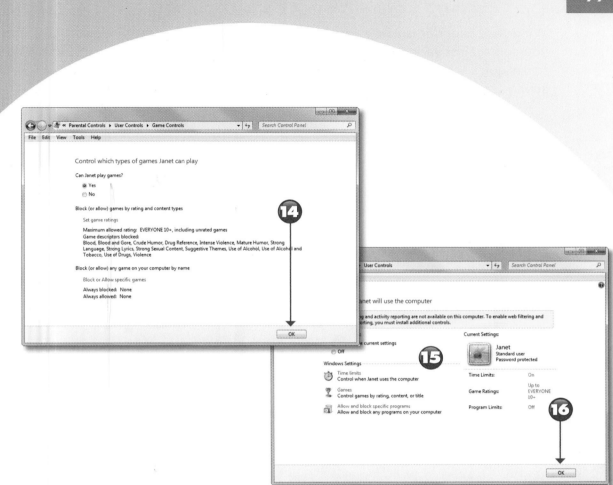

14 Click **OK**.

15 Review settings.

16 Click **OK**.

End

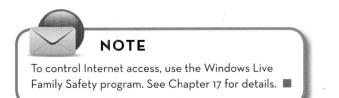

NOTE

To control Internet access, use the Windows Live Family Safety program. See Chapter 17 for details. ■

CHECKING FOR SPYWARE WITH WINDOWS DEFENDER

Windows Defender is a free anti-spyware program included in Windows 7. Use it to protect yourself against various types of spyware and malware. Although Windows Defender performs quick scans daily, you can also use it to perform full scans at your direction. Use this section to learn how to start and run Windows Defender.

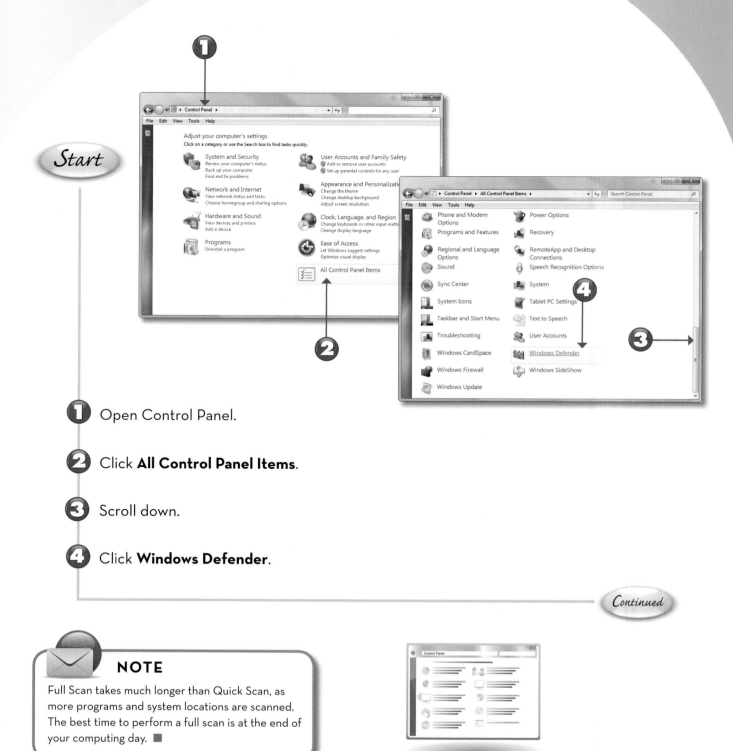

Start

1 Open Control Panel.

2 Click **All Control Panel Items**.

3 Scroll down.

4 Click **Windows Defender**.

Continued

NOTE

Full Scan takes much longer than Quick Scan, as more programs and system locations are scanned. The best time to perform a full scan is at the end of your computing day. ■

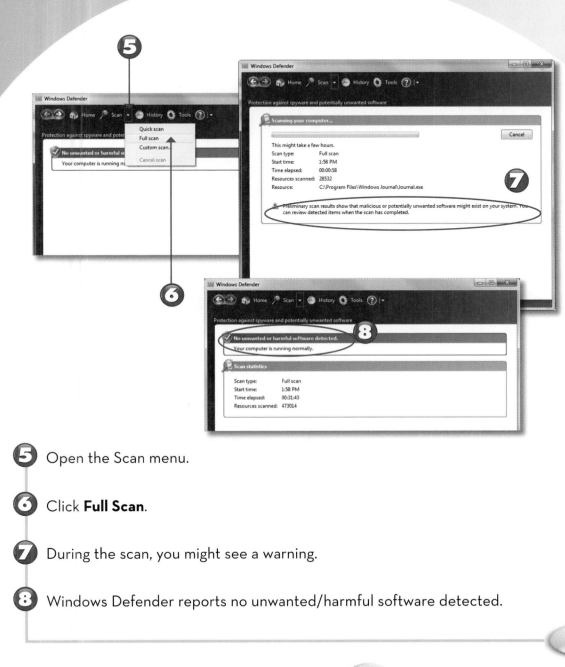

5 Open the Scan menu.

6 Click **Full Scan**.

7 During the scan, you might see a warning.

8 Windows Defender reports no unwanted/harmful software detected.

End

NOTE

By default, Windows Defender performs a quick scan each day at 2:00 AM. Use the Options menu to change the scheduled time and other settings as needed. ■

SETTING WINDOWS DEFENDER OPTIONS

Windows Defender's standard settings work well for most users, but if you want to adjust the protection it provides, you can make changes to those settings. In this tutorial, you learn how to enable additional protection settings.

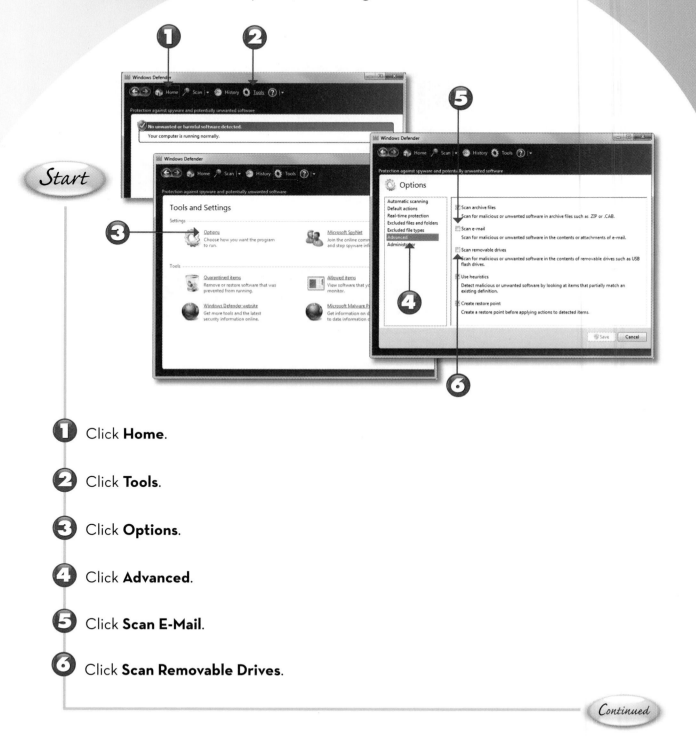

1 Click **Home**.

2 Click **Tools**.

3 Click **Options**.

4 Click **Advanced**.

5 Click **Scan E-Mail**.

6 Click **Scan Removable Drives**.

Continued

7 Click **Save**.

8 Click **Close**.

End

NOTE

When you save changes (Step 7), a UAC prompt might appear. ■

USING ACTION CENTER

Action Center is a new feature of Windows 7, combining security and troubleshooting features. Action Center displays an icon in the notification area if there are problems with your system.

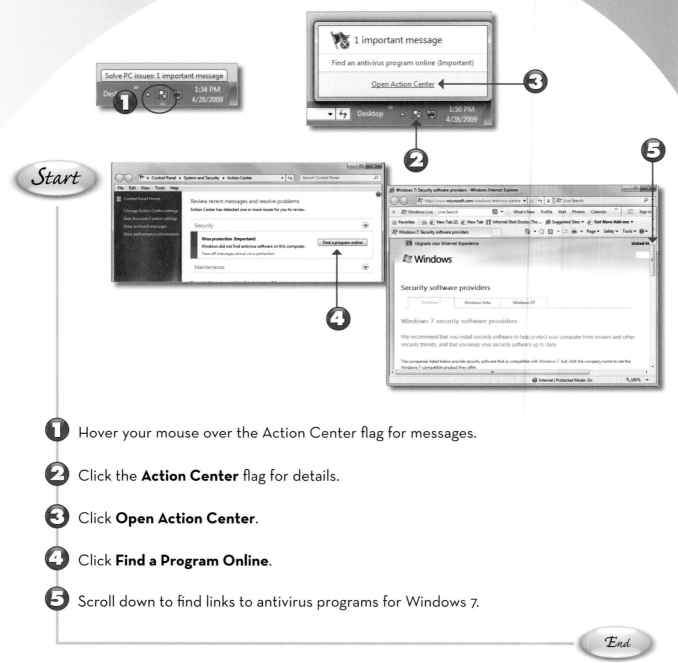

1. Hover your mouse over the Action Center flag for messages.

2. Click the **Action Center** flag for details.

3. Click **Open Action Center**.

4. Click **Find a Program Online**.

5. Scroll down to find links to antivirus programs for Windows 7.

NOTE

To learn more about an antivirus vendor, or to install an antivirus program, scroll down and click a vendor name. ■

NOTE

Action Center will always display a warning if you do not have an antivirus program installed and running. It also checks for unreported problems. ■

REPORTING PROBLEMS WITH ACTION CENTER

Action Center can also be used to report system problems and look for possible solutions.

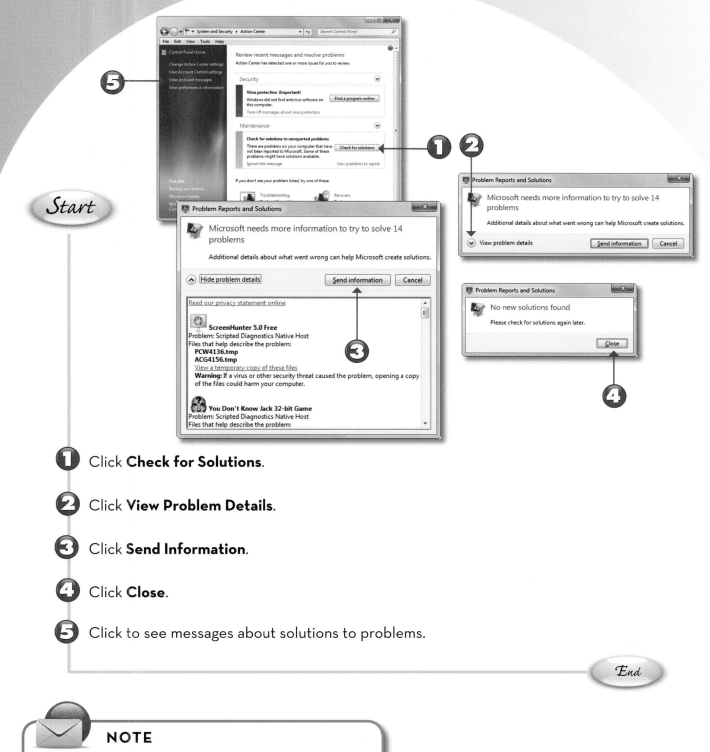

Start

1 Click **Check for Solutions**.

2 Click **View Problem Details**.

3 Click **Send Information**.

4 Click **Close**.

5 Click to see messages about solutions to problems.

End

NOTE

You will be prompted to send information only if Microsoft requests additional information about a problem. ■

Chapter 12

PERSONALIZING WINDOWS 7

Windows 7 makes the process of personalizing your desktop's wallpaper, color scheme, and sound effects easier than ever before. In this chapter, you'll learn how to use the Personalization, Screen Resolution, and Accessibility menus to make the PC running Windows 7 a truly "personal" computer.

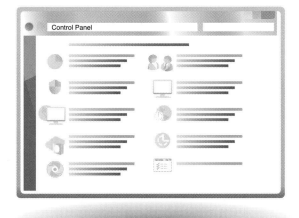

Select the type of desktop background (wallpaper) you want, and save it as part of a theme

Whether you use one or more monitors, use the Screen Resolution dialog to detect, identify, and adjust the settings for each display

OPENING THE PERSONALIZATION MENU FROM THE DESKTOP

The Personalization menu provides the fast track to changing the appearance of the Windows 7 desktop, system sound effects, and other visual and audio features. The Personalization menu can be opened directly from the desktop or from the Control Panel.

1 Right-click an empty space on the desktop.

2 Select **Personalize**.

3 The Personalization menu appears.

End

NOTE

You can also place gadgets on the desktop or adjust screen resolution from the right-click menu shown in Step 2. ■

OPENING THE PERSONALIZATION MENU FROM CONTROL PANEL

Although you might find it faster to open the Personalization menu from the desktop, if you are already working with Control Panel, or if your desktop is covered with open windows, you might find it more convenient to open the Personalization menu from within Control Panel.

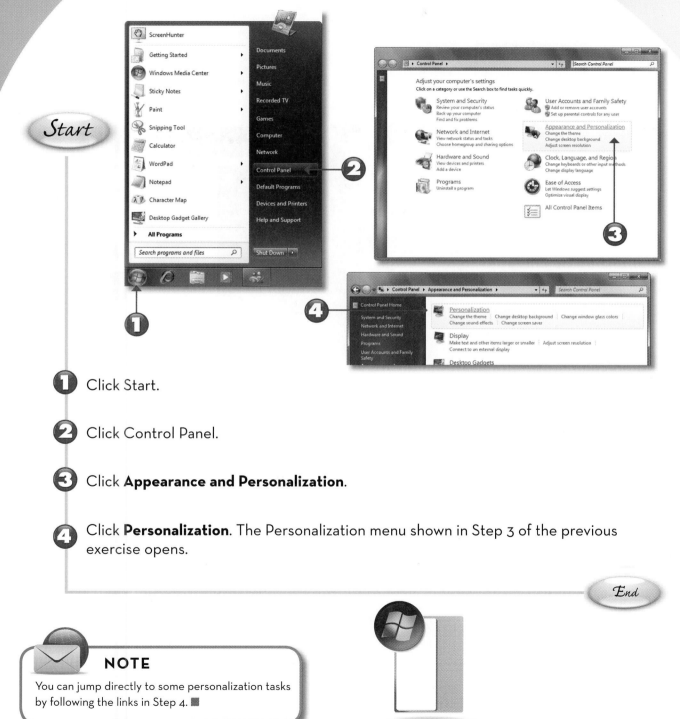

1 Click Start.

2 Click Control Panel.

3 Click **Appearance and Personalization**.

4 Click **Personalization**. The Personalization menu shown in Step 3 of the previous exercise opens.

NOTE

You can jump directly to some personalization tasks by following the links in Step 4. ■

SELECTING A DESKTOP THEME

Windows 7 uses the term "desktop theme" to refer to the combination of the desktop background, window color, sounds, and screen saver. In this exercise, you learn how to select and use an existing theme. You can also create your own desktop theme, as you will see in later exercises.

Start

1. From the Personalization menu, scroll down to view the existing Windows themes.

2. Click a theme.

3. The desktop background changes in accordance with the theme.

4. The window color and other settings might also change.

5. Close the window to retain the changes.

End

NOTE

You can download additional themes by clicking the Get More Themes Online link. ■

CHANGING THE WINDOW COLOR

You can create your own unique theme by changing its components. In this exercise, you learn how to select a new color for the window and how to adjust its transparency (your system must support Windows Aero to support transparent windows).

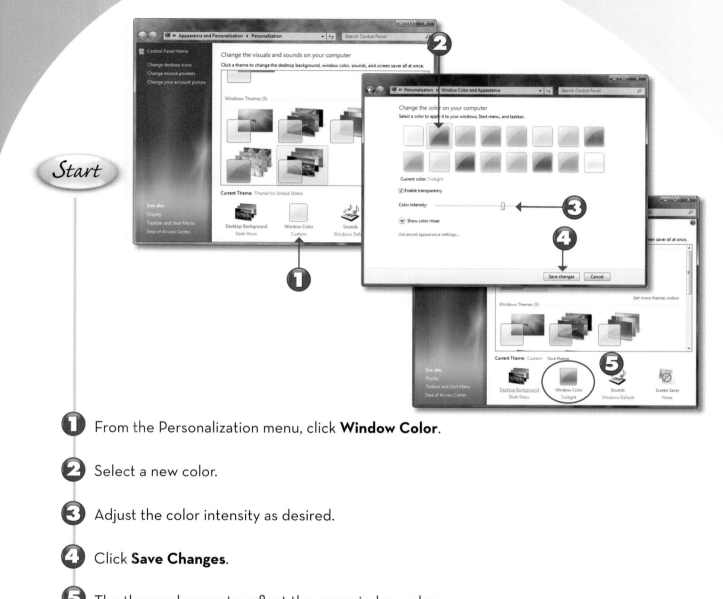

1 From the Personalization menu, click **Window Color**.

2 Select a new color.

3 Adjust the color intensity as desired.

4 Click **Save Changes**.

5 The theme changes to reflect the new window color.

NOTE

You can also choose from additional colors by clicking the Show Color Mixer button before selecting a new color. ■

CHOOSING A DESKTOP BACKGROUND

Your desktop background can be a solid color or can use a photograph, slide show, or a video. Using video as a desktop background adds extra interest to your desktop, but can slow down some systems. This exercise shows you how to select multiple photographs as your desktop background.

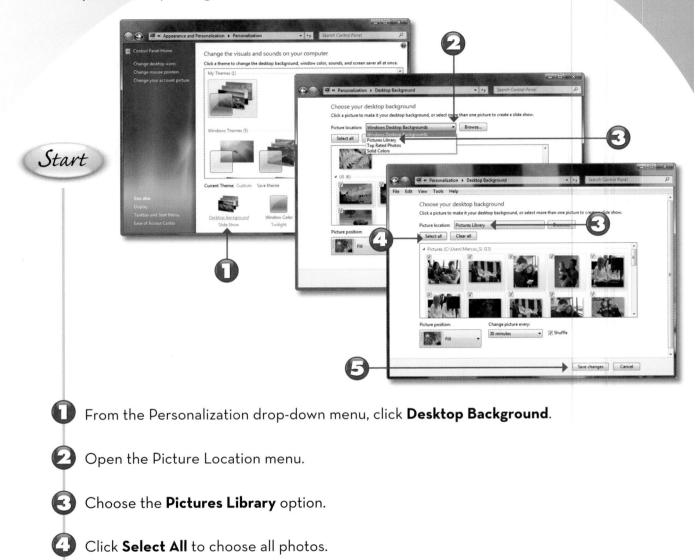

Start

End

1. From the Personalization drop-down menu, click **Desktop Background**.

2. Open the Picture Location menu.

3. Choose the **Pictures Library** option.

4. Click **Select All** to choose all photos.

5. Click **Save Changes**.

NOTE

To choose photos from a different location, click Browse. You can also use the Picture Position and Change Picture menus to change how your desktop will appear. ■

SELECTING A SCREEN SAVER

Monitors and projectors using various technologies can retain images displayed on-screen for long periods of time. To avoid this type of damage, you have two options: enable the screen saver feature built into Windows 7, or set your power management to turn off the screen after a specified period of time (see Chapter 13 for details). Using a screen saver helps you see that your computer is running, and you can configure your system to ask for a password to exit the screen saver. On the other hand, turning off the monitor can save a bit of power.

If you prefer to use a screen saver, keep in mind that some standard themes do not include screen savers. Don't assume that your Windows installation has a screen saver set up unless you do it yourself.

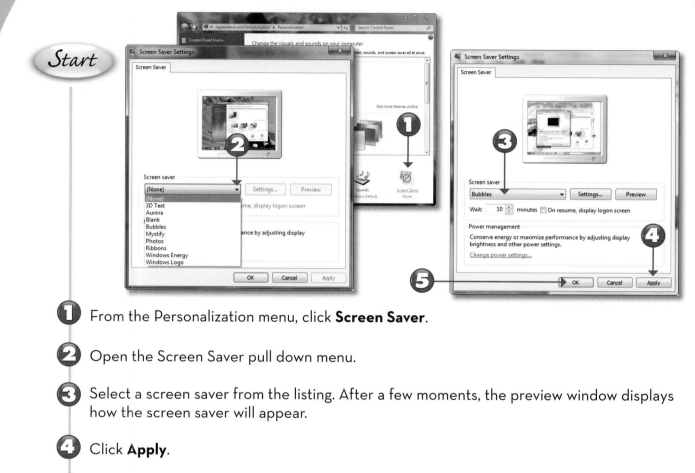

1. From the Personalization menu, click **Screen Saver**.

2. Open the Screen Saver pull down menu.

3. Select a screen saver from the listing. After a few moments, the preview window displays how the screen saver will appear.

4. Click **Apply**.

5. Click **OK**.

NOTE

To protect your system from tampering when you're away from it, enable the On Resume, Display Logon Screen checkbox. ∎

ENABLING AND USING MULTIPLE MONITORS

When you connect an external monitor or projector to a laptop's VGA, DVI, or HDMI port, or you connect a second monitor to a desktop computer, Windows 7 automatically detects the monitor. However, you must enable the additional display and specify how you want to use it before you can use it. In this tutorial, you learn how to extend your desktop to the secondary display.

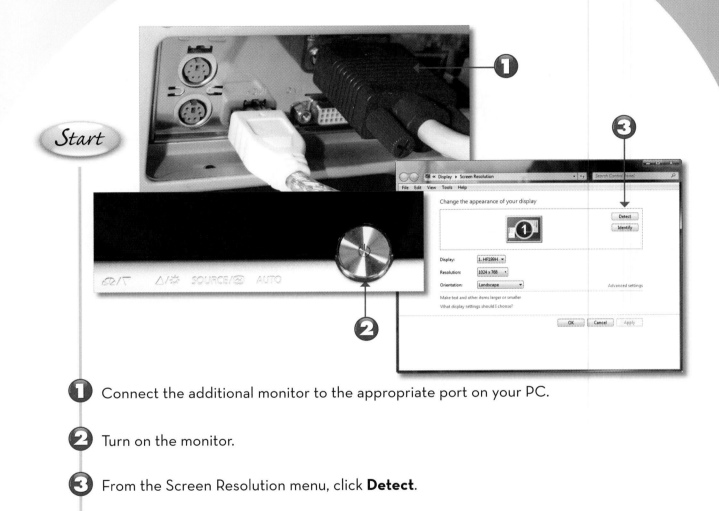

Start

1 Connect the additional monitor to the appropriate port on your PC.

2 Turn on the monitor.

3 From the Screen Resolution menu, click **Detect**.

Continued

NOTE

You can also use this feature with composite, component, or S-video ports. ■

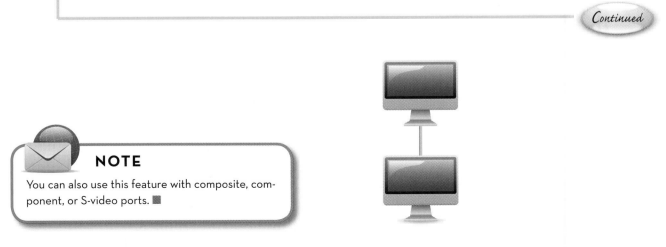

Display Settings

Do you want to keep these display settings?

Keep changes   **Revert**

Reverting to previous display settings in 5 seconds.

4 Select the newly-detected display.

5 Select **Extend These Displays**. The desktop appears on the secondary display, as well as the primary display.

6 Click **Apply**.

7 Click **Keep Changes**.

8 Click **OK**.

End

NOTE

To show the same information on two displays or on a display and a projector, select Duplicate These Displays in Step 5. You might need to set both displays for the same resolution (see next exercise). ■

ADJUSTING SCREEN RESOLUTION

To assure that you are getting the best-quality picture, you should make sure that your monitor is using the recommended screen resolution. If you switch to a larger monitor, you should repeat this process and adjust settings as needed.

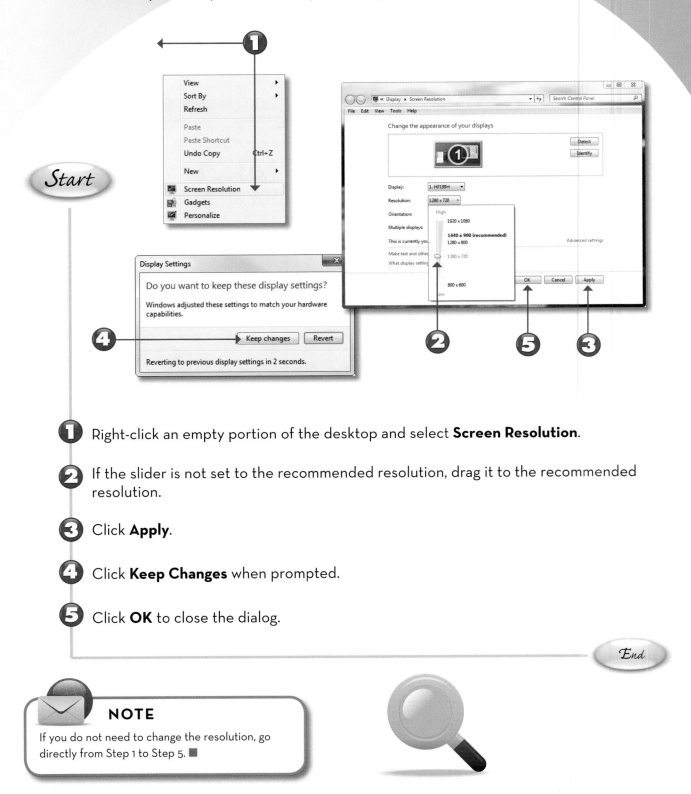

1 Right-click an empty portion of the desktop and select **Screen Resolution**.

2 If the slider is not set to the recommended resolution, drag it to the recommended resolution.

3 Click **Apply**.

4 Click **Keep Changes** when prompted.

5 Click **OK** to close the dialog.

NOTE

If you do not need to change the resolution, go directly from Step 1 to Step 5. ■

ADJUSTING MOUSE SETTINGS

Your mouse or compatible pointing device is a very important part of your Windows experience. To make it better, you can adjust double-click speed, mouse pointer size, and many other settings. In this tutorial, you learn how to change the mouse pointer size.

1 From the Personalization menu, click **Change Mouse Pointers**.

2 To choose a different size or style of mouse pointer, select it from the Scheme menu on the Pointers tab.

3 Click **Apply**.

4 Click **OK**.

NOTE

The Buttons tab is used to change double-click speed and to swap left and right mouse buttons. The Pointer Options tab includes various settings for changing mouse pointer visibility (other than pointer size). The Wheel tab is used to change how the mouse scroll and tilt wheel works. ■

USING A SOUND SCHEME

Windows 7 automatically assigns sounds to events such as starting or closing Windows, errors, and other events. You can assign new sounds to events, add sounds to events, and create a modified sound scheme you can save for reuse.

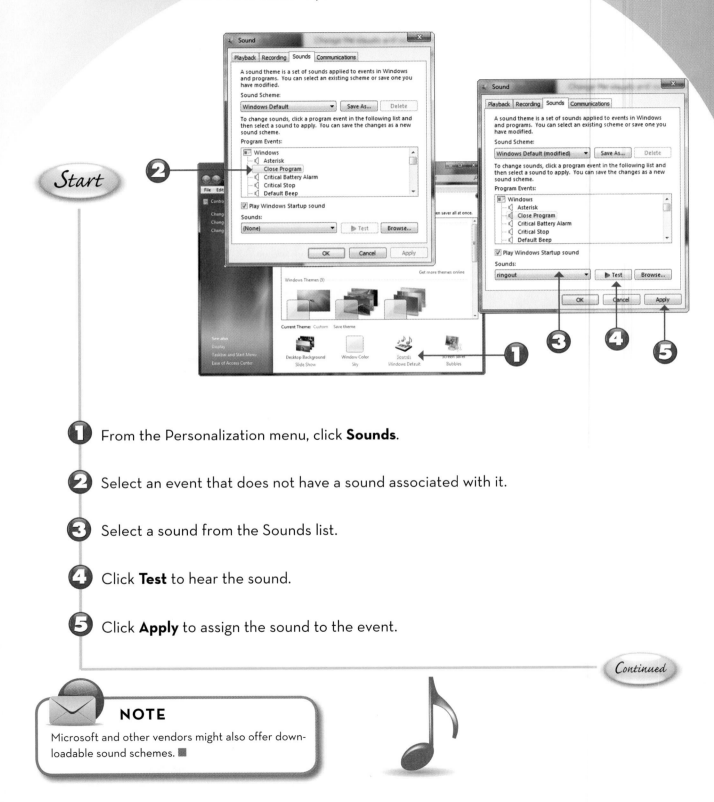

From the Personalization menu, click **Sounds**.

Select an event that does not have a sound associated with it.

Select a sound from the Sounds list.

Click **Test** to hear the sound.

Click **Apply** to assign the sound to the event.

Continued

NOTE

Microsoft and other vendors might also offer down-loadable sound schemes. ■

6 Click **Save As**.

7 Enter a name for the new sound scheme.

8 Click **OK**.

9 The new sound scheme is used in place of the previous one.

End

NOTE

To save the desktop background, window color, sounds, and screen saver as a new theme, click Save Theme and follow the prompts. ■

SETTING THE DATE AND TIME

If your computer doesn't have the correct date and time, all your files will be incorrectly date/time stamped. Use this tutorial to make any changes needed.

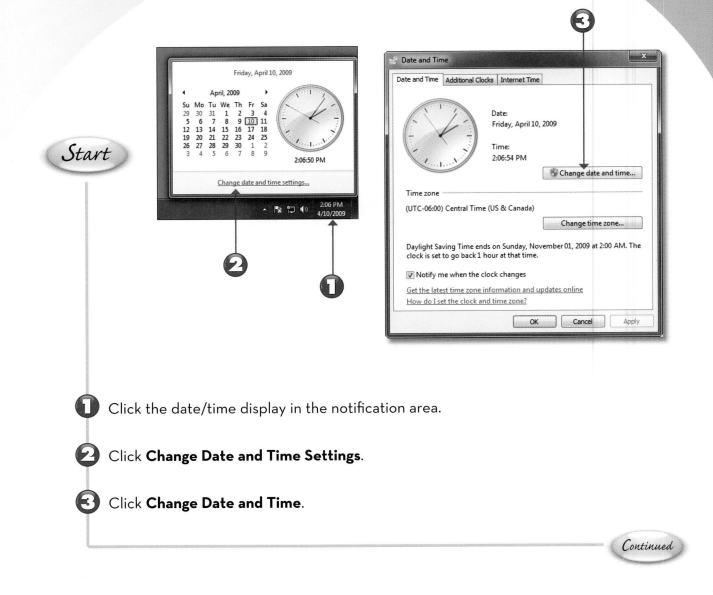

Start

① Click the date/time display in the notification area.

② Click **Change Date and Time Settings**.

③ Click **Change Date and Time**.

Continued

NOTE

Even if the date and time are correct, the time zone setting may be incorrect. The dialog in Step 3 shows the current time zone and a menu for changing the setting. ■

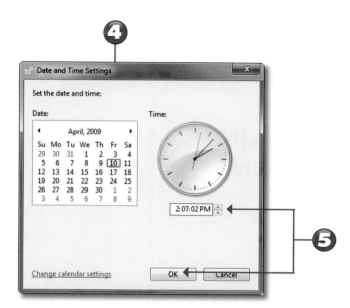

4 Click the new date.

5 Enter the new time by selecting hours, minutes, seconds, AM/PM, and using the arrows.

End

NOTE

To close the dialogs, click OK. ■

NOTE

Use the arrow buttons next to the month and year to change to a different month. Click the correct day to change to a different day. ■

SYSTEM MAINTENANCE AND PERFORMANCE

Windows 7 includes many features designed to help keep your computer running fast and reliably. This chapter discusses the most important features for the typical home user.

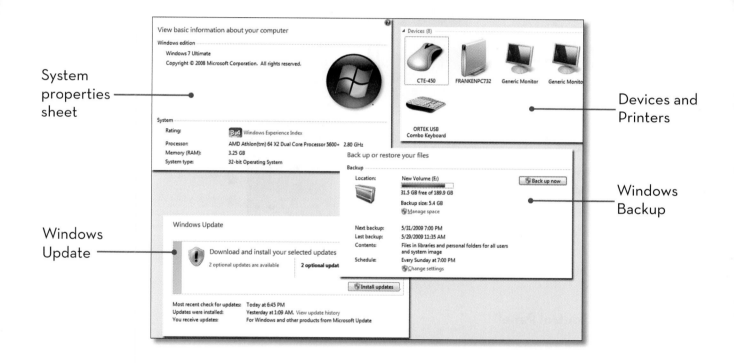

System properties sheet

Devices and Printers

Windows Backup

Windows Update

THE SYSTEM AND SECURITY CATEGORY IN CONTROL PANEL

The System and Security category in Control Panel is the starting point for most of the tasks covered in this chapter. This section shows you how to access this category.

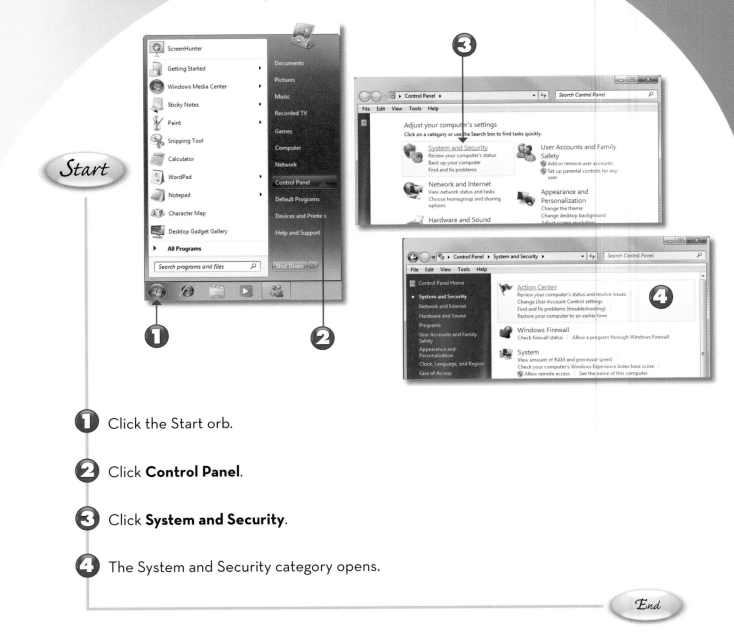

1 Click the Start orb.

2 Click **Control Panel**.

3 Click **System and Security**.

4 The System and Security category opens.

NOTE

Click the blue links shown to go directly to the most common tasks in any Control Panel menu. ■

NOTE

If Control Panel displays individual icons instead of categories, click Control Panel Home in the left pane to display categories. ■

DISPLAYING SYSTEM INFORMATION

Windows 7's System properties sheet provides a one-stop source for important system information, including processor type, speed, memory size, network information, and Windows version. Here's how to access it from the Control Panel.

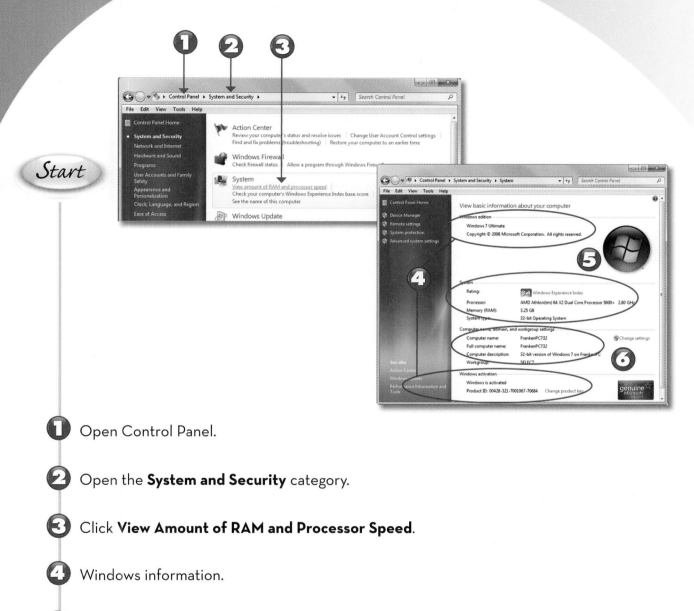

1 Open Control Panel.

2 Open the **System and Security** category.

3 Click **View Amount of RAM and Processor Speed**.

4 Windows information.

5 Hardware information.

6 Network information.

CONFIGURING WINDOWS UPDATE

By default, Windows Update automatically downloads and installs important updates. However, if you prefer to specify when to receive and install updates, you can change Windows Updates' default settings. Here's how.

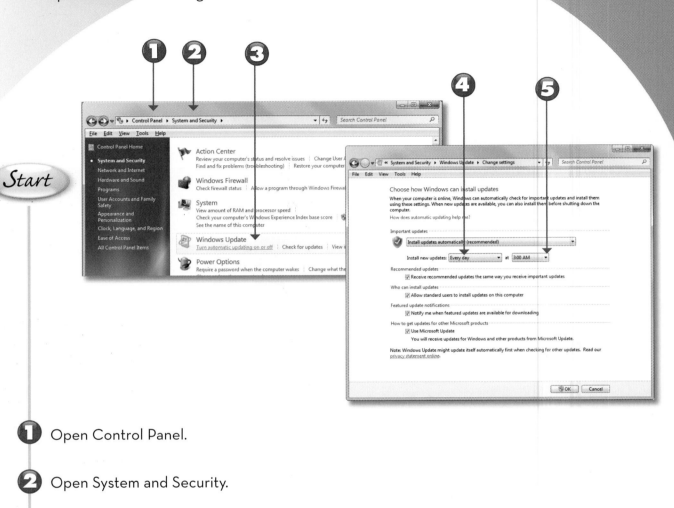

Start

1 Open Control Panel.

2 Open System and Security.

3 Click **Turn Automatic Updating On or Off**.

4 Click to change how often updates are installed.

5 Click to change at what time updates are installed.

Continued

NOTE

Select a time that the computer is on, but is not in use. ■

6

Choose how Windows can install updates

When your computer is online, Windows can automatically check for important updates and install them using these settings. When new updates are available, you can also install them before shutting down the computer.

How does automatic updating help me?

Important updates

Download updates but let me choose whether to install them

Install new updates: Every day   at   3:00 AM

Recommended updates

☑ Receive recommended updates the same way you receive important updates

Who can install updates

☑ Allow standard users to install updates on this computer

Featured update notifications

☑ Notify me when featured updates are available for downloading

How to get updates for other Microsoft products

☑ Use Microsoft Update

You will receive updates for Windows and other products from Microsoft Update.

Note: Windows Update might update itself automatically first when checking for other updates. Read our privacy statement online.

OK   Cancel

7

6 Choose this option if you want to install updates manually.

7 Click to save changes.

End

NOTE

Note the Windows security shield. Depending on how UAC is configured and whether you are an administrator or standard user, you might see an additional UAC prompt appear after you click OK. ■

UPDATING WINDOWS MANUALLY

If you find out about an important Windows update, you don't need to wait until Windows Update runs automatically to download and install the update. This tutorial shows you how to update Windows manually using Windows Update.

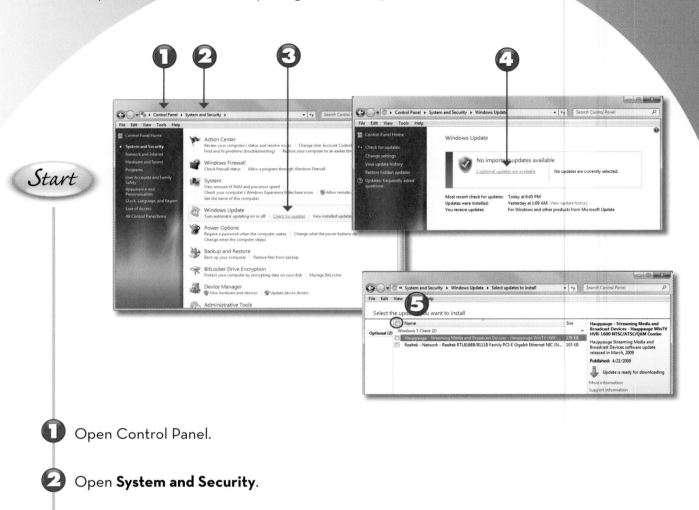

Start

1 Open Control Panel.

2 Open **System and Security**.

3 Click **Check for Updates**.

4 Click to start the installation process.

5 Click to select all updates.

Continued

NOTE

If there are no updates available, you will see a message to that effect in Step 4. ■

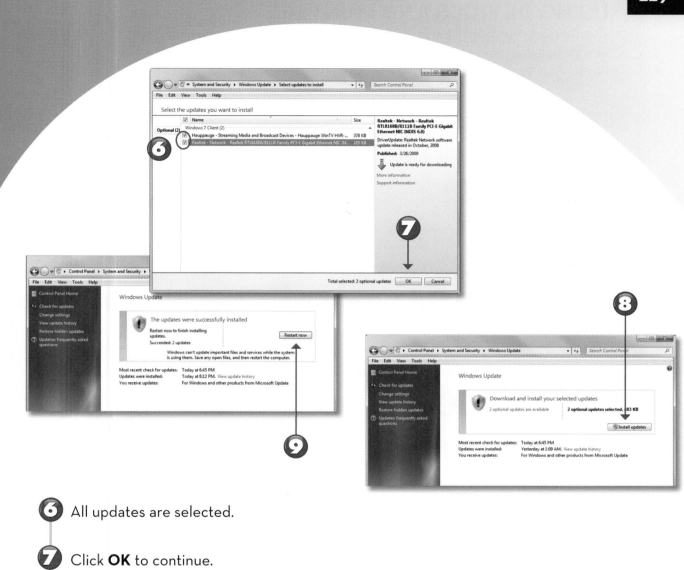

6 All updates are selected.

7 Click **OK** to continue.

8 Click Install Updates.

9 Click **Restart Now** if prompted to complete the process.

End

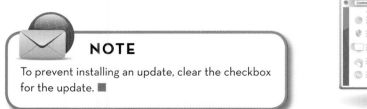

NOTE

To prevent installing an update, clear the checkbox for the update. ■

USING DEVICES AND PRINTERS

The Devices and Printers dialog is a brand-new feature in Windows 7, enabling you to see, at a glance, the drives, printers, and other devices connected to your PC and manage them. Here's how to use it.

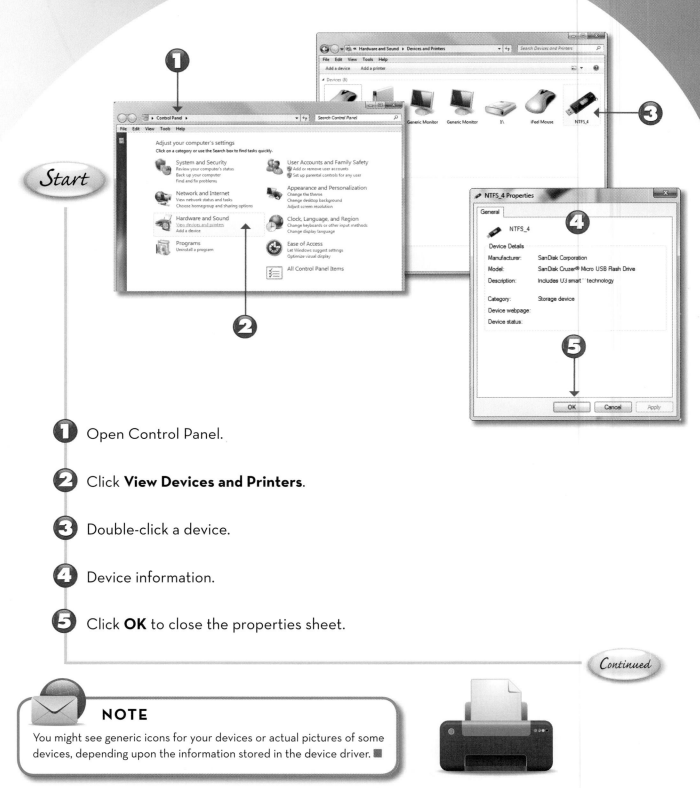

Start

1 Open Control Panel.

2 Click **View Devices and Printers**.

3 Double-click a device.

4 Device information.

5 Click **OK** to close the properties sheet.

Continued

NOTE

You might see generic icons for your devices or actual pictures of some devices, depending upon the information stored in the device driver. ■

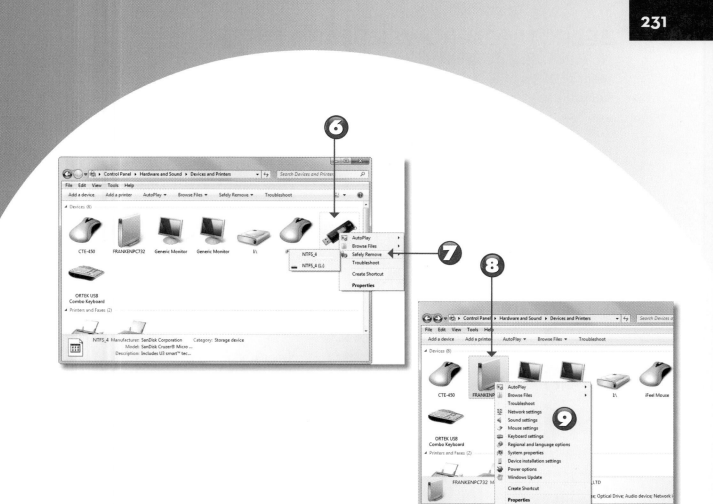

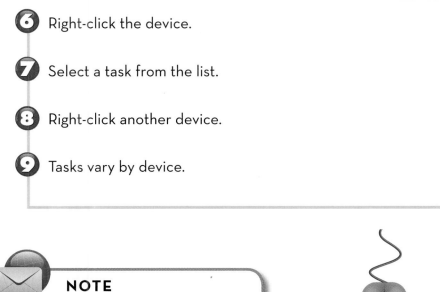

6 Right-click the device.

7 Select a task from the list.

8 Right-click another device.

9 Tasks vary by device.

End

NOTE

Use Devices and Printers to provide a quick way to the most common tasks you need to perform for each device. ■

SELECTING A POWER PLAN

No matter the type of computer you use for Windows 7, you can adjust the power management settings. You can choose to optimize for performance, for longer battery life and less heat (on a laptop) or lower utility bills (on a desktop), or strike a balance. This section shows you how to configure your system for high performance.

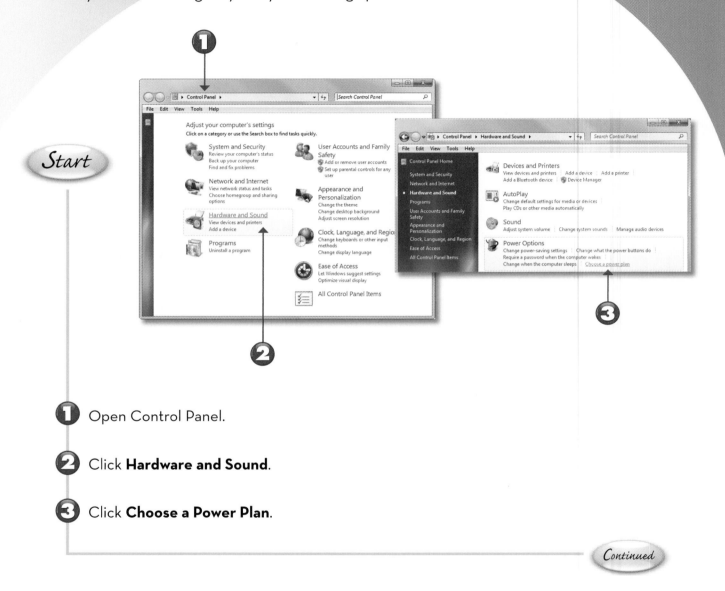

Start

1 Open Control Panel.

2 Click **Hardware and Sound**.

3 Click **Choose a Power Plan**.

Continued

NOTE

By default, Windows 7 uses the Balanced power plan for both desktop and portable computers. ■

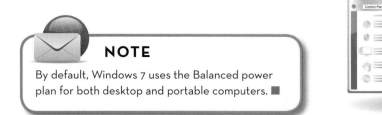

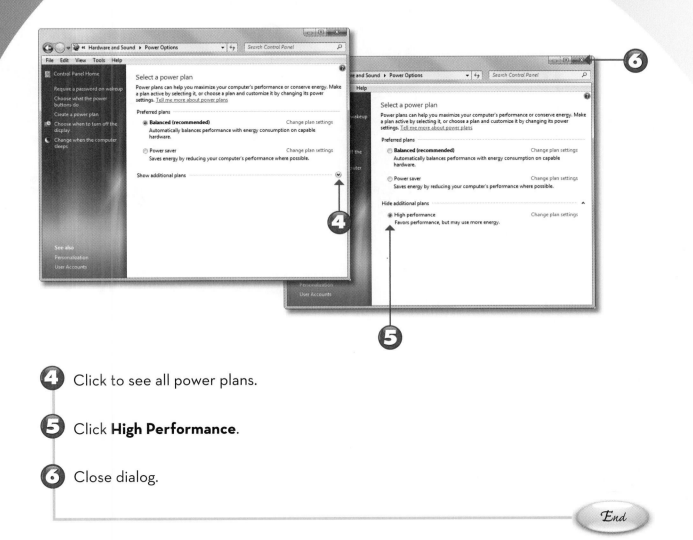

4 Click to see all power plans.

5 Click **High Performance**.

6 Close dialog.

End

NOTE

To change specific settings used by any power plan, click the Change Plan Settings link for the plan. ■

VIEWING DISK INFORMATION

Windows 7's Computer explorer provides several ways to view the drives connected to your computer. This tutorial demonstrates how to access the Computer explorer and change views.

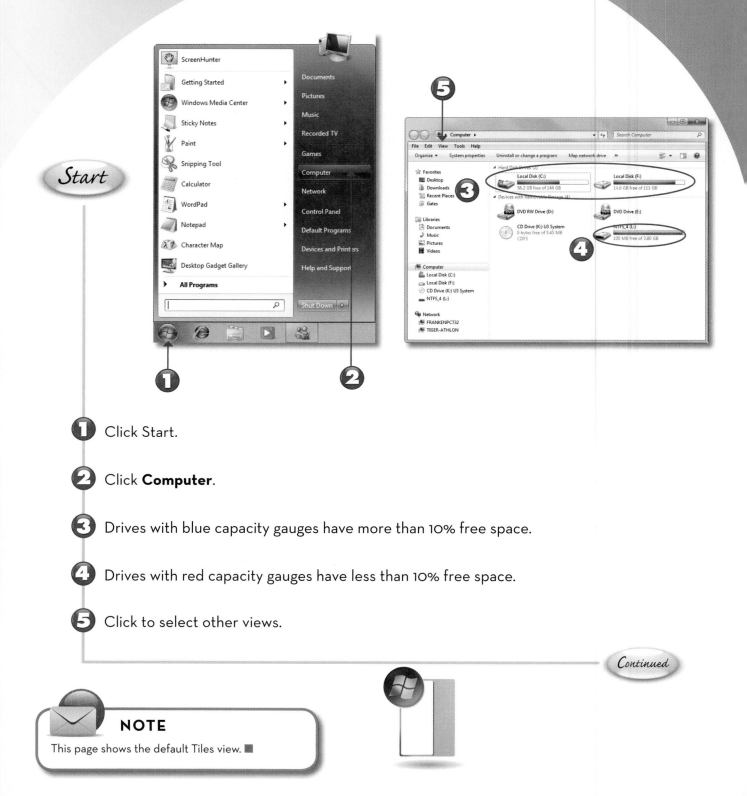

1 Click Start.

2 Click **Computer**.

3 Drives with blue capacity gauges have more than 10% free space.

4 Drives with red capacity gauges have less than 10% free space.

5 Click to select other views.

Continued

NOTE

This page shows the default Tiles view. ■

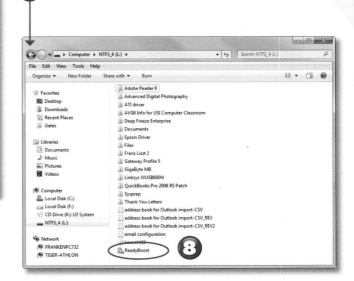

6 Contents view.

7 Double-click to display drive contents.

8 ReadyBoost cache file.

9 Click to return to previous view.

End

NOTE

To learn more about ReadyBoost (Step 8), see the next exercise. ■

USING READYBOOST

For systems with less than 1GB of RAM, adding a USB flash memory drive or flash memory card designed for ReadyBoost can improve memory performance. This tutorial shows you how to set up a USB flash memory drive for ReadyBoost.

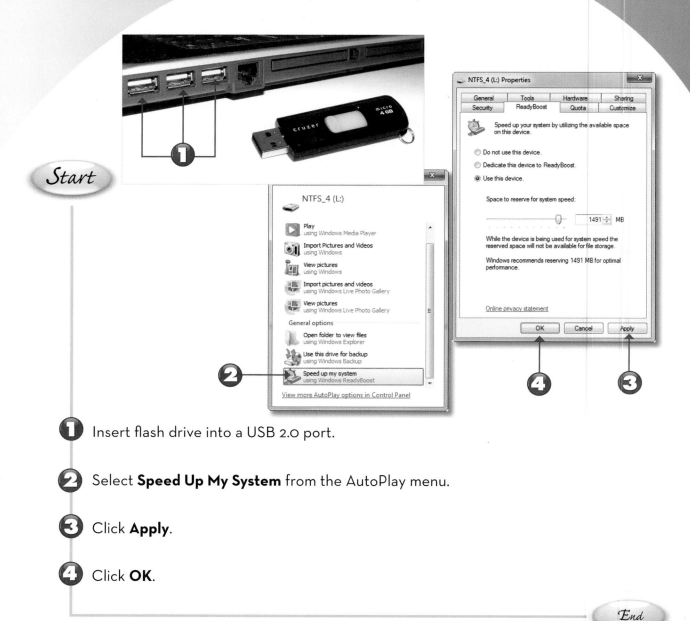

1. Insert flash drive into a USB 2.0 port.

2. Select **Speed Up My System** from the AutoPlay menu.

3. Click **Apply**.

4. Click **OK**.

NOTE

A file called ReadyBoost.sfcache is placed on the flash drive. The file is used to improve memory transfers. ■

NOTE

Some flash memory drives and cards are not fast enough to use with ReadyBoost. Drives and cards that support ReadyBoost are labeled as ReadyBoost-compatible. ■

CLEANING UP UNNECESSARY FILES

If any drive is displayed with a red capacity gauge, it has less than 10% free space remaining. If the free space on any drive drops below 15%, Windows 7 cannot defragment the drive. If the system drive (usually C: drive) runs out of space, temporary files (such as those created for printing) cannot be created, and sending information to and from the paging (swap) file (which is used as a substitute for RAM) becomes very slow. For these reasons, keeping an eye on the free space for your disk drives is important.

You can use the Disk Cleanup tool to remove unnecessary files or compress seldom-used files to gain space. Here's how it works.

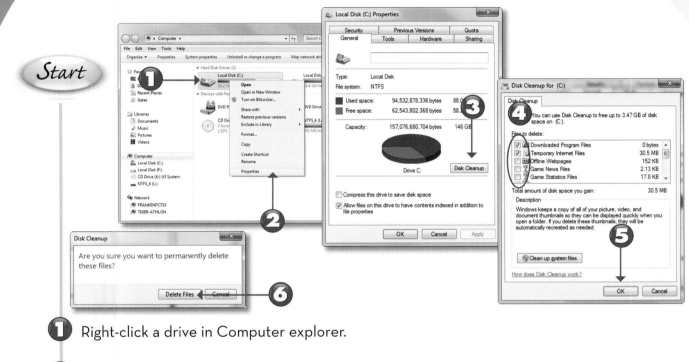

1 Right-click a drive in Computer explorer.

2 Select **Properties**.

3 Click **Disk Cleanup**.

4 Add/remove items by adding/clearing checkboxes.

5 Click to proceed.

6 Click **Delete Files** to clean up selected files.

End

NOTE

A description of each category appears when you select it. Windows 7 selects "safe" categories for deletion. However, you should review the choices and make changes as desired before proceeding. ■

CHECKING DRIVES FOR ERRORS

You should periodically check hard disks and USB flash drives for errors. Windows 7 starts this task from the Drive Properties menu.

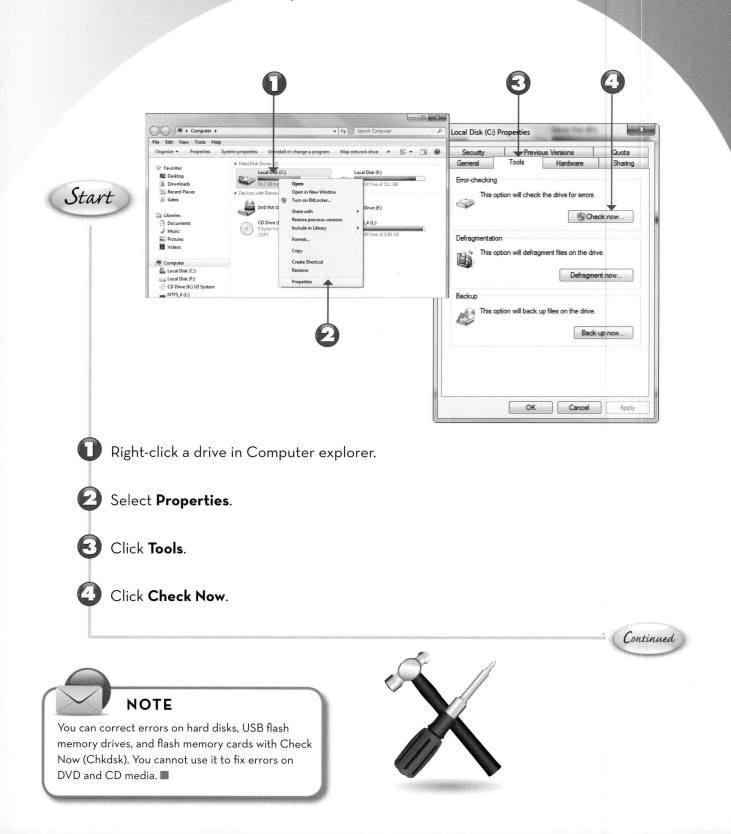

Start

1 Right-click a drive in Computer explorer.

2 Select **Properties**.

3 Click **Tools**.

4 Click **Check Now**.

Continued

NOTE

You can correct errors on hard disks, USB flash memory drives, and flash memory cards with Check Now (Chkdsk). You cannot use it to fix errors on DVD and CD media. ■

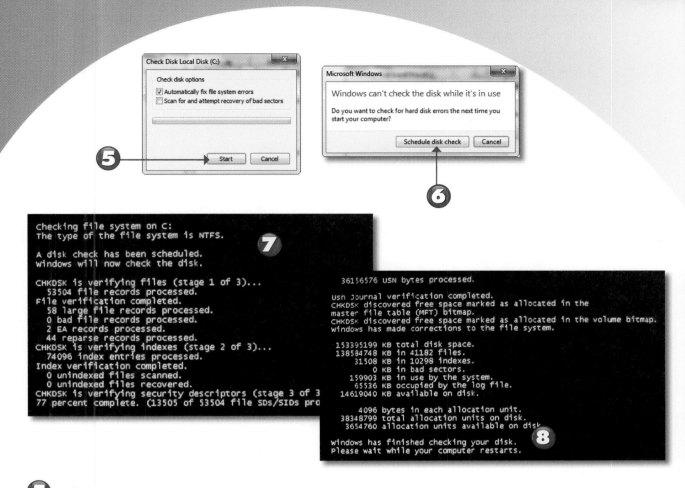

5 Click Start.

6 Click **Schedule Disk Check** if prompted.

7 The next time the system starts, the disk check is performed.

8 After displaying the results, disk check restarts the computer.

End

NOTE

Windows must schedule disk checking of drives containing system files or drives with open files. Non-system drives that are not in use are tested immediately without restarting the system. ■

CONFIGURING DEFRAGMENT

Windows 7's Disk Defragment feature runs automatically to improve disk read-write performance. However, you can control when the defragger runs, and you can also defragment drives manually. In this tutorial, you learn how to change the day of the week used for defragmentation and how to analyze your drives.

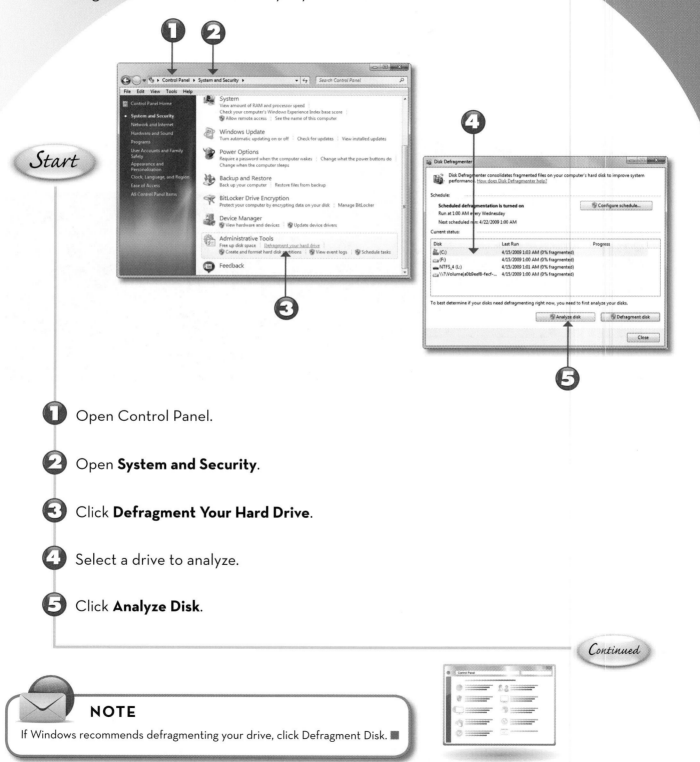

Start

① Open Control Panel.

② Open **System and Security**.

③ Click **Defragment Your Hard Drive**.

④ Select a drive to analyze.

⑤ Click **Analyze Disk**.

Continued

NOTE

If Windows recommends defragmenting your drive, click Defragment Disk. ■

6 To change the defragmentation schedule, click **Configure Schedule**.

7 Open the day menu.

8 Select **Sunday**.

9 Click **OK**.

10 Click **Close**.

End

NOTE

By default, Disk Defragmenter automatically defragments all hard disks and USB flash memory drives. If you are using a solid-state drive (SSD) instead of a hard disk, you should disable defragmenting for the SSD. Do this by opening the Choose Disks menu and unchecking the drive letter for the SSD. SSDs are most commonly used in netbook systems. ■

TROUBLESHOOTING

Windows 7 contains a large number of troubleshooters designed to help you solve system problems. This section shows you how to locate the troubleshooters and solve a problem with Internet connectivity by using the Internet Connection troubleshooter.

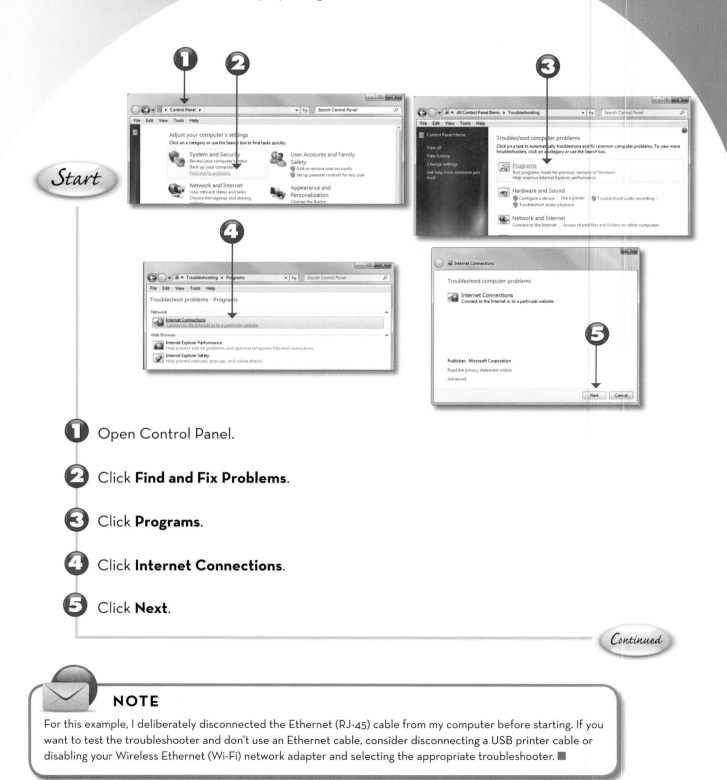

Start

1 Open Control Panel.

2 Click **Find and Fix Problems**.

3 Click **Programs**.

4 Click **Internet Connections**.

5 Click **Next**.

Continued

NOTE

For this example, I deliberately disconnected the Ethernet (RJ-45) cable from my computer before starting. If you want to test the troubleshooter and don't use an Ethernet cable, consider disconnecting a USB printer cable or disabling your Wireless Ethernet (Wi-Fi) network adapter and selecting the appropriate troubleshooter. ■

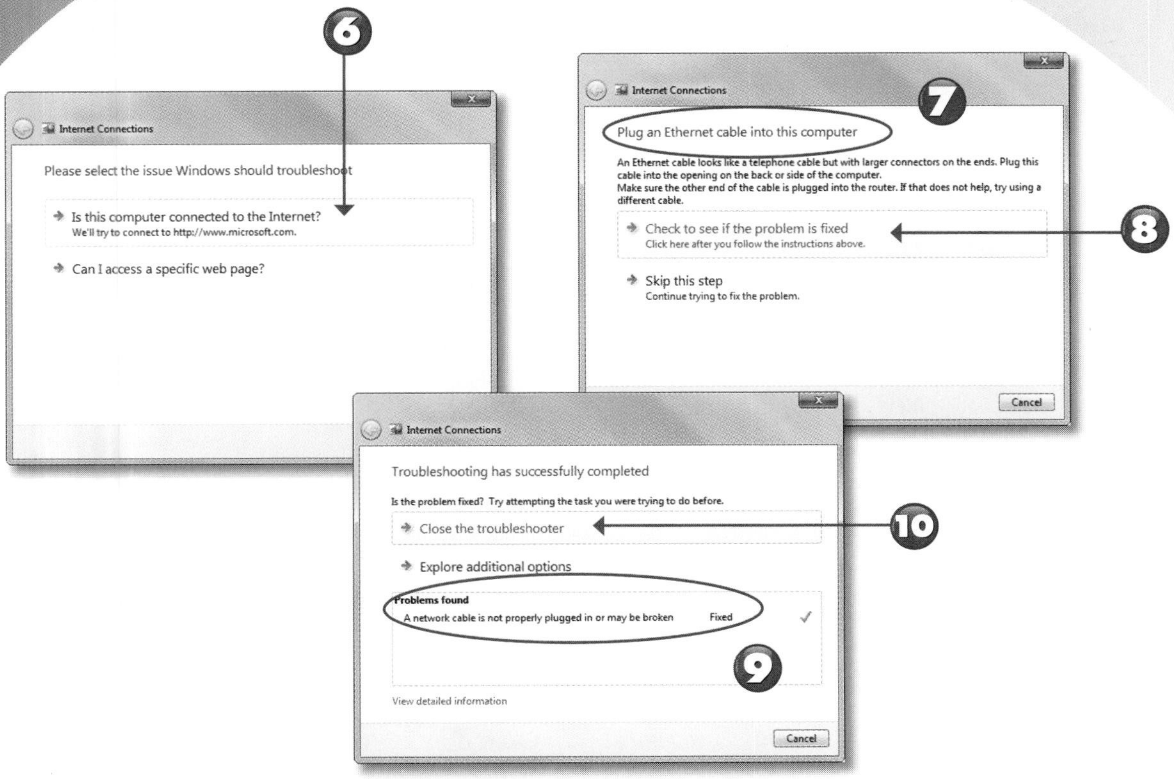

6 Click the issue you need to troubleshoot.

7 If Windows offers a solution, make the change suggested.

8 Click to see if the problem is fixed.

9 Review the list of problems checked.

10 Click Close.

End

NOTE

If you deliberately disable a device or remove a cable to trigger the trouble-shooter, make sure you enable the device or reconnect the cable afterwards. ■

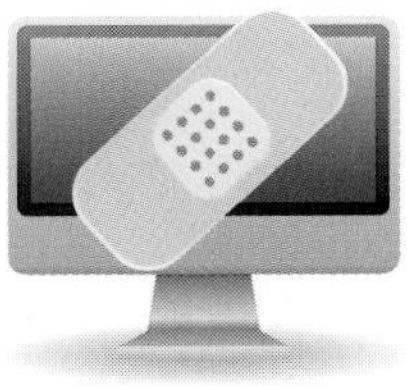

FIXING PROBLEMS WITH SYSTEM RESTORE

If a computer problem appears to be caused by a program installation, hardware upgrade, or Windows upgrade, you can return your computer to a previous condition with System Restore. System Restore resets the Windows Registry to its state as of the date/time you select, and in Windows 7, System Restore can also check to see what programs will be affected by running System Restore. Here's how to use System Restore to send your computer back in time.

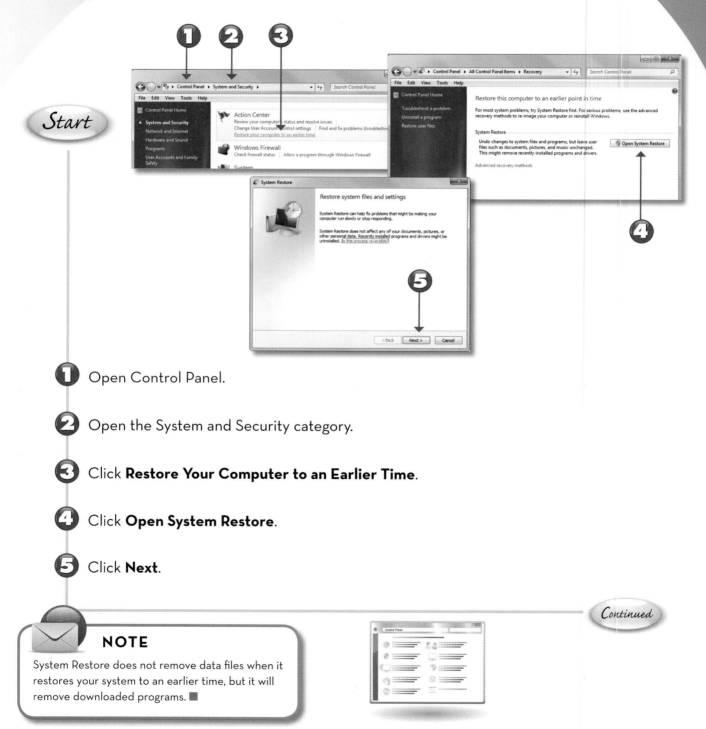

Start

1. Open Control Panel.

2. Open the System and Security category.

3. Click **Restore Your Computer to an Earlier Time**.

4. Click **Open System Restore**.

5. Click **Next**.

Continued

NOTE

System Restore does not remove data files when it restores your system to an earlier time, but it will remove downloaded programs. ■

6 Select a restore point.

7 Click **Scan for Affected Programs**.

8 After reviewing the list of affected programs and drivers, click **Close**.

9 Click **Next**.

10 Click **Finish**.

11 Click **Yes**.

12 After your system restarts, click **Close**.

End

NOTE

If you want to use affected programs and drivers after running System Restore, you must reinstall them. If possible, get updated versions from the vendor. ■

CREATING A SYSTEM REPAIR DISC

Windows 7 includes a program that creates a system repair disc. This disc can be used to start the system if it will not boot and provides access to system restore, backup image restore, and other advanced repair features. This tutorial shows you how to create a system repair disc.

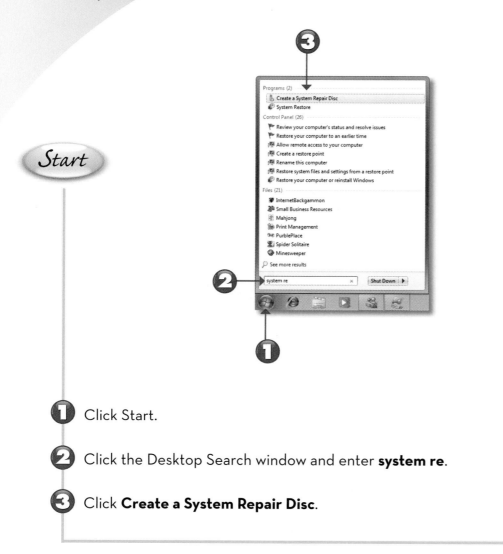

Click **Start**.

Click the Desktop Search window and enter **system re**.

Click **Create a System Repair Disc**.

Continued

NOTE

Be sure to label the disc and put it in a safe place after the process is complete. ■

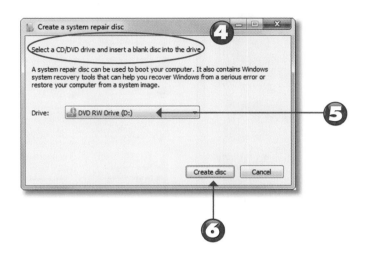

4 Insert a blank CD or DVD.

5 Select the correct drive if you have more than one CD/DVD drive.

6 Click **Create Disc**.

End

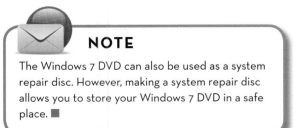

NOTE

The Windows 7 DVD can also be used as a system repair disc. However, making a system repair disc allows you to store your Windows 7 DVD in a safe place. ■

BACKING UP YOUR FILES

Windows 7 Home Premium, Business, and Ultimate editions include a backup utility that does two backups in one: it backs up your entire computer's contents, including Windows, so you can restore it to a formatted or brand-new hard disk in case of a serious system crash, and it also backs up your data files. Microsoft recommends using an external hard disk with enough space for your backup, and in this tutorial, that is what we're using.

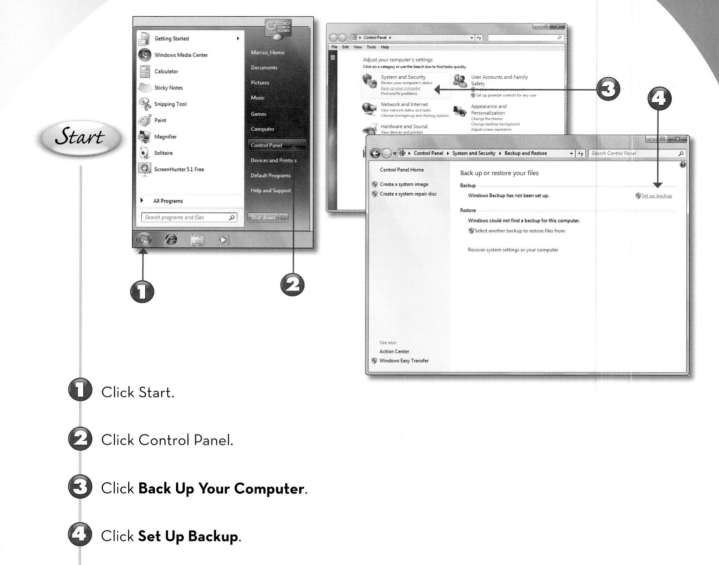

1. Click Start.

2. Click Control Panel.

3. Click **Back Up Your Computer**.

4. Click **Set Up Backup**.

Continued

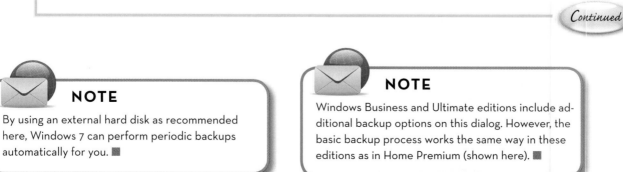

NOTE

By using an external hard disk as recommended here, Windows 7 can perform periodic backups automatically for you. ■

NOTE

Windows Business and Ultimate editions include additional backup options on this dialog. However, the basic backup process works the same way in these editions as in Home Premium (shown here). ■

5 Select your external hard disk.

6 Click **Next**.

7 Select **Let Windows Choose**.

8 Click **Next**.

Continued

NOTE

Make sure the external hard disk you select has enough room for your initial backup and additional backups. I recommend an external hard disk that's at least twice the capacity of your computer's hard disk. ■

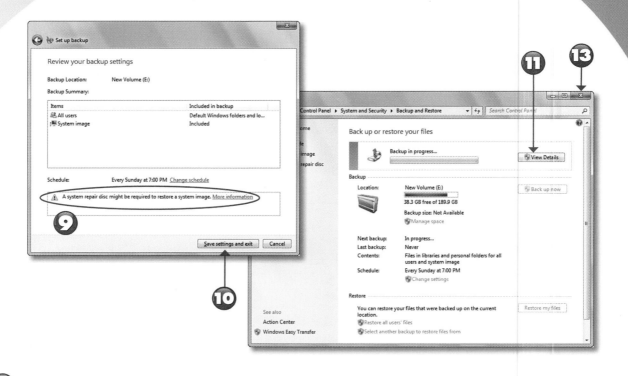

9 Note the reminder to create a system repair disc if you haven't made one already.

10 Click **Save Settings and Run Backup**.

11 To see the backup status, click **View Details**.

Continued

NOTE

To restore a system image, you need to use the Windows 7 DVD or a system repair disc. If you have a preinstalled copy of Windows 7 without a DVD, be sure to make a repair disc right away. ■

Windows Backup...100% complete

Windows Backup has completed successfully

Finished

Open the Backup and Restore Control Panel to view settings

Close

12

12 At the end of the backup, click **Close**.

13 Click **Close** to close the backup window.

End

NOTE

By default, the Windows 7 backup program runs
every Sunday night at 7:00 PM. If you typically use
your computer at that time, click the View Details
link (see Step 11) and select a different date and/or
time. ■

RESTORING FILES FROM A BACKUP

Oops! You erased the birthday party pictures—or your family budget. If you use Windows 7's backup, though, there's a good chance you can retrieve a backup copy and save the day. In this tutorial, you learn how to test your backup by retrieving individual files from a backup and restoring them to a different location.

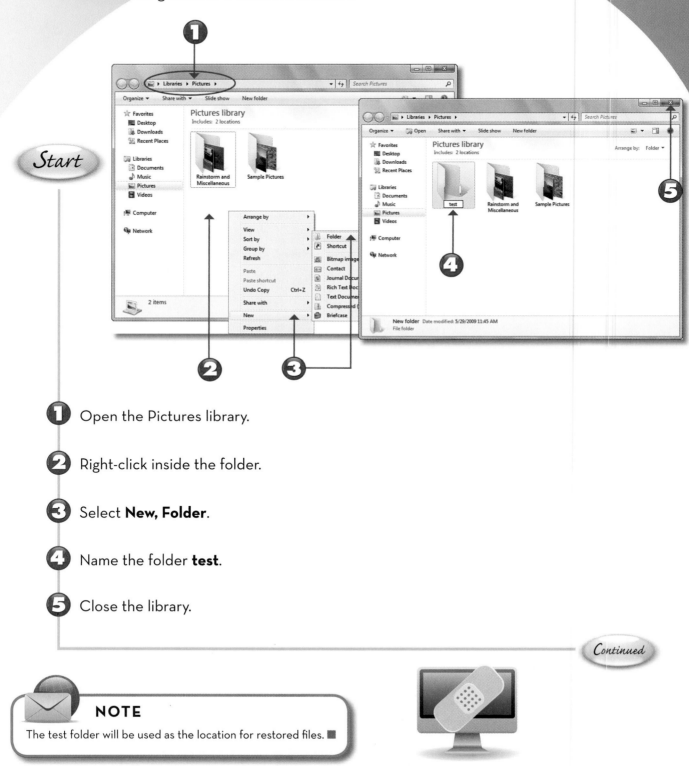

1 Open the Pictures library.

2 Right-click inside the folder.

3 Select **New, Folder**.

4 Name the folder **test**.

5 Close the library.

Continued

NOTE

The test folder will be used as the location for restored files. ∎

6 Click Start.

7 Click **Control Panel**.

8 Click **Back Up Your Computer**.

9 Click **Restore My Files**.

10 Click **Browse** for Files.

Continued

NOTE

Testing a backup (as in this exercise) assures you that your backup can be restored in case of an emergency. ■

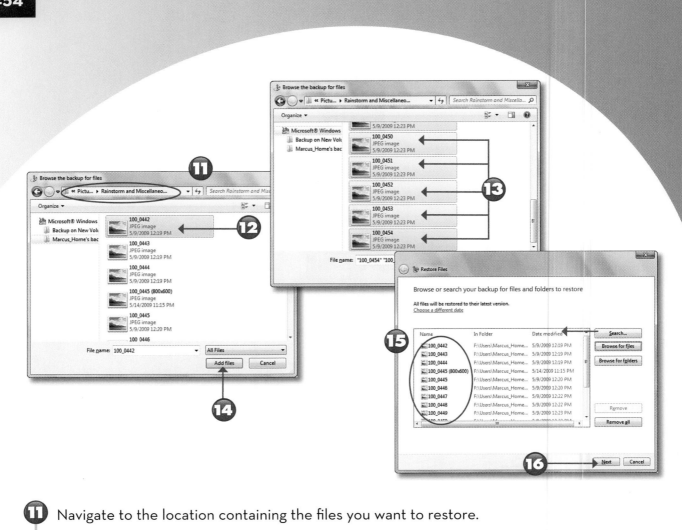

11. Navigate to the location containing the files you want to restore.

12. Click the first file.

13. Press and hold **Shift or Ctrl** while clicking other files.

14. Click **Add Files**.

15. The files you have selected to restore are listed.

16. Click **Next**.

Continued

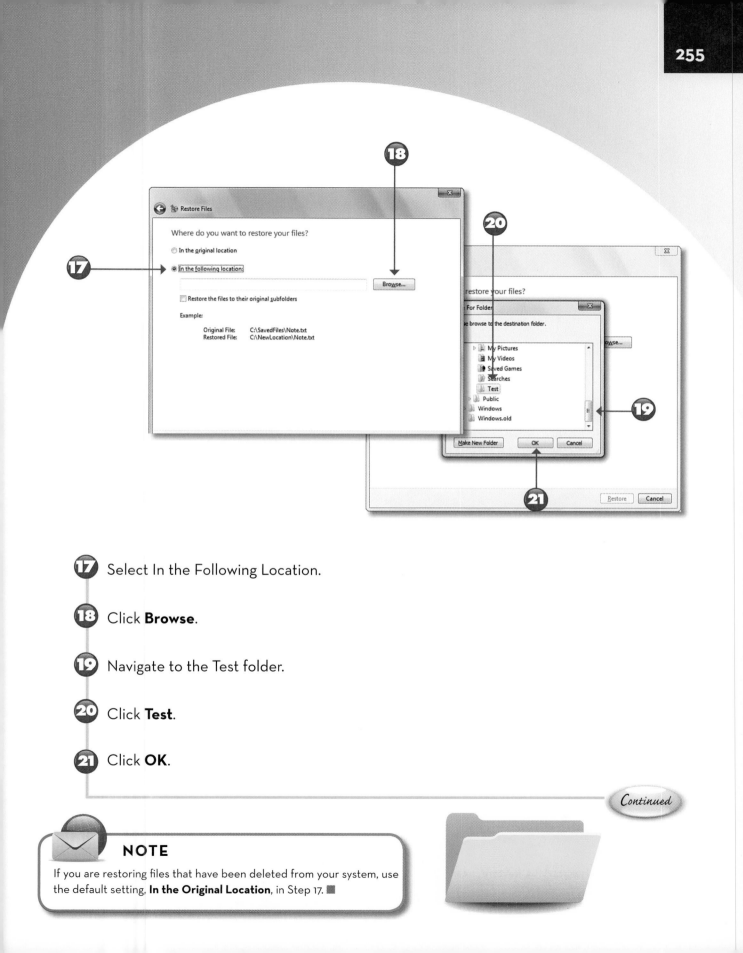

17 Select In the Following Location.

18 Click **Browse**.

19 Navigate to the Test folder.

20 Click **Test**.

21 Click **OK**.

Continued

NOTE

If you are restoring files that have been deleted from your system, use the default setting, **In the Original Location**, in Step 17. ■

22 Click **Restore**.

Continued

NOTE

Depending upon the number of files you are restoring, it might take a while after you click **Restore** before the next dialog appears. ■

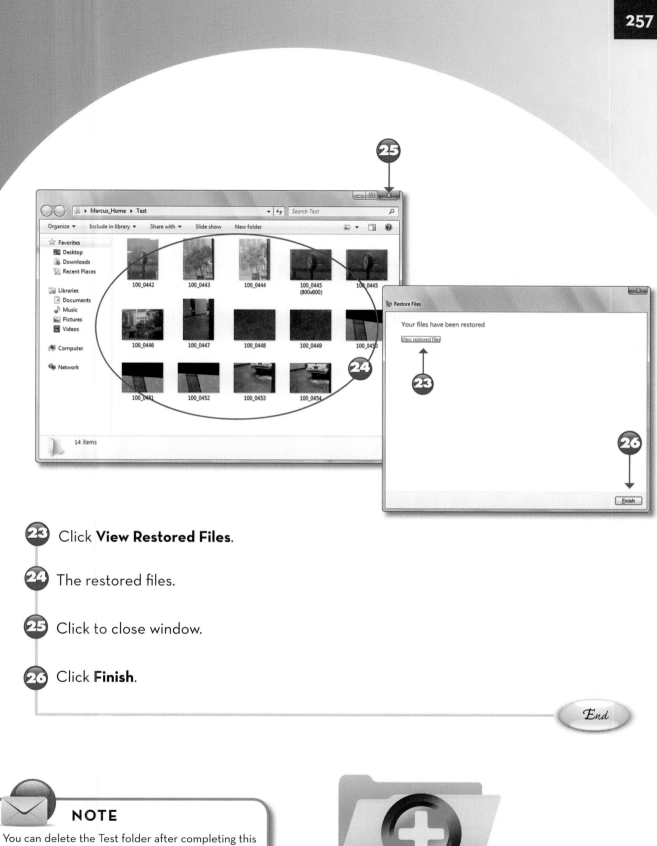

23 Click **View Restored Files**.

24 The restored files.

25 Click to close window.

26 Click **Finish**.

End

NOTE

You can delete the Test folder after completing this exercise. ■

Chapter 14

SETTING UP PROGRAMS

Windows 7 provides many ways to control how programs work. From placing program shortcuts where you want them, enabling older programs to run properly under Windows 7, to customizing the Start menu, taskbar, and notification area, Windows 7 makes it possible to make the process of adding, using, and removing programs easier than with previous versions.

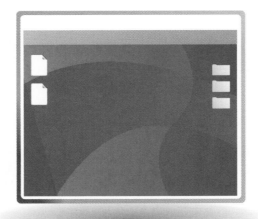

You can customize both the taskbar and the notification area through the Taskbar properties sheet

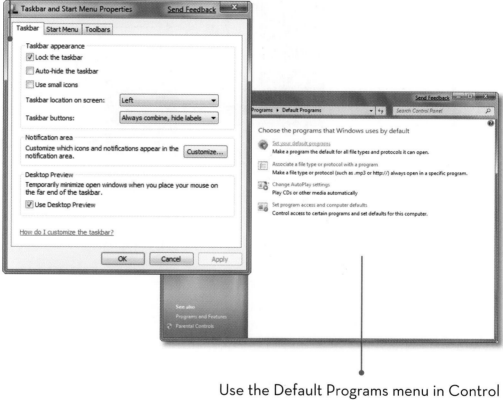

Use the Default Programs menu in Control Panel to select the programs you want to use to perform different types of actions and to configure AutoPlay

CONTROL PANEL'S PROGRAMS MENU

The Programs menu in the Control Panel provides a convenient jumping-off place for installing, uninstalling, and setting up default programs. In this chapter, you'll learn about the Programs and Features and Default Programs submenus.

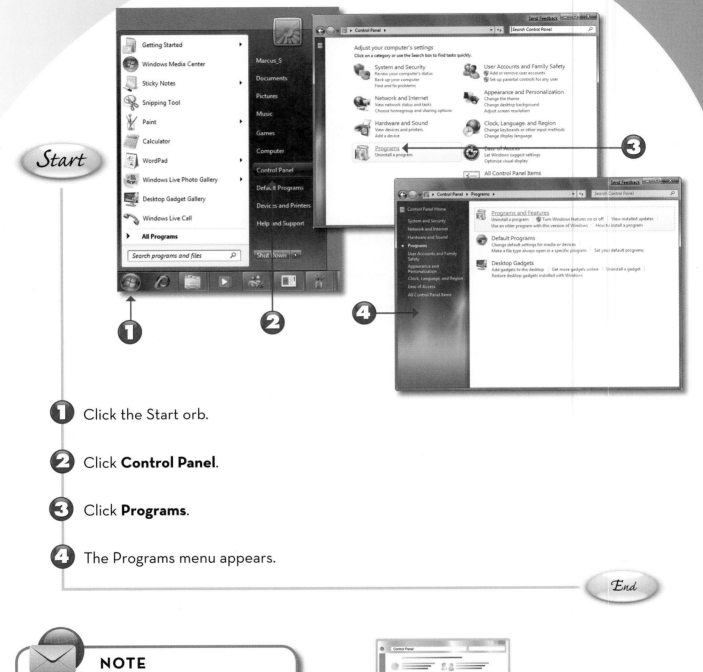

1 Click the Start orb.

2 Click **Control Panel**.

3 Click **Programs**.

4 The Programs menu appears.

End

NOTE

The Programs menu also includes the Desktop Gadgets submenu. To learn more about desktop gadgets, see Chapter 3, "Using the Windows 7 Desktop." ■

INSTALLING A CD OR DVD PROGRAM FROM THE AUTOPLAY MENU

When you insert most recent CD- and DVD-based commercial programs, they display an AutoPlay menu that provides immediate access to the installation program.

1 Insert the CD or DVD, and an AutoPlay menu appears in a few seconds.

2 Select the option listed in the Install or Run Program section.

3 The installation program appears. Select Install from the menu and follow the prompts to complete the installation process.

NOTE

For a reminder of how to install programs from different types of sources, click the How to Install a Program link in the Programs and Features submenu. ▪

INSTALLING A PROGRAM MANUALLY

When you install a program on a CD or DVD manually (common with older programs) or a program you have downloaded from the Internet, you might see a User Account Control (UAC) prompt. You must provide the information requested to finish the installation successfully.

Start

End

① If you are installing from a CD, and an Open Folder to View Files option appears in the AutoPlay menu instead of an Install or Run Program option, select it.

① If you are installing a downloaded program, navigate to the file location.

② Scroll down the file listing until you find the Setup program (usually called Setup).

③ Double-click the **Setup** program to start it.

④ When the User Account Control (UAC) prompt appears, asking if you want to install the program, click **Yes** or provide the administrator's password as prompted.

NOTE

When you download a program, you should save it to your Downloads folder to make it easier to locate. ■

NOTE

User Account Control might display a UAC shield icon in the taskbar. Click it to display the UAC prompt shown in Step 4. ■

ADDING A PROGRAM SHORTCUT TO THE START MENU

Most of the time, a Windows program installs a shortcut to the Start menu automatically.
However, if it doesn't, or you want to have the program shortcut visible as soon as you click
the Start orb, it's an easy change to make in Windows 7.

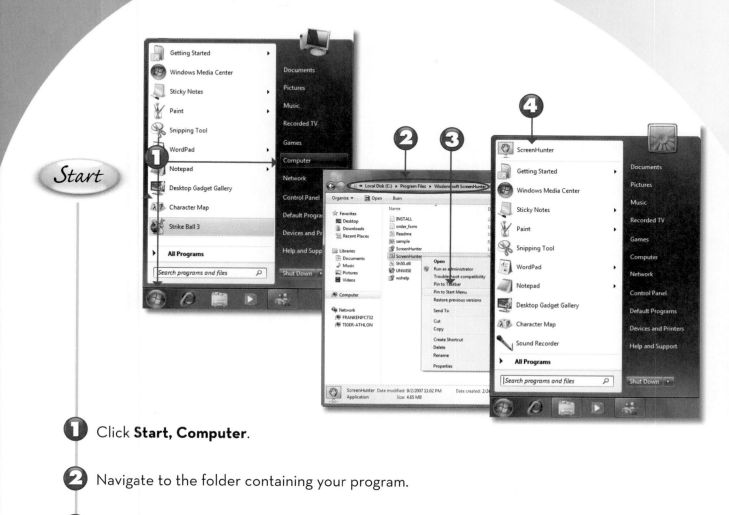

1 Click **Start, Computer**.

2 Navigate to the folder containing your program.

3 Right-click the program's executable file and select Pin to Start Menu.

4 The program appears on the top of the Start menu.

End

NOTE

Most programs are installed to a subfolder of the C:
drive's Program Files folder. ■

ADDING A PROGRAM SHORTCUT TO THE DESKTOP

If you prefer to run programs from desktop shortcuts, but you don't have a desktop shortcut for a favorite program, it's easy to add one with Windows 7 by using drag and drop.

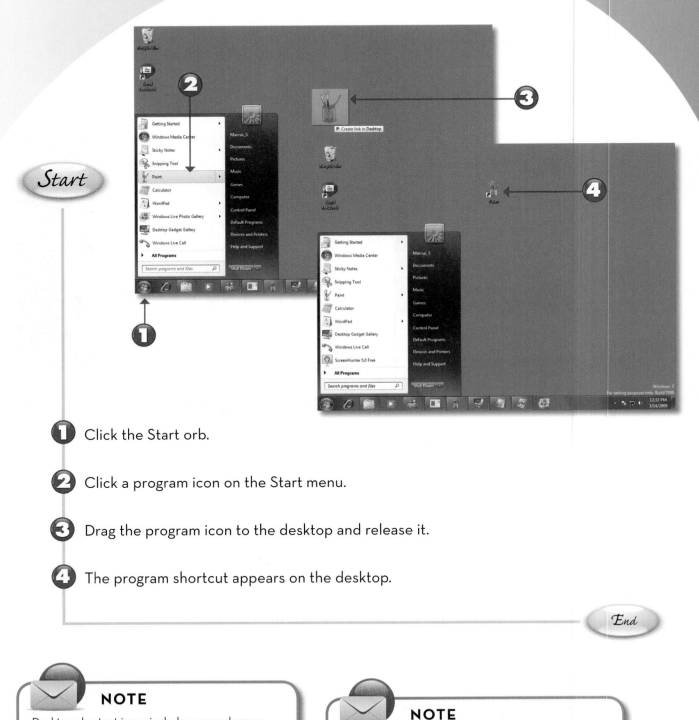

Start

1 Click the Start orb.

2 Click a program icon on the Start menu.

3 Drag the program icon to the desktop and release it.

4 The program shortcut appears on the desktop.

End

NOTE

Desktop shortcut icons include a curved arrow
in the lower left-hand corner. Compare the Paint
shortcut icon to the Recycle Bin icon. ■

NOTE

If you don't see the shortcut appear in Step 4, right-
click the desktop, select View, Show Desktop Icons. ■

ADDING A PROGRAM SHORTCUT TO THE TASKBAR

As you use programs in Windows 7, they are automatically placed on the taskbar. However, you can also place a program on the taskbar, even before you run it.

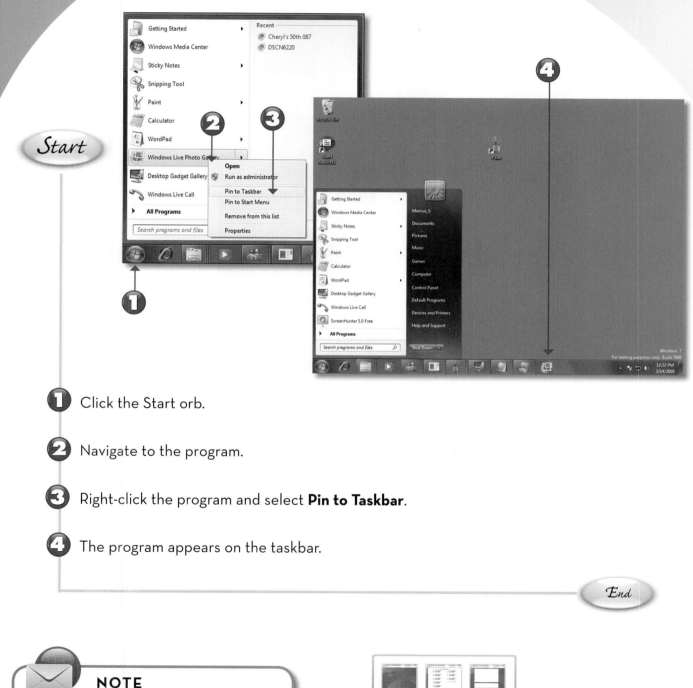

① Click the Start orb.

② Navigate to the program.

③ Right-click the program and select **Pin to Taskbar**.

④ The program appears on the taskbar.

End

NOTE

Place frequently-used programs on the Taskbar so you can launch them more quickly and easily. ■

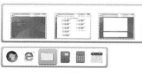

HELPING AN OLDER PROGRAM TO RUN PROPERLY

Although recent Windows programs automatically run in full-screen, programs written for older versions of Windows might run in a window or might not run at all. The Program compatibility wizard built into Windows 7 provides an easy way to help older Windows programs to run properly in Windows 7.

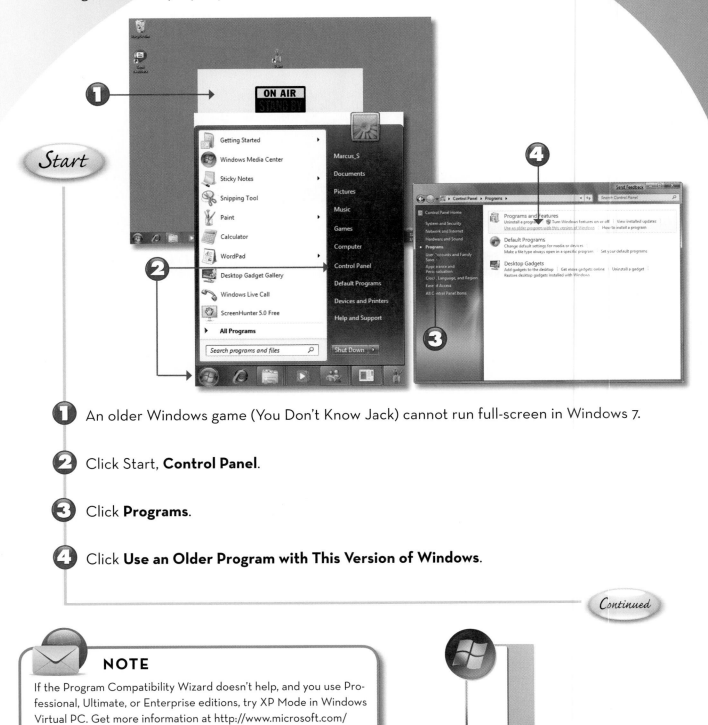

Start

1 An older Windows game (You Don't Know Jack) cannot run full-screen in Windows 7.

2 Click Start, **Control Panel**.

3 Click **Programs**.

4 Click **Use an Older Program with This Version of Windows**.

Continued

NOTE

If the Program Compatibility Wizard doesn't help, and you use Professional, Ultimate, or Enterprise editions, try XP Mode in Windows Virtual PC. Get more information at http://www.microsoft.com/windows/virtual-pc/download.aspx. ■

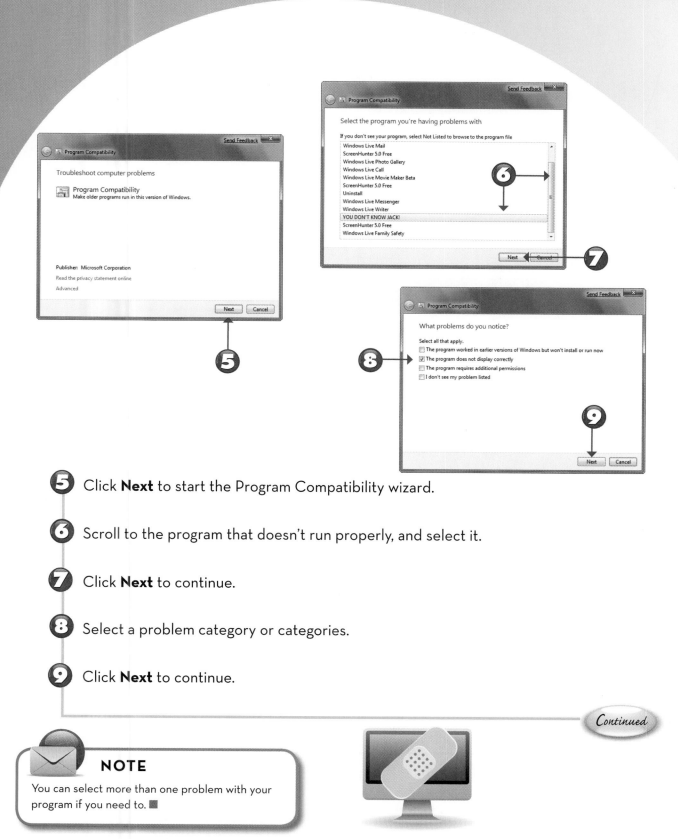

5 Click **Next** to start the Program Compatibility wizard.

6 Scroll to the program that doesn't run properly, and select it.

7 Click **Next** to continue.

8 Select a problem category or categories.

9 Click **Next** to continue.

Continued

NOTE

You can select more than one problem with your program if you need to. ■

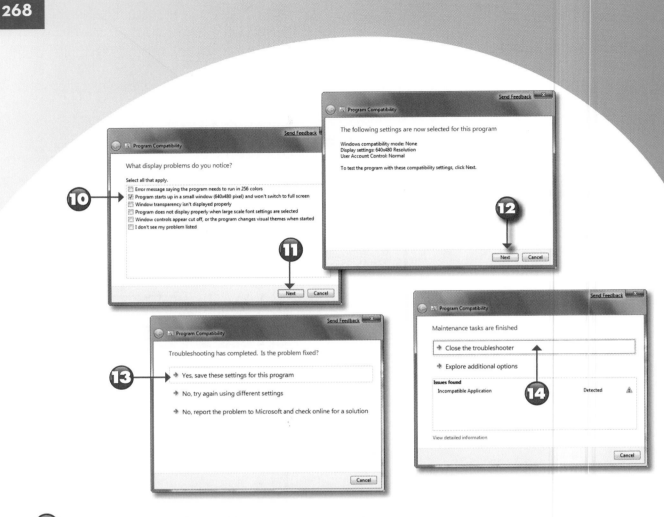

10 Choose the specific problems your program has.

11 Click **Next** to continue.

12 The wizard lists the settings that will be used. Click **Next** to test your program.

13 The program runs. Exit the program, and if the program runs correctly, select **Yes, Save These Settings....**

14 Click **Close the Troubleshooter** to finish the process.

End

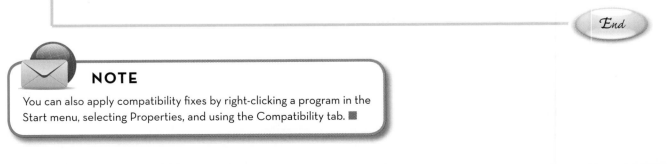

NOTE

You can also apply compatibility fixes by right-clicking a program in the Start menu, selecting Properties, and using the Compatibility tab. ■

REMOVING (UNINSTALLING) A PROGRAM

Windows 7 includes a program-removal feature very similar to the ones found in earlier Windows versions. If you want to uninstall a program, be sure to use this procedure, as it helps to ensure that references to the program are removed as well as program files themselves.

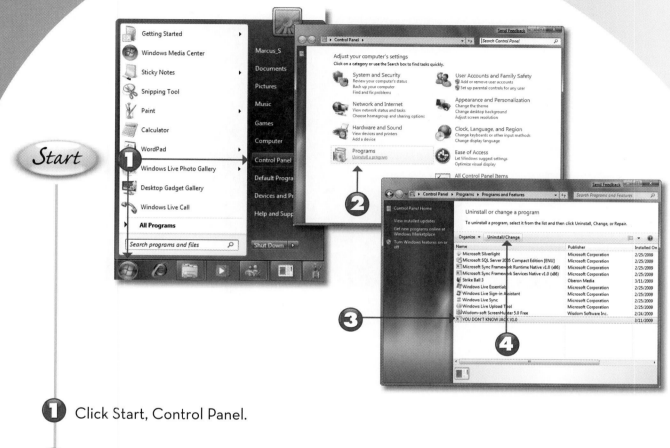

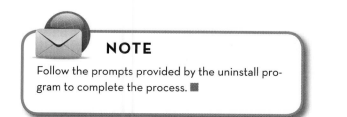

1 Click Start, Control Panel.

2 Click **Uninstall a Program**.

3 Select the program you want to uninstall.

4 Click **Uninstall/Change**.

End

NOTE

Follow the prompts provided by the uninstall program to complete the process. ■

DELETING A DESKTOP SHORTCUT

If you no longer want a shortcut to appear on the desktop, but you don't want to uninstall the program, you can remove it very quickly.

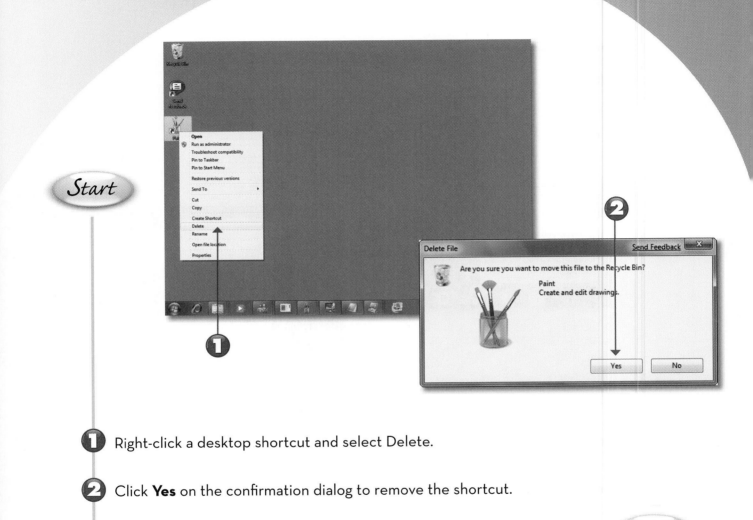

Start

1 Right-click a desktop shortcut and select Delete.

2 Click **Yes** on the confirmation dialog to remove the shortcut.

End

NOTE

If you don't want the deleted shortcut to go to the Recycle Bin, hold down either Shift key before you select Delete from the right-click menu. Items removed with Shift-Delete bypass the Recycle Bin, freeing up disk space immediately for reuse. ■

CUSTOMIZING THE START MENU

Windows 7 makes it easy to change the shortcuts listed on the right pane of the Start menu.

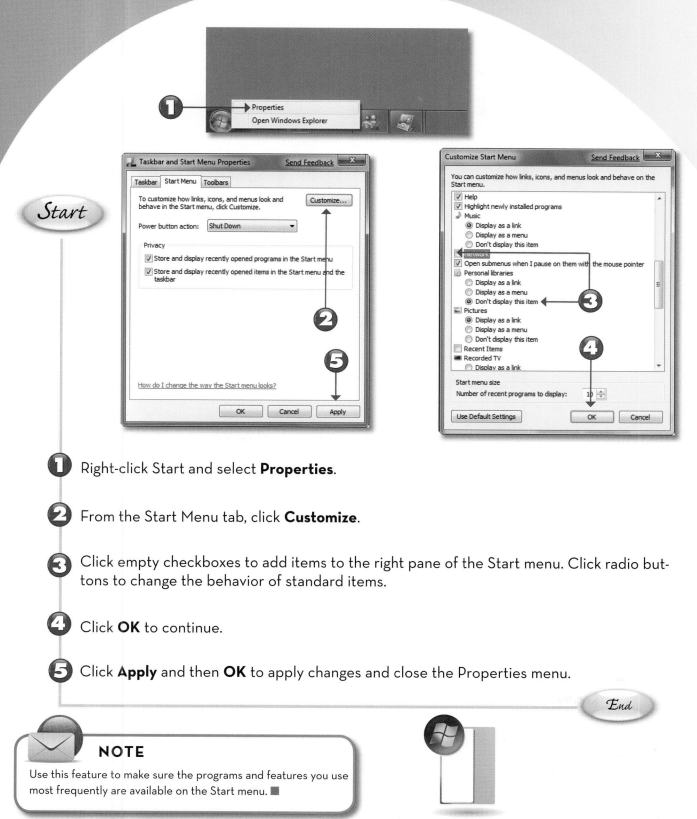

Start

End

1 Right-click Start and select **Properties**.

2 From the Start Menu tab, click **Customize**.

3 Click empty checkboxes to add items to the right pane of the Start menu. Click radio buttons to change the behavior of standard items.

4 Click **OK** to continue.

5 Click **Apply** and then **OK** to apply changes and close the Properties menu.

NOTE

Use this feature to make sure the programs and features you use most frequently are available on the Start menu. ■

CUSTOMIZING THE TASKBAR

If you don't like the new look of the taskbar in Windows 7, you can change how it works and change its location by using the Taskbar tab of the Taskbar and Start Menu Properties sheet.

Start

① Right-click the Start orb and select **Properties**.

② Select the Taskbar tab. After selecting the desired option(s), click **Apply** to use them. Here, the Small Icons option is selected.

③ Using the Combine When Taskbar is Full option.

Continued

NOTE

You can also use Small Icons (Step 2) in conjunction with other taskbar settings. ∎

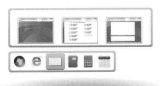

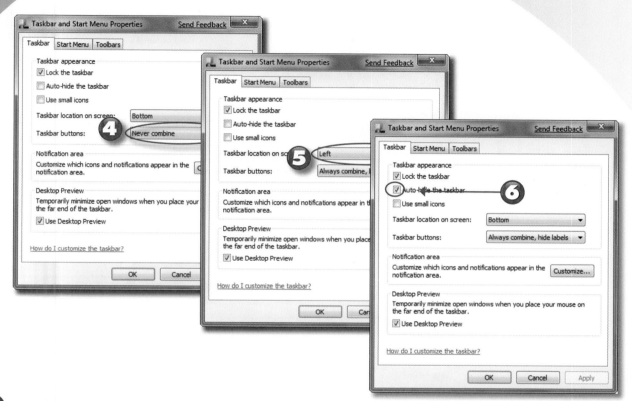

4 Using the Never Combine Taskbar option.

5 Using the Taskbar Left Location option.

6 Using the Auto-Hide the Taskbar option.

End

NOTE

When Auto-Hide is enabled, the taskbar becomes visible only when the mouse pointer is moved to the edge of the screen where the taskbar is. ■

CUSTOMIZING NOTIFICATION ICONS WITH CONTROL PANEL

The notification area (also known as the system tray or systray) refers to the icons between the clock and the taskbar. These icons are used to display information about processes, and Windows 7 provides new ways to manage and customize these icons.

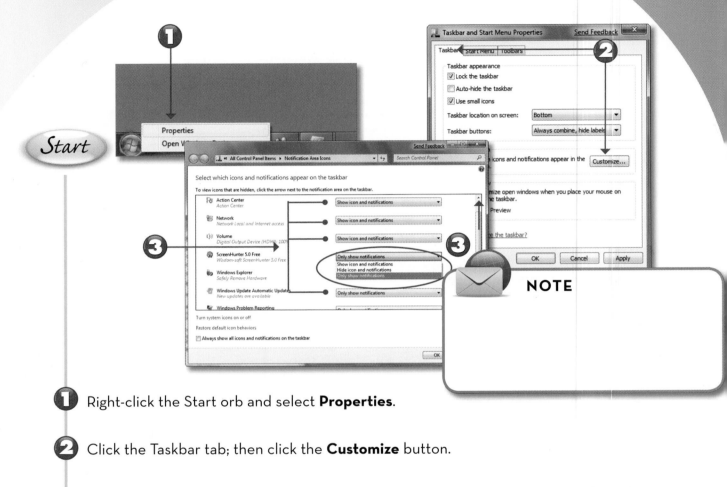

1 Right-click the Start orb and select **Properties**.

2 Click the Taskbar tab; then click the **Customize** button.

3 Scroll as needed to see all icons. For each icon, select whether you want to show the icon and notifications, hide icon and notifications, or only show notifications.

Continued

NOTE

Select the Icon or Icon and Notification options for items you interact with, such as Safely Remove Hardware or Volume. ■

4 To turn system icons on or off, click the link shown in Step 3; then select on or off for each listed icon.

5 Click **OK** on each dialog to save changes.

End

NOTE

To turn on or turn off icons from third-party programs using the Notification Area, use those programs' setup options. ■

SETTING AUTOPLAY OPTIONS

The AutoPlay features enable Windows to play various types of media files found on removable media drives such as USB flash memory cards, USB flash memory drives, CDs, and DVDs. Windows 7, like Windows Vista, enables you to select AutoPlay defaults based on the type of media files found on a drive.

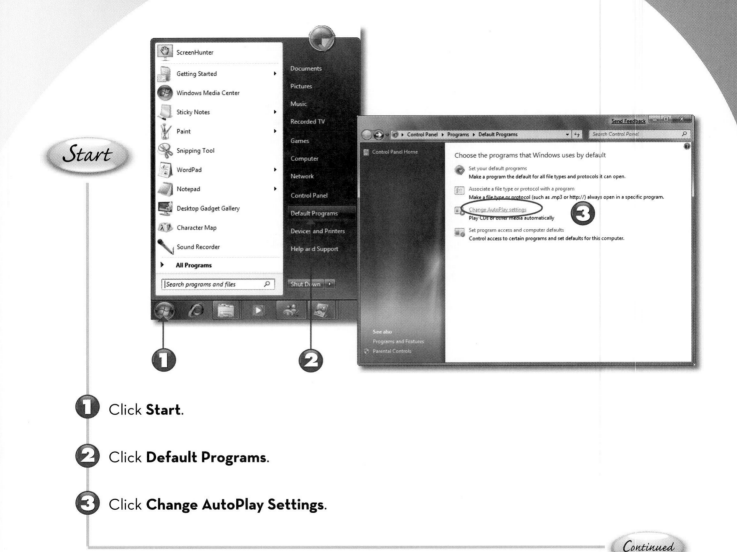

1 Click **Start**.

2 Click **Default Programs**.

3 Click **Change AutoPlay Settings**.

Continued

NOTE

AutoPlay refers to the popup menu of options that appears when you plug in an external USB drive, insert a CD or DVD, or insert other types of removable media. Options vary by media type (see Step 4). ■

4 Open the pull-down menu next to each media type to choose a default action (in this example, Audio CD).

5 Scroll as needed to see all media types.

6 Choosing a default action for DVD movie.

7 Choosing a default action for Pictures.

8 Click **Save** to save changes.

End

NOTE

If you prefer to have the option of selecting what to do each time a particular type of media is found on a removable-media drive, choose Ask Me Every Time. ■

Chapter 15

WINDOWS ACCESSORIES

Windows 7, as in previous versions, includes a collection of small applications you can use for various tasks. Although some familiar from Windows Vista (Calendar and Contacts) have now been replaced with optional Windows Live components (see Chapter 17, "Using Windows Live Essentials," for details), others have been spiffed up with new features and new user interfaces. Whether you're a longtime Windows user or a Windows newcomer, this chapter will be helpful in learning the new features of these tools.

The Windows 7 Calculator includes new modes and new features for technical and business users

WordPad now includes a ribbon bar interface inspired by Word 2009

Use Windows Photo Viewer to view your pictures, burn them to disc, or start the process of making a DVD

VIEWING THE ACCESSORIES MENU

Windows 7 includes an Accessories folder you can access from the All Programs shortcut of the Start menu.

1 Click the Start orb.

2 Hover the mouse over **All Programs**.

3 Click **Accessories**; the Accessories menu appears.

End

NOTE

This book covers only the most frequently used accessories, and some are covered in other chapters. For coverage of Getting Started, see Chapter 2, "Getting Started with Windows 7." For coverage of Windows Explorer, see Chapter 4, "Working with Your Folders." ■

WORKING WITH CALCULATOR

In Windows 7, Calculator has gone through a significant upgrade, offering two new modes (programmer and statistics) and a more refined visual design.

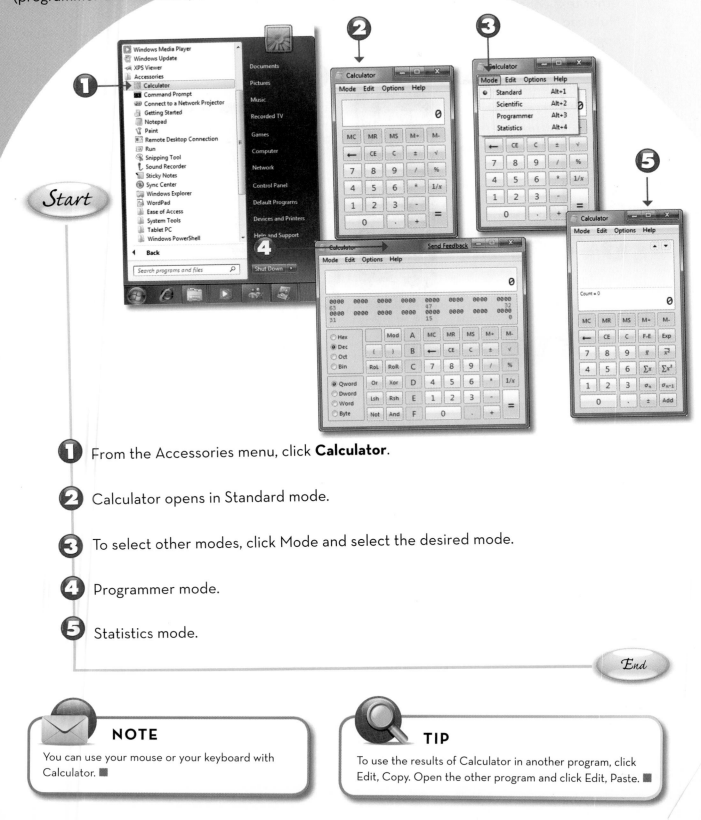

Start

1 From the Accessories menu, click **Calculator**.

2 Calculator opens in Standard mode.

3 To select other modes, click Mode and select the desired mode.

4 Programmer mode.

5 Statistics mode.

End

NOTE

You can use your mouse or your keyboard with Calculator. ■

TIP

To use the results of Calculator in another program, click Edit, Copy. Open the other program and click Edit, Paste. ■

USING WORDPAD

You can use the WordPad word processor to create new documents and to view and edit several of the most common word-processing file formats. You can also add fonts and other text enhancements to documents originally created with plain-text editors, such as Notepad. In Windows 7, the WordPad word processor has gone through an extensive visual upgrade and added new features.

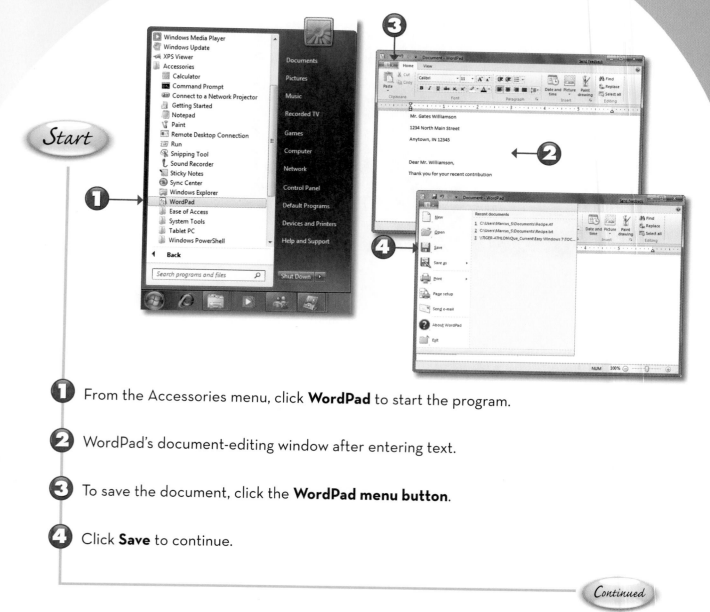

Start

1. From the Accessories menu, click **WordPad** to start the program.

2. WordPad's document-editing window after entering text.

3. To save the document, click the **WordPad menu button**.

4. Click **Save** to continue.

Continued

TIP

The first time you save a new document, you can use Save or Save As to save the document. If you use Save to save changes after you save the document the first time, you will replace the previous version. If you want to preserve the previous version of the document, use Save As and use a different name for the new version of the document. ■

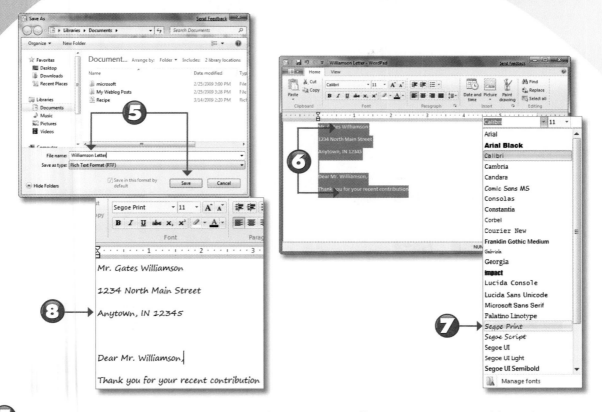

5 To save the document in the current location (usually your Documents library), enter a new name for the document and click Save.

6 To change font, font size, or text attributes, highlight text. Move the mouse to the start of the text, and when the arrow changes to an i-beam icon, click and drag to the end of the text to highlight it.

7 Select the font and other attributes from the Font menu.

8 The document reflects the changes.

Continued

NOTE

By default, WordPad saves files in Rich Text Format (RTF), which can be opened by almost any word processor or other programs that work with text, such as photo editors, draw-type graphics programs, and publishing programs. To choose from other formats, open the Save As Type menu and select the format needed. ■

NOTE

To save a file to a different location, use the left pane to navigate to the location desired, open it, and then click Save. ■

9 To add a picture to the document, place the cursor at the beginning of a blank line in the document and select **Picture** from the Picture menu.

10 Select a picture from the Picture folder or other location and click **Open**.

11 The picture appears in the document. Scroll up to see the text above the picture.

End

TIP

For more help with WordPad, open the WordPad menu and select About WordPad. ■

USING NOTEPAD

The Notepad text editor is designed to create and edit plain-text files. It's changed very little from previous Windows versions, but it might have some features you've overlooked.

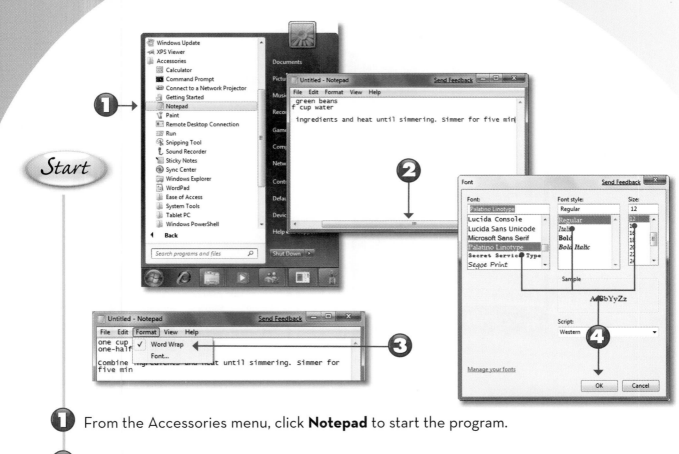

Start

1. From the Accessories menu, click **Notepad** to start the program.

2. When entering text in Notepad, word wrap is turned off, so you might need to scroll horizontally to see your text.

3. Select **Format, Word Wrap** to make the text fit into the window.

4. To change the font, click **Format, Font**, and choose the font and size you prefer. Click **OK** when done.

End

NOTE

Use the Edit menu to find and replace text, to insert the current date and time, to undo the last edit, and to go to a specific line number in the file. ■

NOTE

Use File, Save, or File, Save As, to save your document. See the WordPad tutorial for details. ■

USING PAINT

Like WordPad, Paint is also using a new ribbon-style interface that makes access to new features easier. Although it's designed primarily as a painting program, it does include some features useful to photographers, such as resizing and skewing images.

Start

① From the Accessories menu, click **Paint** to open the program.

② To open an existing picture or photo, click the Paint menu and select **Open**.

③ Select a picture and click **Open**.

Continued

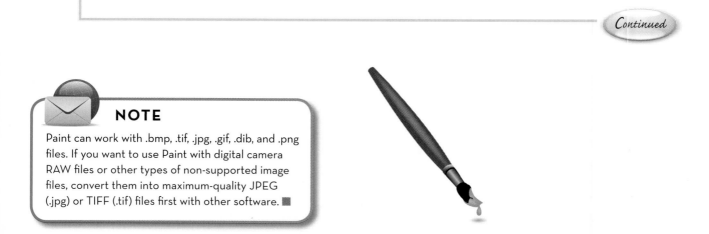

NOTE

Paint can work with .bmp, .tif, .jpg, .gif, .dib, and .png files. If you want to use Paint with digital camera RAW files or other types of non-supported image files, convert them into maximum-quality JPEG (.jpg) or TIFF (.tif) files first with other software. ∎

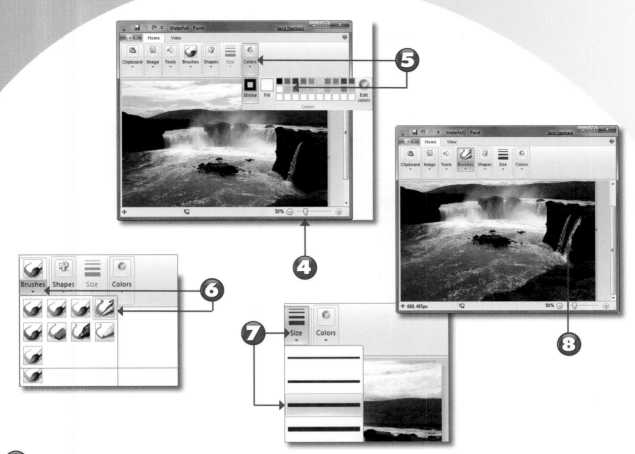

4 Adjust the zoom control until the picture fits the window.

5 To select a color for painting, open the Colors menu and select a color from the Stroke menu.

6 To select a brush type for painting, open the Brushes menu and select a brush.

7 To select a brush size for painting, open the Size menu and select a line thickness.

8 To paint on the picture, use the mouse to click and drag.

Continued

NOTE

Click the down-arrow below each item in the menu to view menu options. ■

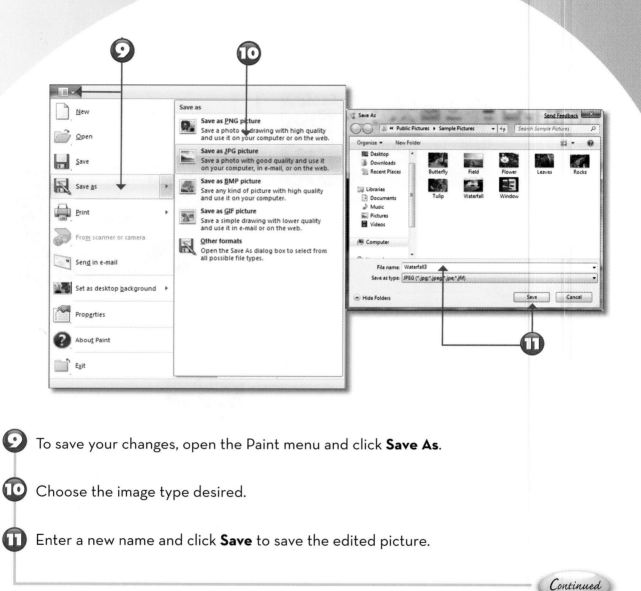

9 To save your changes, open the Paint menu and click **Save As**.

10 Choose the image type desired.

11 Enter a new name and click **Save** to save the edited picture.

Continued

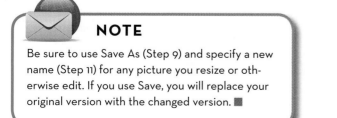

NOTE

Be sure to use Save As (Step 9) and specify a new name (Step 11) for any picture you resize or otherwise edit. If you use Save, you will replace your original version with the changed version. ■

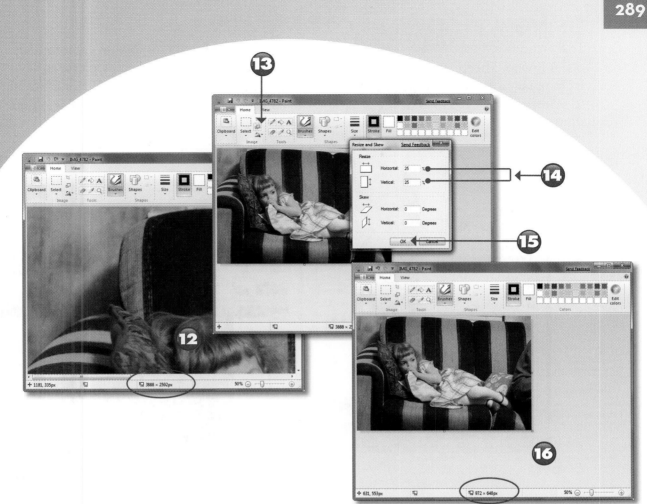

12 Many photos are too large to work well in email (this picture is 3888×2592 pixels). A width of no more than 1024 pixels is recommended for emailed photos.

13 To resize a picture, click the **Resize and Skew** button on the Home ribbon in the Image section.

14 Select the same percentage for horizontal and vertical in the Resize menu (I used 25%).

15 Click **OK** to resize the picture.

16 The picture is now 972×648 pixels, which will work nicely for emailing.

End

USING WINDOWS PHOTO VIEWER

The Windows Photo Viewer enables you to view the most common digital camera and other image types supported by Windows 7. You can also use it to display pictures saved from email or from the web, to print your photos, to burn your photos to CD or DVD, and to open your photos in another program. Unlike other accessories in this chapter, Windows Photo Viewer works from the right-click (also known as context) menu.

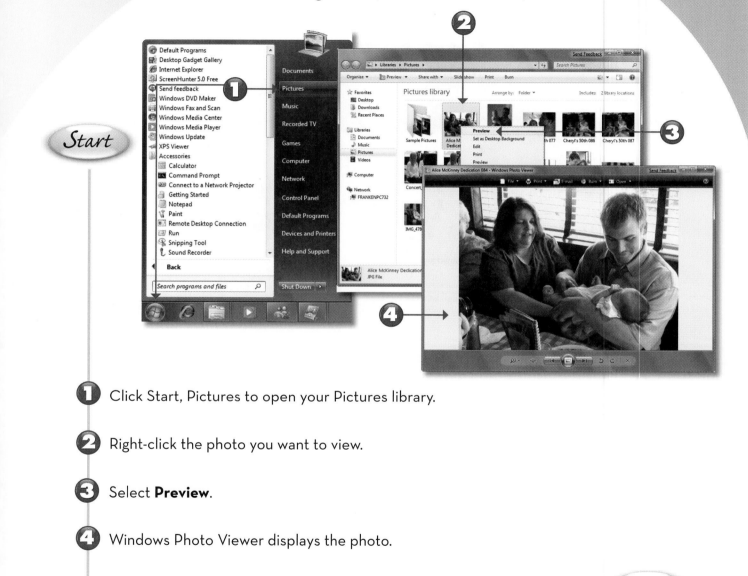

Start

1 Click Start, Pictures to open your Pictures library.

2 Right-click the photo you want to view.

3 Select **Preview**.

4 Windows Photo Viewer displays the photo.

Continued

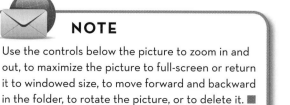

NOTE

Use the controls below the picture to zoom in and out, to maximize the picture to full-screen or return it to windowed size, to move forward and backward in the folder, to rotate the picture, or to delete it. ■

5 To see exposure and camera information, click **File, Properties**.

6 Camera and exposure information. Click **OK** to close the window.

7 To reduce a picture for emailing and send it, click **Email**.

8 Select the size desired and click Attach.

End

NOTE

Before using the Email feature, you need to have an email account set up. See Chapter 17, "Using Windows Live Essentials," to learn more about setting up an email account with Windows Live Mail. ■

NOTE

To learn more about printing photos and documents, see Chapter 6, "Printing." See Chapter 17 to learn more about burning CDs or DVDs of your photos. ■

Chapter 16

NETWORKING YOUR HOME

Windows 7 makes networking your home easier than ever before. In this chapter, you'll learn how to connect your computer to wired and wireless networks, how to share folders and printers, how to use the new HomeGroup feature, and how to use Windows Easy Transfer to move files from your old computer to your new computer via the network.

In this chapter, we assume that your computer has wired (Ethernet) or wireless Ethernet (Wi-Fi) adapters installed in your computer.

HomeGroup setup

Windows Firewall setup for wireless connections

Wireless network detection

Network and Sharing Center

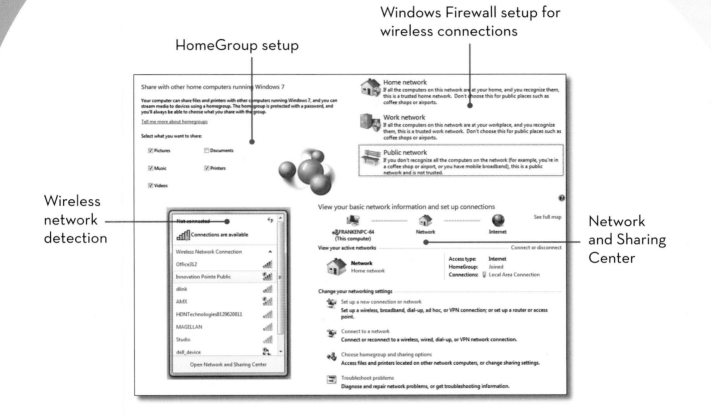

Share with other home computers running Windows 7

Your computer can share files and printers with other computers running Windows 7, and you can stream media to devices using a homegroup. The homegroup is protected with a password, and you'll always be able to choose what you share with the group.

Tell me more about homegroups

Select what you want to share:

☑ Pictures   ☐ Documents
☑ Music   ☑ Printers
☑ Videos

Home network
If all the computers on this network are at your home, and you recognize them, this is a trusted home network. Don't choose this for public places such as coffee shops or airports.

Work network
If all the computers on this network are at your workplace, and you recognize them, this is a trusted work network. Don't choose this for public places such as coffee shops or airports.

Public network
If you don't recognize all the computers on the network (for example, you're in a coffee shop or airport, or you have mobile broadband), this is a public network and is not trusted.

View your basic network information and set up connections

See full map

FRANKENPC-64   Network   Internet
(This computer)

View your active networks   Connect or disconnect

Network   Access type: Internet
Home network   HomeGroup: Joined
                            Connections: Local Area Connection

Change your networking settings

Set up a new connection or network
Set up a wireless, broadband, dial-up, ad hoc, or VPN connection; or set up a router or access point.

Connect to a network
Connect or reconnect to a wireless, wired, dial-up, or VPN network connection.

Choose homegroup and sharing options
Access files and printers located on other network computers, or change sharing settings.

Troubleshoot problems
Diagnose and repair network problems, or get troubleshooting information.

Not connected
Connections are available

Wireless Network Connection
Office312
Innovation Pointe Public
dlink
AMX
HDNTechnologies8129620811
MAGELLAN
Studio
dell_device

Open Network and Sharing Center

CONNECTING TO AN UNSECURED WIRELESS NETWORK

If you use your laptop or portable computer at public locations, such as restaurants or coffee shops, you are connecting to an unsecured wireless network. Here's how to connect safely and protect your system from intrusions.

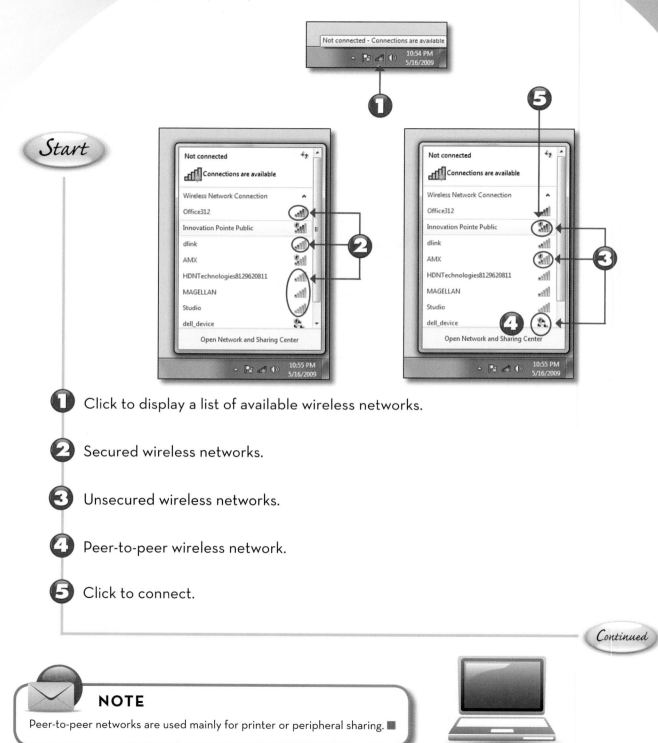

Start

1 Click to display a list of available wireless networks.

2 Secured wireless networks.

3 Unsecured wireless networks.

4 Peer-to-peer wireless network.

5 Click to connect.

Continued

NOTE

Peer-to-peer networks are used mainly for printer or peripheral sharing. ■

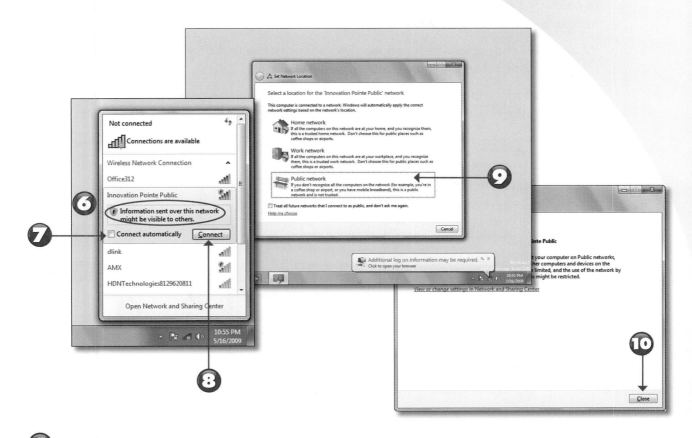

6 Note the warning that your connection is not secure.

7 Click the checkbox to connect automatically if you will use this network again.

8 Click to connect.

9 Click **Public Network**.

10 Click **Close**.

End

NOTE

Some public networks might require you to perform additional steps before you can use the network. In those cases, you will see a notification such as "Additional log on information may be required." Click the notification to open your web browser and provide the information needed. ■

NOTE

By selecting Public Network, you are configuring Windows Firewall to block all unsolicited incoming traffic. This prevents any shared resources on your system from being used by other computers. ■

CONNECTING TO A SECURED WIRELESS NETWORK

Wireless networks at home and office should be secure—meaning that the wireless router should be configured with WPA2 (preferred) or WPA encryption, and a strong passphrase (a password with a mixture of letters, numbers, and symbols) should be used to prevent access by unauthorized users.

When you connect to a secured wireless network the first time, you must provide this information, as this tutorial demonstrates.

If you need more information about how to set up a secure network, see http://www.homeserverland.com/blogs/hslblog/pages/securing-your-whs-network.aspx.

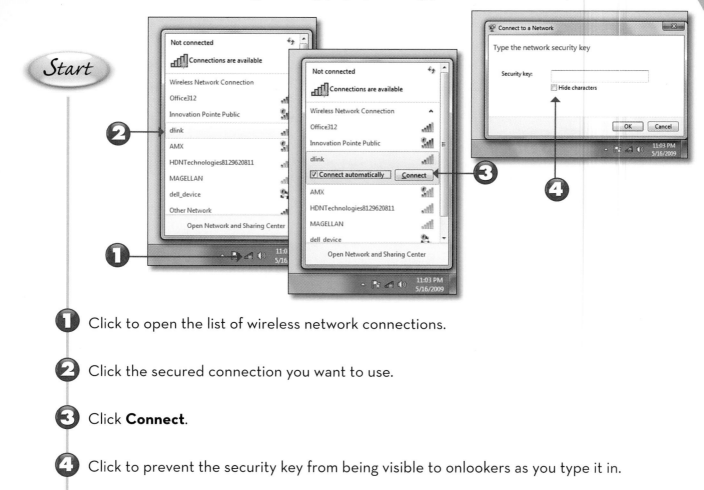

① Click to open the list of wireless network connections.

② Click the secured connection you want to use.

③ Click **Connect**.

④ Click to prevent the security key from being visible to onlookers as you type it in.

Continued

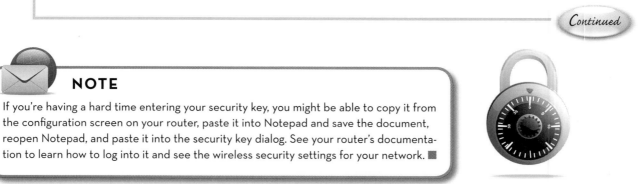

NOTE

If you're having a hard time entering your security key, you might be able to copy it from the configuration screen on your router, paste it into Notepad and save the document, reopen Notepad, and paste it into the security key dialog. See your router's documentation to learn how to log into it and see the wireless security settings for your network. ■

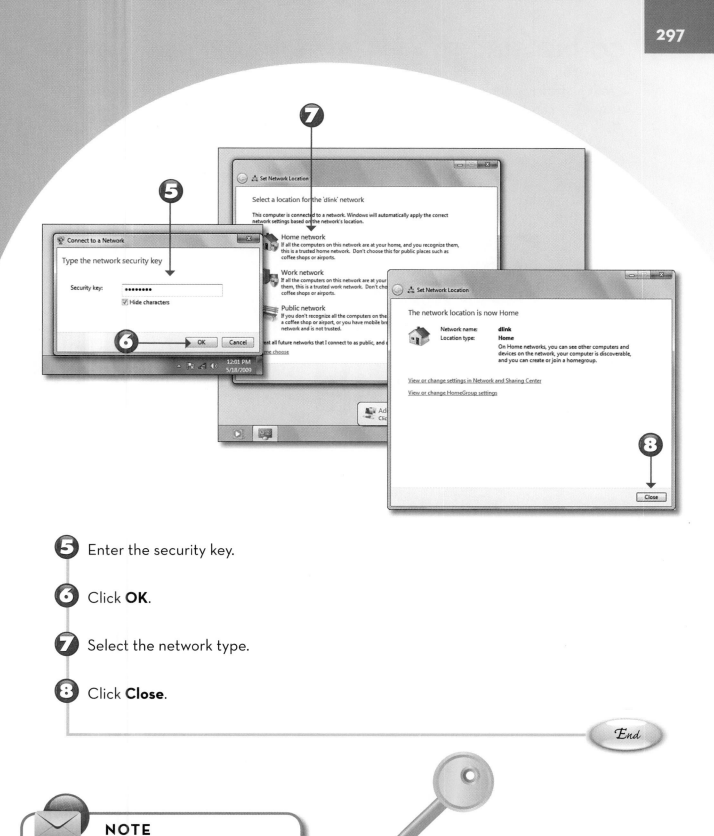

5 Enter the security key.

6 Click **OK**.

7 Select the network type.

8 Click **Close**.

End

NOTE

If you enter the incorrect key in Steps 5 and 6, you will be prompted to enter the correct key. ■

CONNECTING TO A WIRED NETWORK

If your home uses a wired network, you can connect almost any computer running Windows 7 to it just by connecting a network cable to your computer. This tutorial shows you how easy it is to add your new computer to a wired (Ethernet) network.

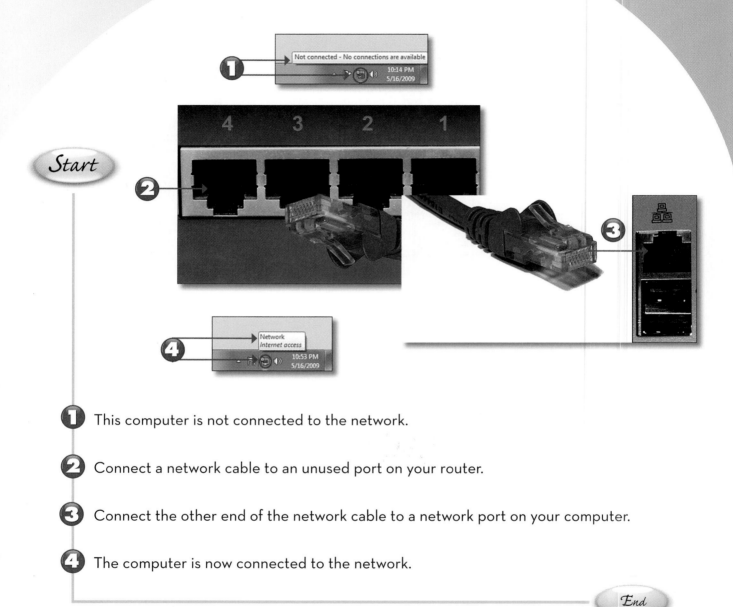

Start

1 This computer is not connected to the network.

2 Connect a network cable to an unused port on your router.

3 Connect the other end of the network cable to a network port on your computer.

4 The computer is now connected to the network.

End

NOTE

If your home or small office has built-in Ethernet cable, you can connect your computer to an RJ-45 port in a wall jack in Step 3. ■

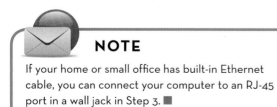

OPENING THE NETWORK AND SHARING CENTER

After you connect to a wired or wireless network, what's next? Use the Network and Sharing Center to see the status of your connection and to determine if you can connect to shared folders and printers on other computers on the network.

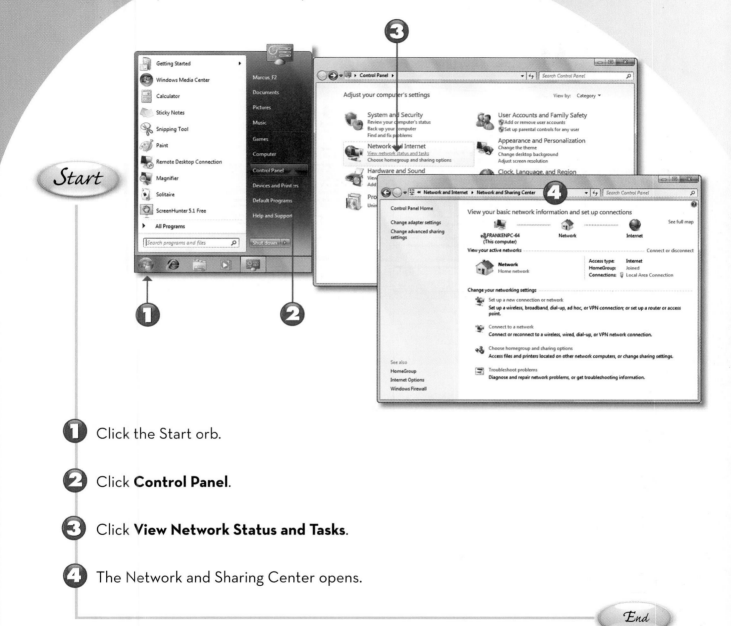

1. Click the Start orb.

2. Click **Control Panel**.

3. Click **View Network Status and Tasks**.

4. The Network and Sharing Center opens.

End

NOTE

The following exercises provide more information about the Network and Sharing Center information in Step 4. ■

VIEWING COMPUTERS ON YOUR NETWORK

Network and Sharing Center can show you the computers on your network and the resources they share. Here's how.

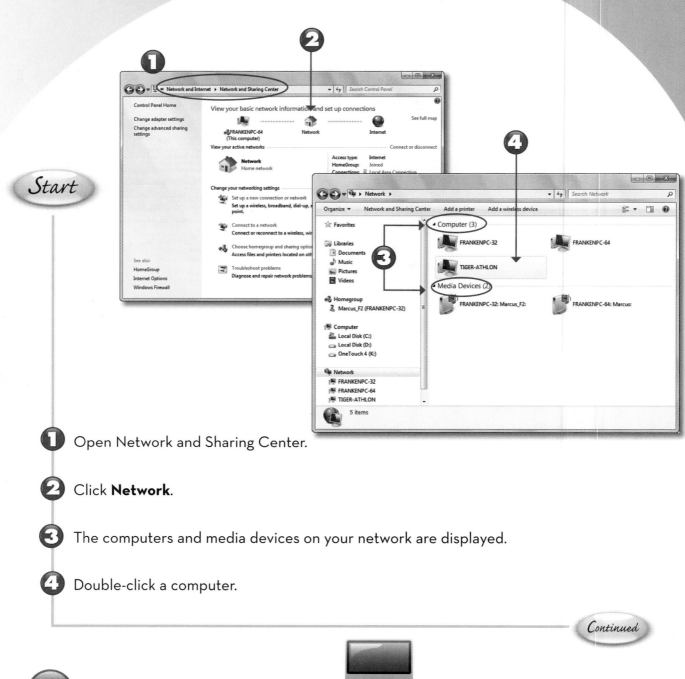

Start

1. Open Network and Sharing Center.

2. Click **Network**.

3. The computers and media devices on your network are displayed.

4. Double-click a computer.

Continued

NOTE

Media Devices (see Step 4) refer to computers or other devices set up to share media with other computers and devices. ■

 A shared folder.

6 A shared printer.

End

 NOTE

The icon for network (Step 2) changes according to whether you have a home, business, or public network. ■

USING THE NETWORK MAP TO DIAGRAM YOUR NETWORK

Network and Sharing Center's Network Map can be a useful tool in visualizing how your network fits together. Here's how to open it and understand what it is telling you.

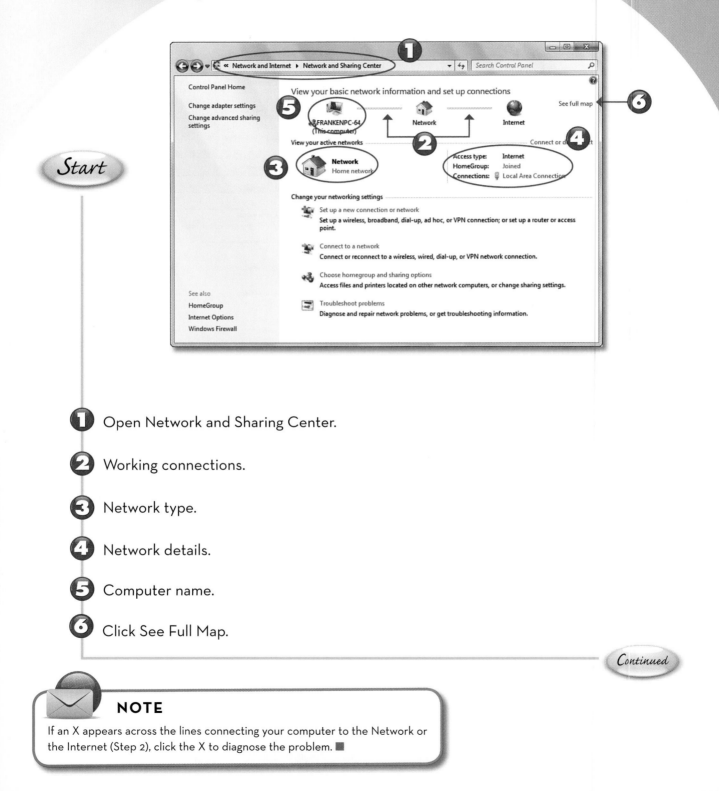

Start

1 Open Network and Sharing Center.

2 Working connections.

3 Network type.

4 Network details.

5 Computer name.

6 Click See Full Map.

Continued

NOTE

If an X appears across the lines connecting your computer to the Network or the Internet (Step 2), click the X to diagnose the problem. ■

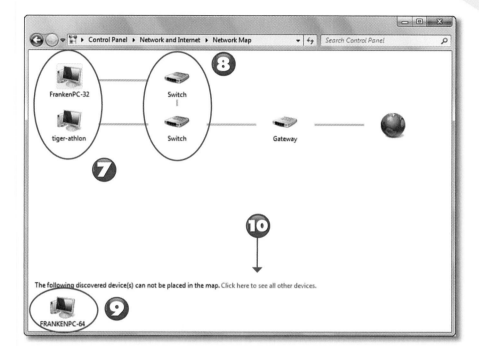

7 Mapped Computers.

8 Connection devices.

9 Non-mapped computers.

10 Click to see all devices.

End

TIP

If your network includes Windows XP computers and you want them to appear on the Network Map, go to http://support.microsoft.com/?kbid=922120 and download LLTD Responder. This file enables Windows XP-based systems to show up on the Network Map feature in Windows 7 as well as Windows Vista. ■

CHANGING YOUR WORKGROUP

Windows 7 views networks in two different ways. If you have only a physical connection to a network (a working wired or wireless connection), you can access the Internet. However, unless you also have the correct workgroup, homegroup, or domain setting, you might not be able to "see" other computers on the network and cannot use their shared resources.

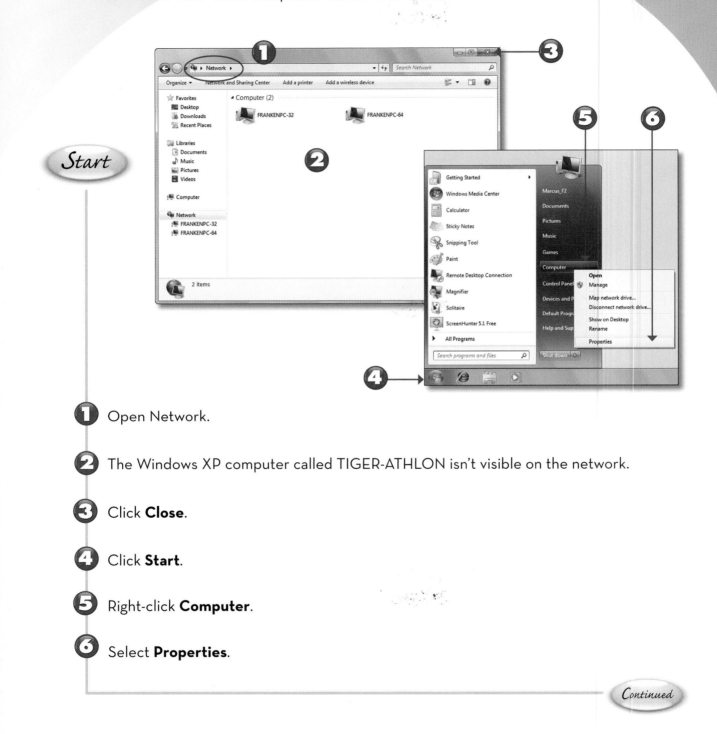

Start

1 Open Network.

2 The Windows XP computer called TIGER-ATHLON isn't visible on the network.

3 Click **Close**.

4 Click **Start**.

5 Right-click **Computer**.

6 Select **Properties**.

Continued

Windows 7 computers can access shared resources on other Windows 7 or Windows Vista computers without being in the same workgroup. However, if your network contains computers running Windows XP, you need to use the same workgroup setting on all computers so you can view the computers and share resources. Windows computers use WORKGROUP as the default workgroup, but if your home or work network uses a different workgroup name and you cannot access shares on those computers, here's how to find out the correct setting and change it on your new Windows 7 computer.

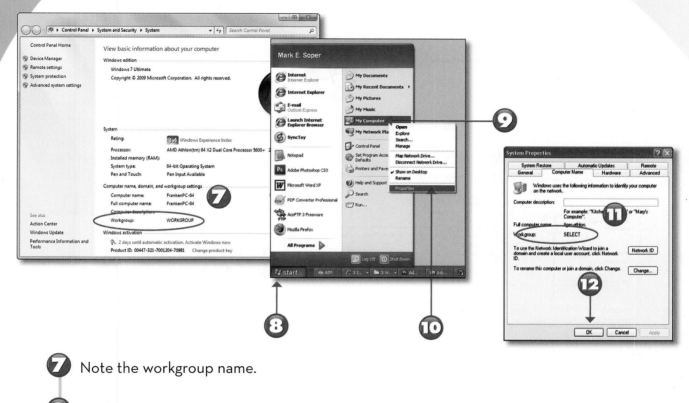

7 Note the workgroup name.

8 On the Windows XP computer, click **Start**.

9 Right-click **My Computer**.

10 Click **Properties**.

11 Note the different workgroup name.

12 Click **OK**.

Continued

NOTE

If you used the Home Networking Wizard included in Windows XP at an earlier time, keep in mind that the wizard uses MSHOME as the default workgroup name. ■

13 Return to the Windows 7 computer and click **Change Settings**.

14 Click **Change**.

15 Enter the new workgroup name.

16 Click **OK**.

17 Click **OK**.

18 Click **OK**.

Continued

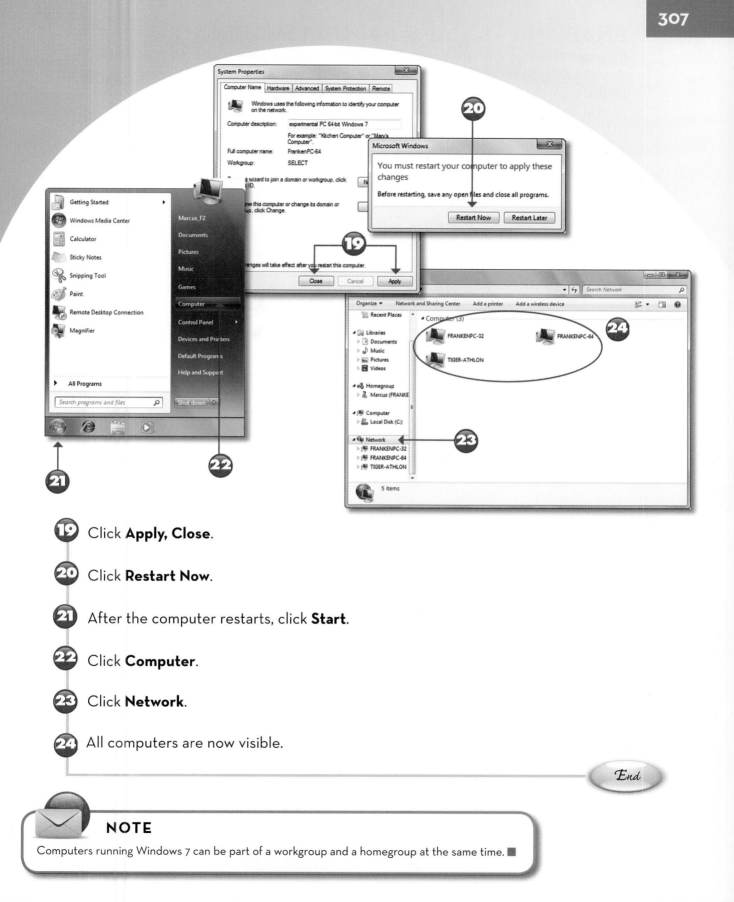

19 Click **Apply, Close**.

20 Click **Restart Now**.

21 After the computer restarts, click **Start**.

22 Click **Computer**.

23 Click **Network**.

24 All computers are now visible.

End

NOTE

Computers running Windows 7 can be part of a workgroup and a homegroup at the same time. ■

ENABLING FILE AND PRINTER SHARING

It's important to understand these facts about file and printer sharing: You don't need to share resources on your system to use resources on other systems. However, if you want to share any folder, printer, or other resource on your computer, you must enable file and printer sharing before you select what you want to share. Here's an easy way to do it.

Start

1 Open the Network and Sharing Center.

2 Click **Network**.

3 If the File Sharing is Turned Off... banner appears, click it to enable sharing.

4 Click the back arrow.

End

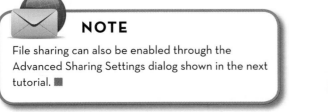

NOTE

File sharing can also be enabled through the Advanced Sharing Settings dialog shown in the next tutorial. ■

SHARING PUBLIC FOLDERS

Windows 7 uses the Public folder and subfolders (Public Pictures, and so on) in two ways: to share files between different users on the same system, or to share files between different PCs. Here's how to enable folder sharing for Public folders.

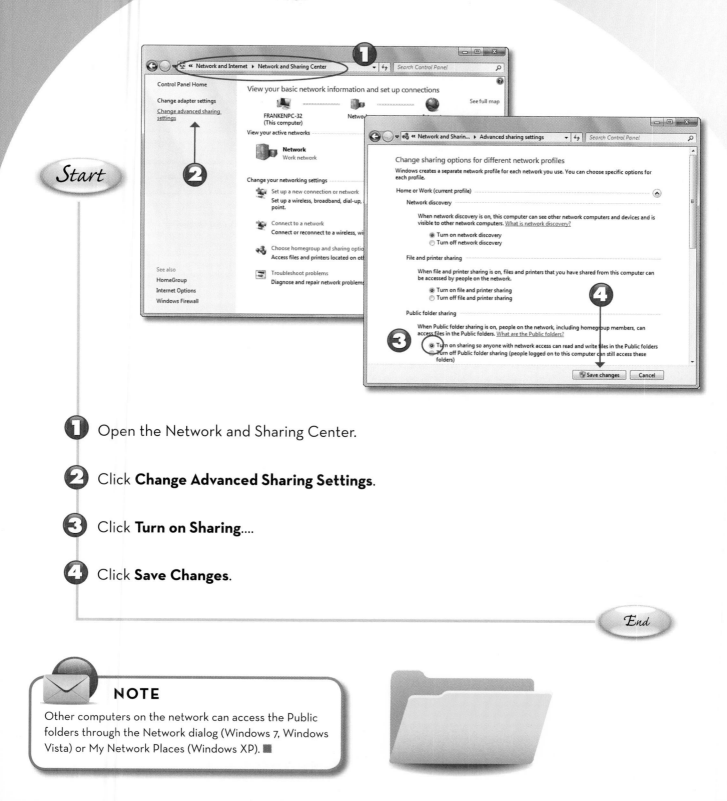

Start

1. Open the Network and Sharing Center.

2. Click **Change Advanced Sharing Settings**.

3. Click **Turn on Sharing**....

4. Click **Save Changes**.

End

NOTE

Other computers on the network can access the Public folders through the Network dialog (Windows 7, Windows Vista) or My Network Places (Windows XP). ■

SHARING PRINTERS

When you set up file and printer sharing, you can share any printer on your system. Here's how.

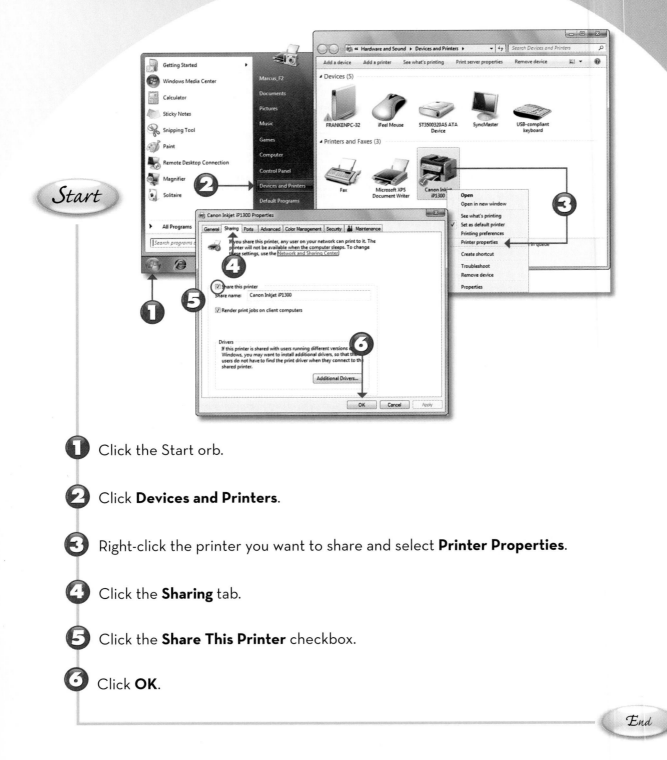

1 Click the Start orb.

2 Click **Devices and Printers**.

3 Right-click the printer you want to share and select **Printer Properties**.

4 Click the **Sharing** tab.

5 Click the **Share This Printer** checkbox.

6 Click **OK**.

End

SETTING UP A HOMEGROUP

If you have two or more Windows 7-based systems on your network, you can set up a home-group, a new type of secured network configuration. A homegroup provides a combination of high security and ease of use. Here's how to set up your own homegroup.

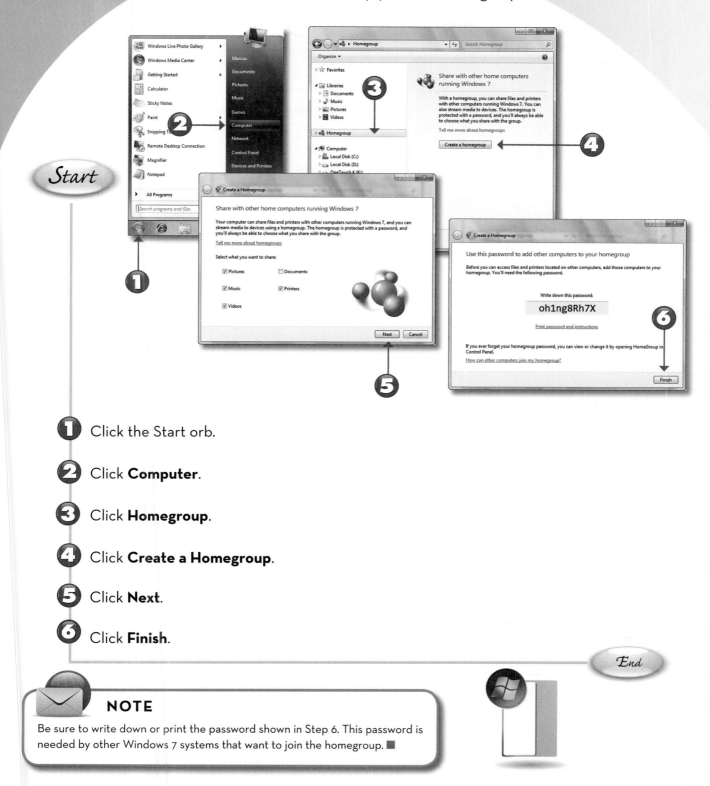

1 Click the Start orb.

2 Click **Computer**.

3 Click **Homegroup**.

4 Click **Create a Homegroup**.

5 Click **Next**.

6 Click **Finish**.

NOTE

Be sure to write down or print the password shown in Step 6. This password is needed by other Windows 7 systems that want to join the homegroup. ■

JOINING A HOMEGROUP

After you create a homegroup on one Windows 7-based computer on your network, wait a few minutes for the homegroup creation process to finish. Then, other Windows 7-based computers can join the homegroup. Here's how.

Start

1 Open **Control Panel**.

2 Click **Choose Homegroup and Sharing Options**.

3 Click **Join Now**.

4 Click **Next**.

Continued

NOTE

You can specify a different combination of file types on each computer that joins the HomeGroup (see Step 4). ■

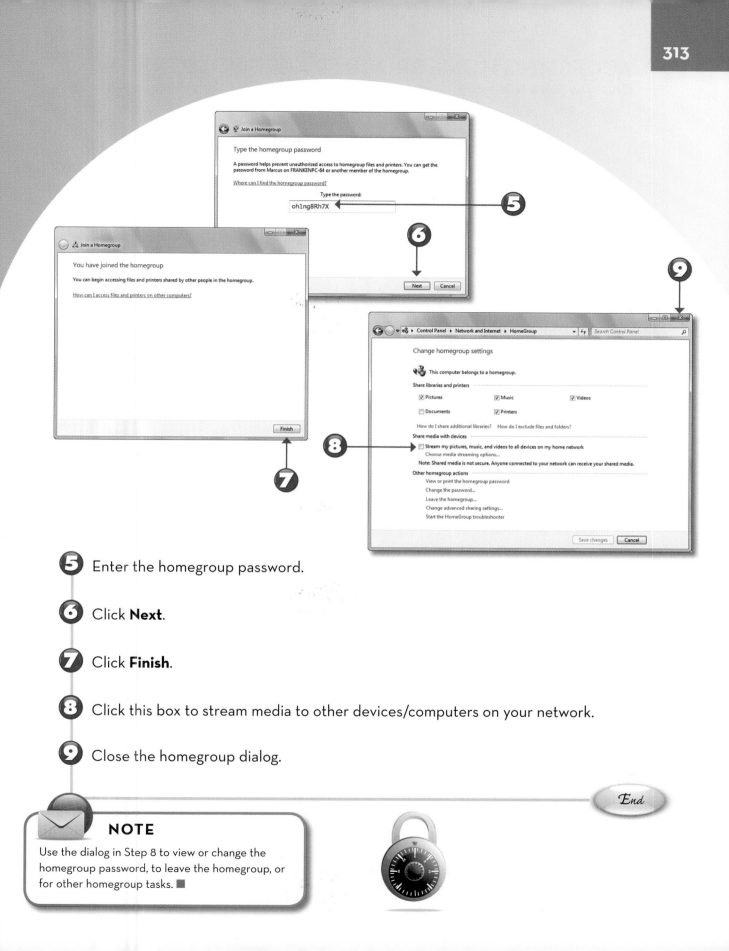

5 Enter the homegroup password.

6 Click **Next**.

7 Click **Finish**.

8 Click this box to stream media to other devices/computers on your network.

9 Close the homegroup dialog.

End

NOTE

Use the dialog in Step 8 to view or change the homegroup password, to leave the homegroup, or for other homegroup tasks. ■

ACCESSING HOMEGROUP SHARED FOLDERS

Once you join a homegroup, you can access other computers' shared folders. Here's how.

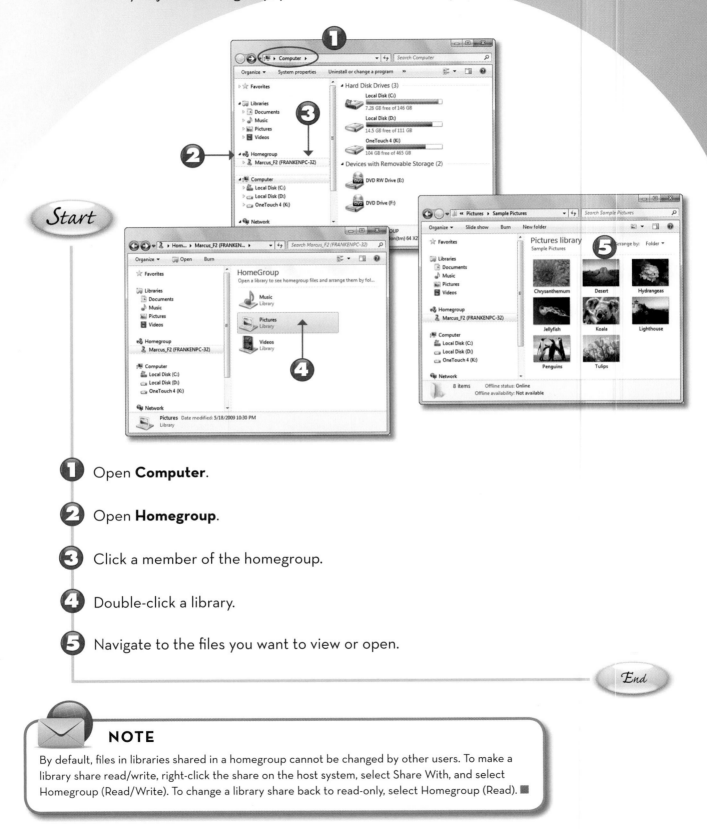

Start

1. Open **Computer**.

2. Open **Homegroup**.

3. Click a member of the homegroup.

4. Double-click a library.

5. Navigate to the files you want to view or open.

End

NOTE

By default, files in libraries shared in a homegroup cannot be changed by other users. To make a library share read/write, right-click the share on the host system, select Share With, and select Homegroup (Read/Write). To change a library share back to read-only, select Homegroup (Read). ■

CHANGING HOMEGROUP SETTINGS

The normal (default) settings used for homegroups might not be exactly what you want. Here's how to make changes on any system that's part of a homegroup. In this example, we'll enable the option to stream media to other devices on the network.

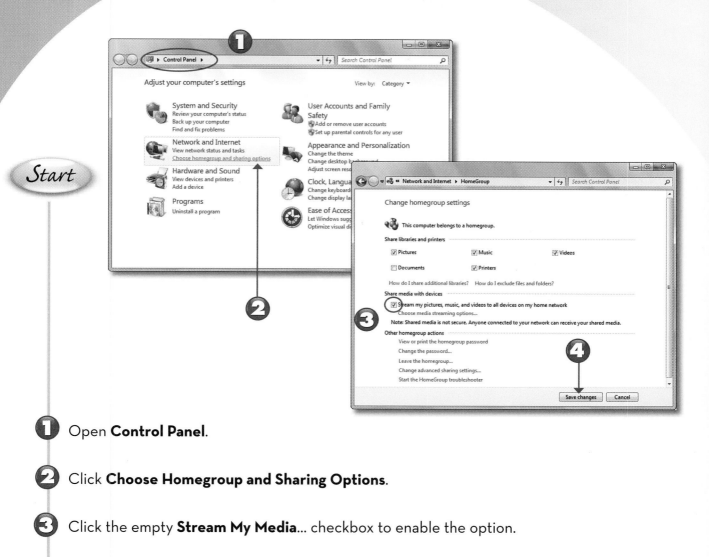

Start

1. Open **Control Panel**.

2. Click **Choose Homegroup and Sharing Options**.

3. Click the empty **Stream My Media**... checkbox to enable the option.

4. Click **Save Changes**.

End

NOTE

To make other changes, follow the appropriate links. ■

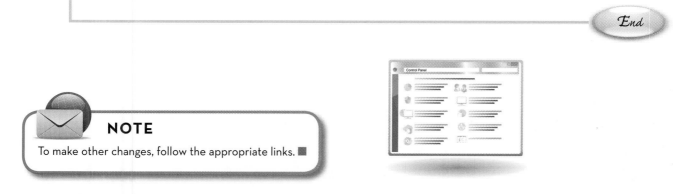

USING WINDOWS EASY TRANSFER

Windows Easy Transfer enables you to transfer files and program settings (but not actual programs) between a Windows 7 PC and a PC running Windows 7, Windows Vista, or Windows XP. Windows Easy Transfer is very useful for making a move to a new computer. Windows Easy Transfer can transfer data from an old computer to a new Windows 7 computer via a Windows Easy Transfer cable, an external hard disk, or a network connection. In this example, we'll show you how to use a network connection to transfer all your files to the new PC.

Start

1 Click the Start orb.

2 Open **Getting Started**.

3 Click **Transfer Your Files**.

4 Click **Next**.

5 Click a network.

Continued

NOTE

You will have the fastest network transfer if you use a gigabit Ethernet wired network. The next fastest transfer is via a Wireless-N (802.11n) network, followed by a Fast Ethernet wired network, and then a Wireless-G (802.11g) or Wireless-A (802.11a) network. The slowest transfers are performed by a 10Base-T wired network or a Wireless-B (802.11a) network. ■

6 Click **This is My New Computer**.

7 Click **I Need to Install It Now**.

8 Click **External Hard Disk or Shared Network Folder**.

9 Navigate to the network folder where you want to install the program.

10 Click **OK**.

Continued

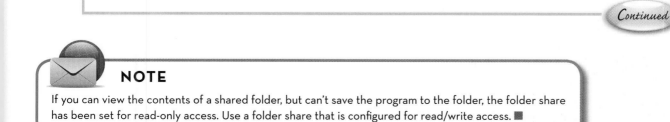

NOTE

If you can view the contents of a shared folder, but can't save the program to the folder, the folder share has been set for read-only access. Use a folder share that is configured for read/write access. ■

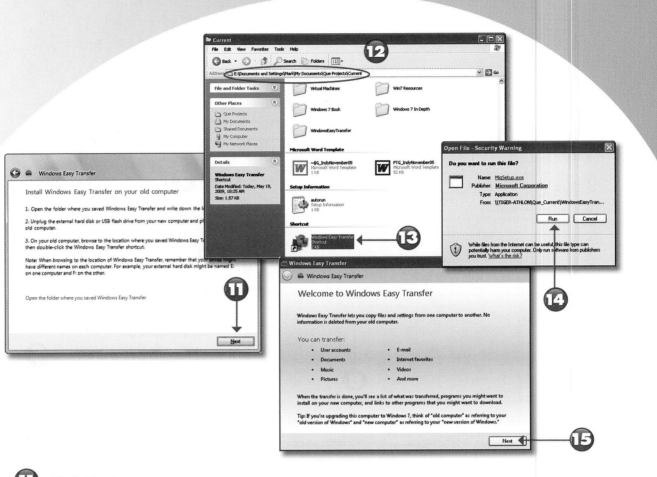

11 Click **Next**.

12 Go to the old computer and navigate to the location where Windows Easy Transfer is installed.

13 Double-click the shortcut.

14 Click **Run**.

15 Click **Next**.

Continued

NOTE

This example uses Windows XP, but Windows Easy Transfer can also transfer files from computers running Windows Vista or Windows 7. ■

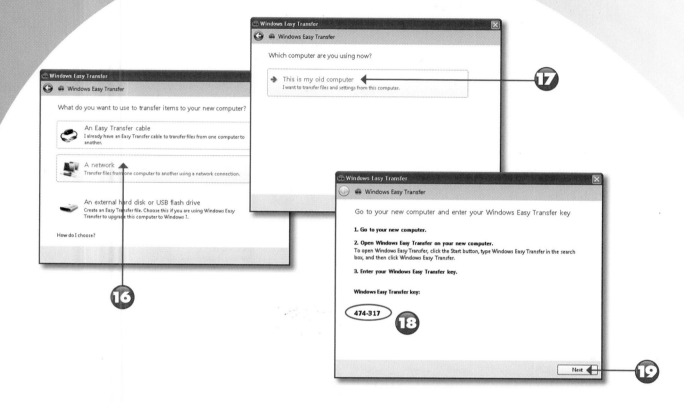

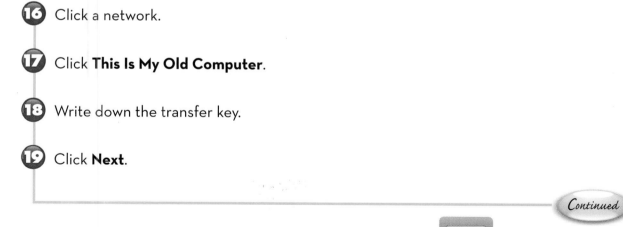

16 Click a network.

17 Click **This Is My Old Computer**.

18 Write down the transfer key.

19 Click **Next**.

Continued

NOTE

If you need to restart the process for some reason, you must create a new transfer key by rerunning the Windows Easy Transfer program on the old PC. ∎

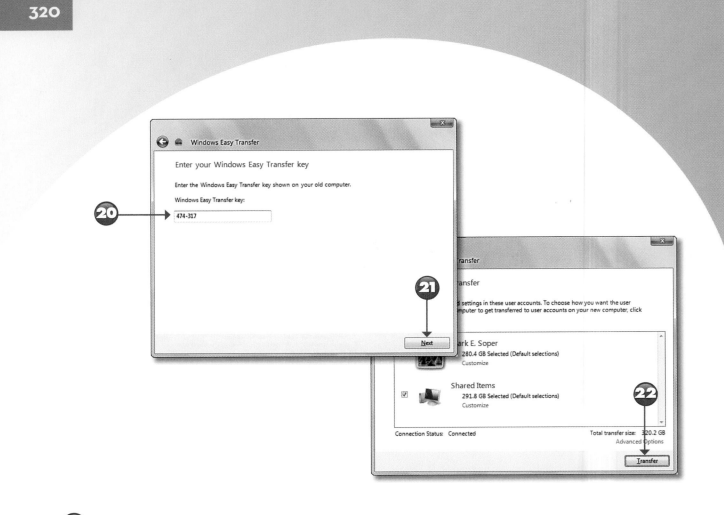

20 Go to the new computer and enter the transfer key.

21 Click **Next**.

22 To transfer all files, click **Transfer**.

Continued

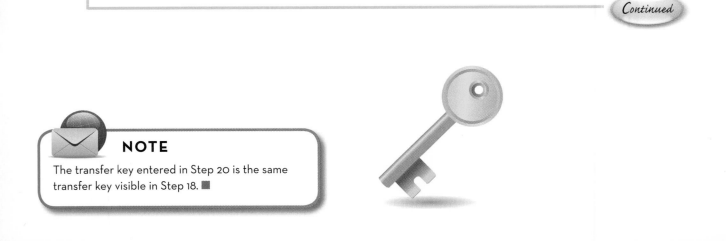

NOTE

The transfer key entered in Step 20 is the same transfer key visible in Step 18. ■

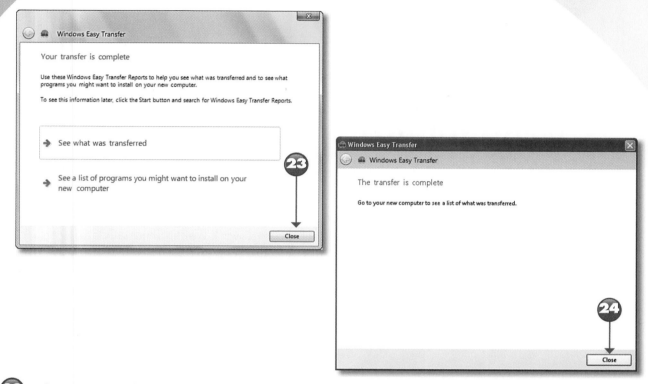

23 After the transfer is complete, click to close.

24 Return to the old computer and click **Close**.

End

NOTE

At Step 22, you can specify which files to transfer by clearing checkboxes or clicking Customize. At Step 23, you can get a detailed list of files transferred and programs to install on the new computer. ■

Chapter 17

USING WINDOWS LIVE ESSENTIALS

For Windows 7, Microsoft has removed the built-in photo editing and organizing, video editing, email, and messaging features found in previous Windows versions and replaced them with the optional Windows Live Essentials family.

Although Windows 7 users are not required to use Windows Live Essentials, the programs it includes provide useful features, work well individually and with each other, integrate well with Windows, and are free to use. This chapter concentrates on the Windows Live Essential components that most users will find helpful: Windows Live Photo Gallery, Windows Live Mail, and Windows Live Family Safety.

Windows DVD Maker

Windows Live program
selection menu

Windows Live
Family Safety
blocked website
message

Windows Live
Mail calendar
module

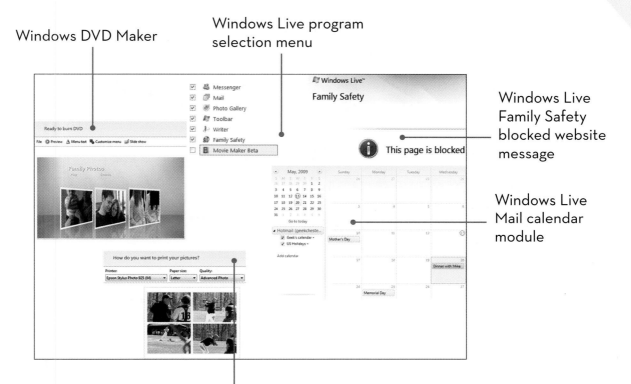

Windows Photo Printing wizard

DOWNLOADING AND INSTALLING WINDOWS LIVE ESSENTIALS

Windows Live Essentials is easy to get: It can be downloaded by using a link on the Windows 7 Getting Started menu. In this tutorial, you learn how to download and install the Windows Live Essentials components you want to use.

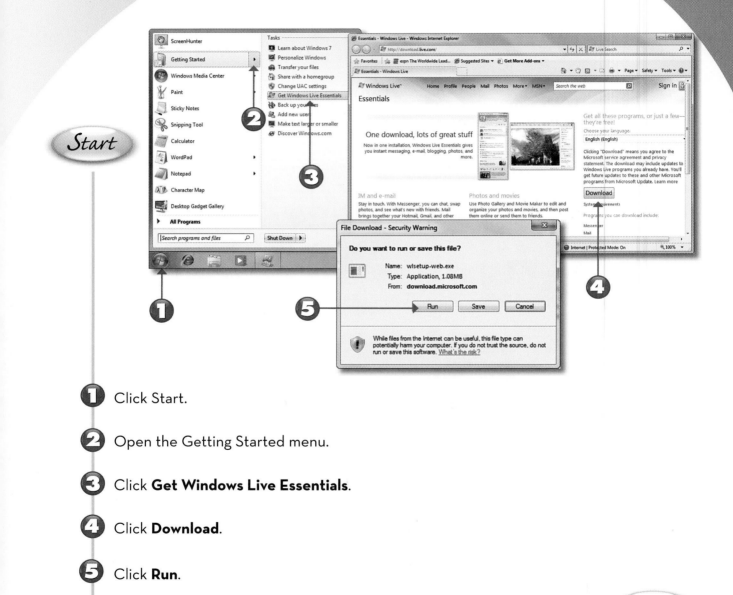

Start

1. Click Start.

2. Open the Getting Started menu.

3. Click **Get Windows Live Essentials**.

4. Click **Download**.

5. Click **Run**.

Continued

 NOTE

If Getting Started is not visible in the left-hand menu, you can start it by opening the All Programs menu and launching it from the shortcut in that menu. ■

 **NOTE**

To install Microsoft Office Outlook Connector or Office Live Add-in, follow steps 1-3, then scroll down and select each of these programs separately. ■

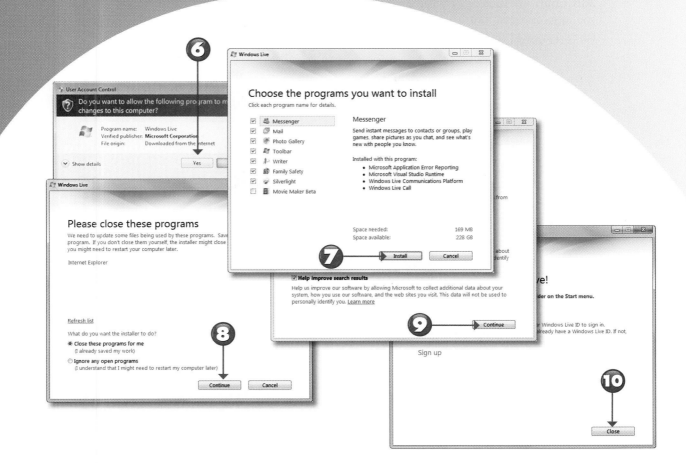

6 Click Yes on the UAC prompt.

7 Click **Install**.

8 You may be prompted to close programs. Click **Continue**.

9 Click **Continue**.

10 Click **Close**.

End

NOTE

If you want to skip installing some programs, clear their checkboxes. To install unchecked programs, click inside the checkbox. ∎

NOTE

At Step 9, you also have the option of enabling or disabling options before continuing. You can also change your search provider and home page settings later through the Internet Options icon in Control Panel. ∎

VIEWING PHOTOS IN GALLERY VIEW

Although Windows 7 includes the Windows Photo Viewer, Windows Live Photo Gallery provides more viewing options. In this tutorial, you learn how to view photos by folder and by date and how to change preview size.

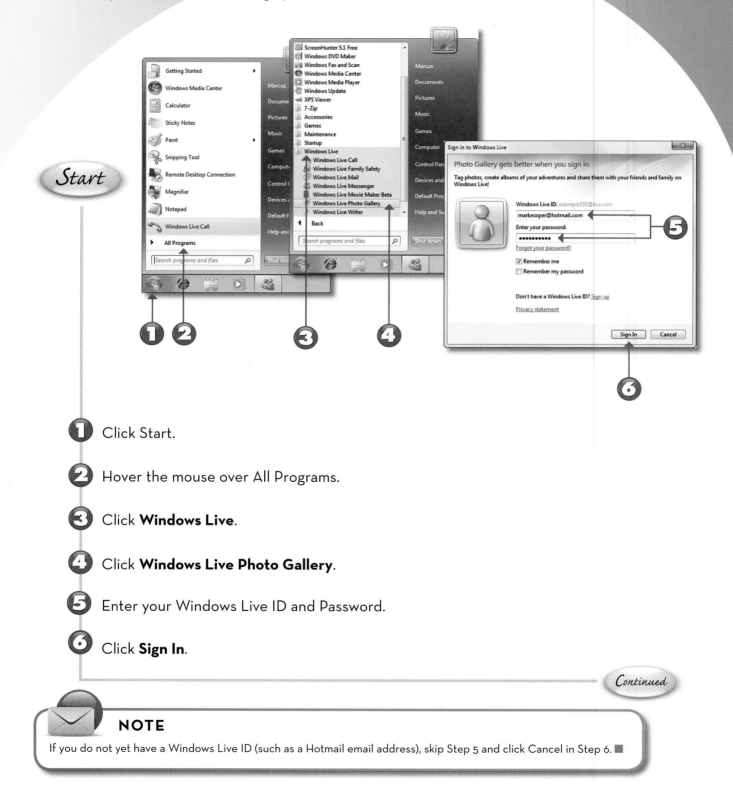

1 Click Start.

2 Hover the mouse over All Programs.

3 Click **Windows Live**.

4 Click **Windows Live Photo Gallery**.

5 Enter your Windows Live ID and Password.

6 Click **Sign In**.

Continued

NOTE

If you do not yet have a Windows Live ID (such as a Hotmail email address), skip Step 5 and click Cancel in Step 6. ∎

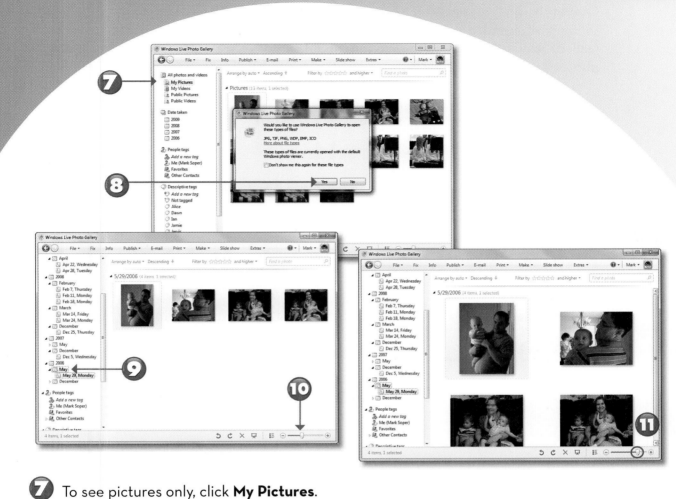

7 To see pictures only, click **My Pictures**.

8 Click **Yes**.

9 To see only pictures taken at a particular time, click the year, month, or day.

10 Move the slider to adjust the size of picture thumbnails.

11 Larger thumbnails.

End

NOTE

If you are unable to view some types of picture or video files, you will be prompted to download and install the appropriate codecs. ■

ADDING AND USING TAGS

One of the best reasons to add Windows Live Photo Gallery to your system is the ability to tag photos and videos by people, subject, location, or other events. Windows Live Photo Gallery now includes both people tags and descriptive tags. Here's how to add them to your photos and videos and use them to filter your collection.

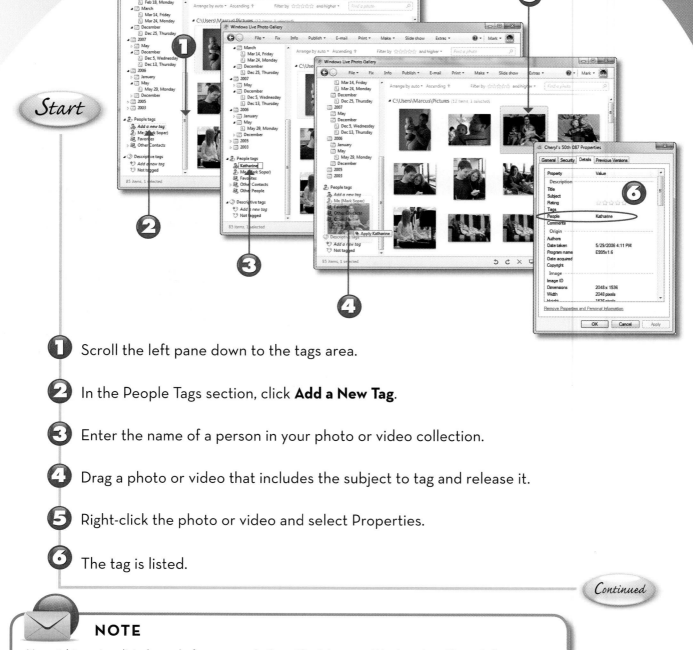

Start

1 Scroll the left pane down to the tags area.

2 In the People Tags section, click **Add a New Tag**.

3 Enter the name of a person in your photo or video collection.

4 Drag a photo or video that includes the subject to tag and release it.

5 Right-click the photo or video and select Properties.

6 The tag is listed.

Continued

NOTE

You might see tags listed even before you apply them. That's because Windows Live Photo Gallery recognizes tags that may have been applied when photos were imported by Windows Photo Gallery in Windows Vista, by Windows Live's picture import function, or tags applied through the properties sheet for a file. ■

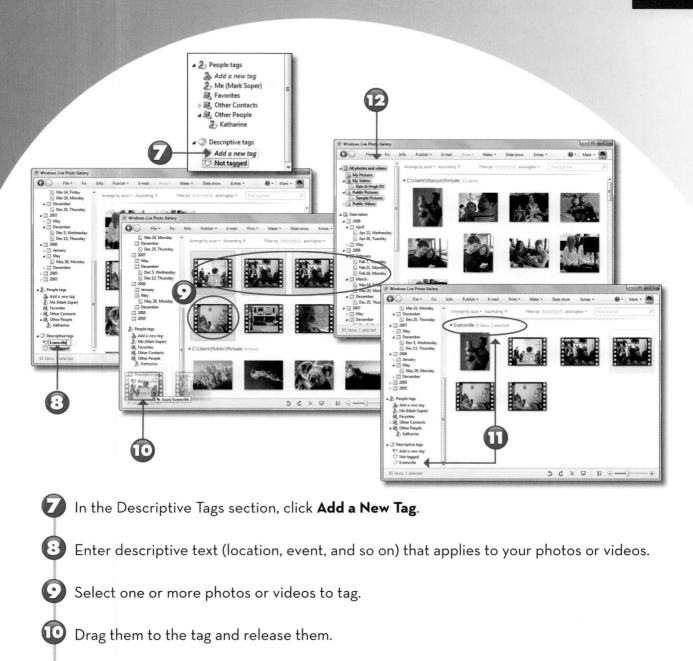

7 In the Descriptive Tags section, click **Add a New Tag**.

8 Enter descriptive text (location, event, and so on) that applies to your photos or videos.

9 Select one or more photos or videos to tag.

10 Drag them to the tag and release them.

11 Click a tag to see only the photos or videos with the tag.

12 Click **All Photos and Videos** to see everything.

End

NOTE

To select multiple photos or videos for tagging, click the first one and then hold down either Ctrl key and click the remainder. Release the Ctrl key when done, and drag the selected files to the tag. ∎

PLAYING A SLIDE SHOW

Windows Live Photo Gallery provides many slide show playback styles when your system supports the Aero desktop. Here's how to start a slide show and select from different options.

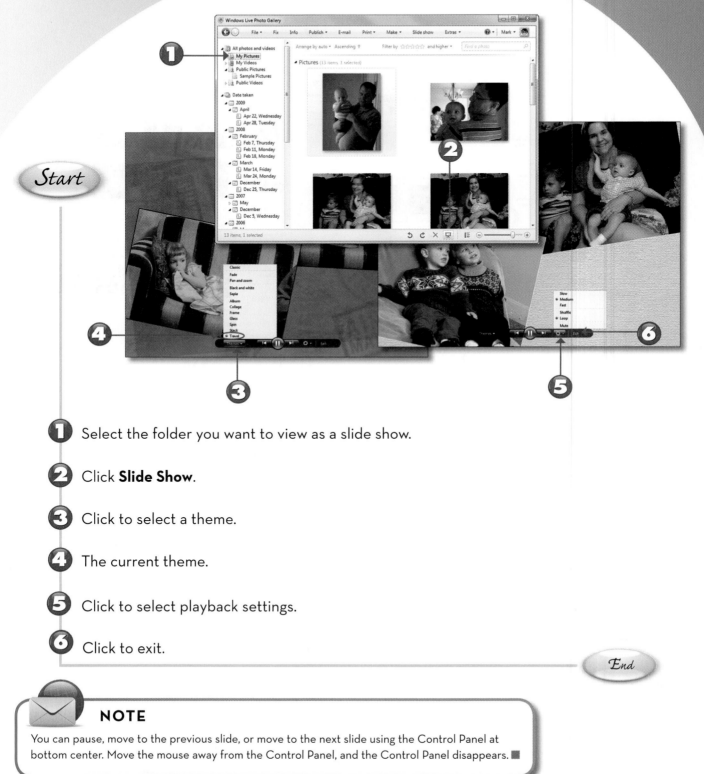

Start

End

1. Select the folder you want to view as a slide show.

2. Click **Slide Show**.

3. Click to select a theme.

4. The current theme.

5. Click to select playback settings.

6. Click to exit.

NOTE

You can pause, move to the previous slide, or move to the next slide using the Control Panel at bottom center. Move the mouse away from the Control Panel, and the Control Panel disappears. ∎

FIXING PHOTOS

Windows Live Photo Gallery includes several powerful photo-repair tools. Here's how to access those tools to fix common photo problems. In this example, we'll use the Auto Adjust tool.

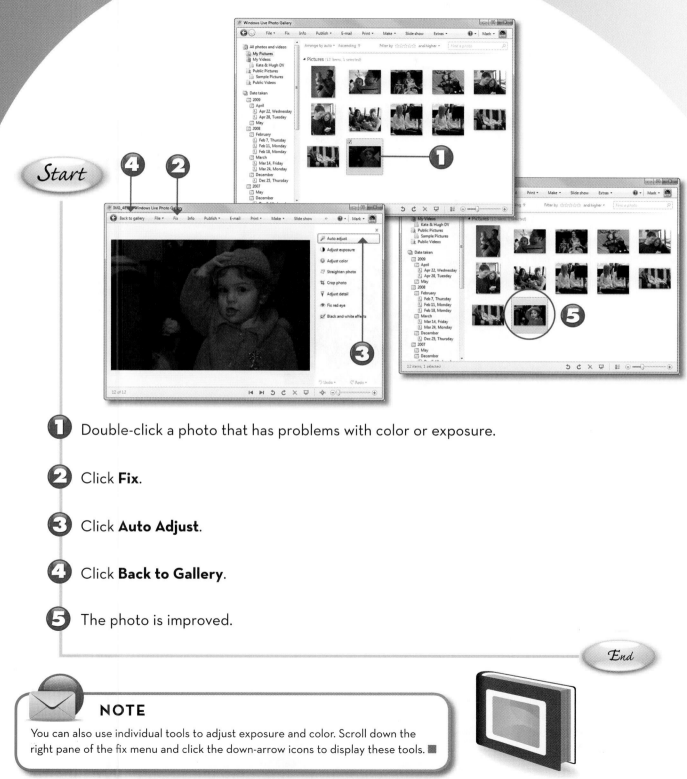

1. Double-click a photo that has problems with color or exposure.

2. Click **Fix**.

3. Click **Auto Adjust**.

4. Click **Back to Gallery**.

5. The photo is improved.

NOTE

You can also use individual tools to adjust exposure and color. Scroll down the right pane of the fix menu and click the down-arrow icons to display these tools. ■

CROPPING A PHOTO AND UNDOING CHANGES

You can also crop a photo with Windows Live Photo Gallery, and undo cropping or other changes. This tutorial shows you how.

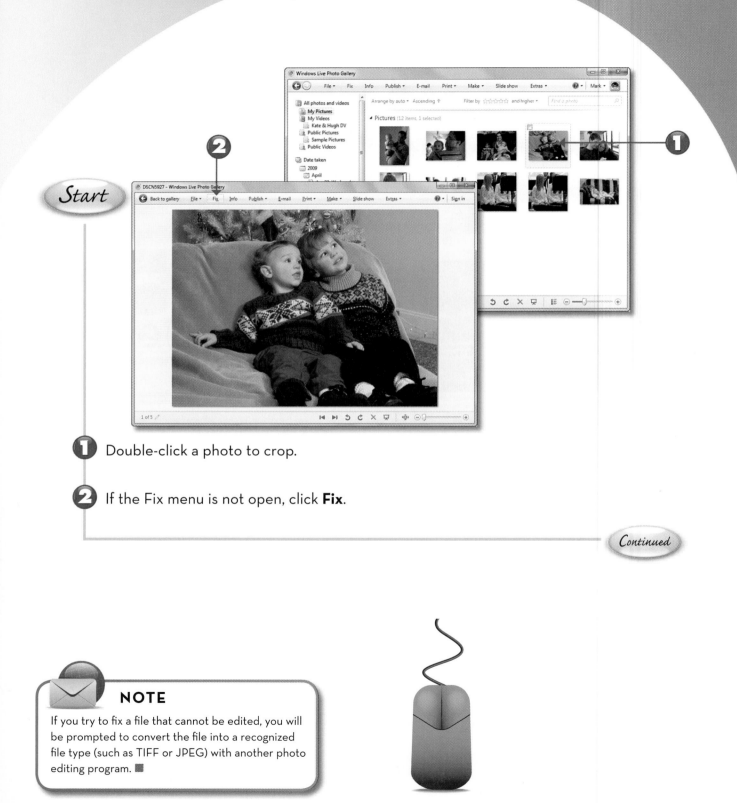

Start

1 Double-click a photo to crop.

2 If the Fix menu is not open, click **Fix**.

Continued

NOTE

If you try to fix a file that cannot be edited, you will be prompted to convert the file into a recognized file type (such as TIFF or JPEG) with another photo editing program. ■

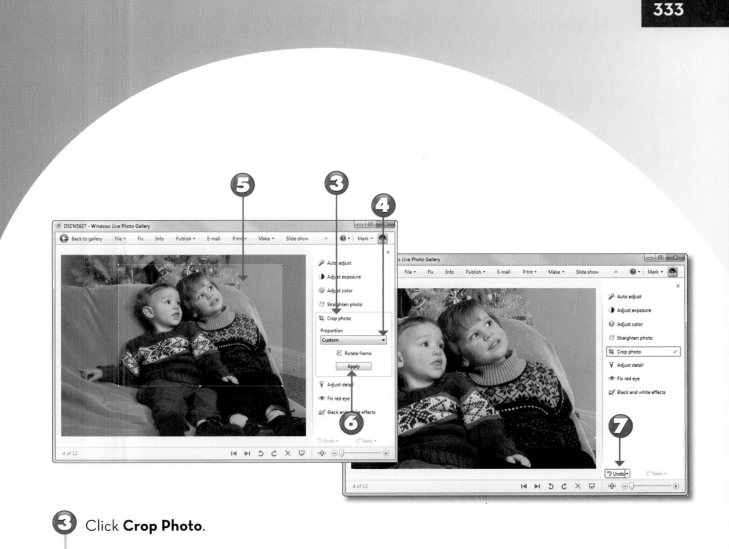

3 Click **Crop Photo**.

4 Select a proportion.

5 Drag cropping mask into position.

6 Click **Apply**.

7 Click **Undo**.

End

TIP

Drag the crop mask as desired to fit your subject by clicking inside the mask or by dragging the crop marks. ■

NOTE

You can also remove changes after returning to Gallery View. Open the photo, select Fix, and choose Revert to Original from the Undo menu. ■

SHARING PHOTOS WITH FLICKR

Windows Live Photo Gallery also enables you to share your photos with Flickr. Here's how to select photos to share and start the sharing process. In this tutorial, we assume you already have a Flickr account.

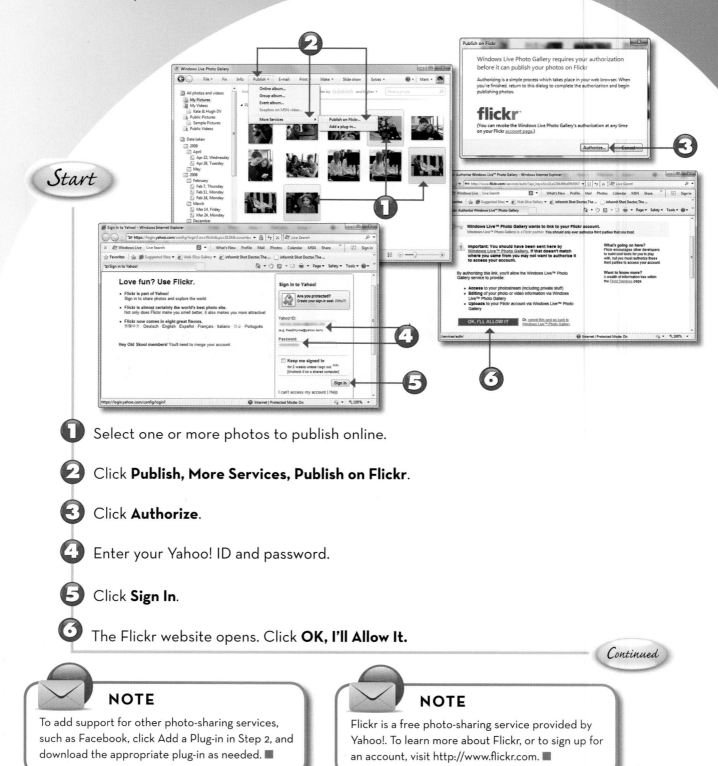

Start

1. Select one or more photos to publish online.

2. Click **Publish, More Services, Publish on Flickr**.

3. Click **Authorize**.

4. Enter your Yahoo! ID and password.

5. Click **Sign In**.

6. The Flickr website opens. Click **OK, I'll Allow It.**

Continued

NOTE

To add support for other photo-sharing services, such as Facebook, click Add a Plug-in in Step 2, and download the appropriate plug-in as needed. ■

NOTE

Flickr is a free photo-sharing service provided by Yahoo!. To learn more about Flickr, or to sign up for an account, visit http://www.flickr.com. ■

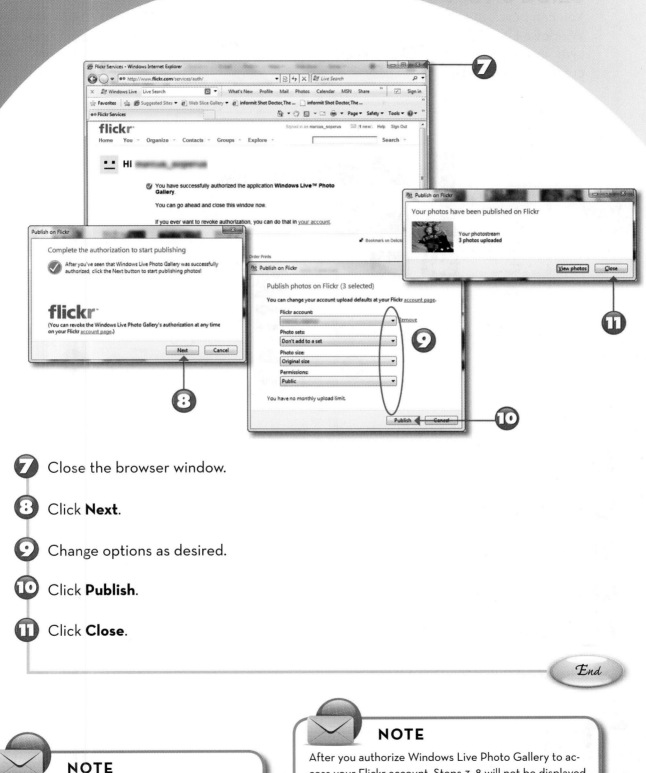

7 Close the browser window.

8 Click **Next**.

9 Change options as desired.

10 Click **Publish**.

11 Click **Close**.

End

NOTE

To see your photos on Flickr, click View Photos. ■

NOTE

After you authorize Windows Live Photo Gallery to access your Flickr account, Steps 3–8 will not be displayed the next time you publish your photos to Flickr. ■

BURNING PHOTOS AND VIDEOS TO A DVD SLIDE SHOW

You can burn your photos and videos to CD or DVD from either Windows Photo Viewer or Windows Live Photo Gallery. However, I recommend starting the process from Windows Live Photo Gallery, as it makes selecting the photos and videos easier. In this example, we'll create a video DVD.

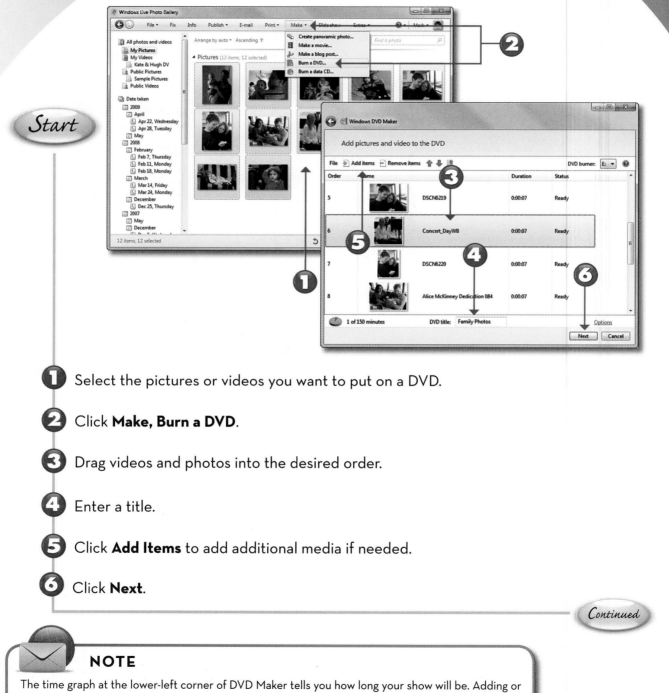

Start

1. Select the pictures or videos you want to put on a DVD.

2. Click **Make, Burn a DVD**.

3. Drag videos and photos into the desired order.

4. Enter a title.

5. Click **Add Items** to add additional media if needed.

6. Click **Next**.

Continued

NOTE

The time graph at the lower-left corner of DVD Maker tells you how long your show will be. Adding or deleting photos and videos and adjusting the playback time of each photo changes the time graph. ■

7 Select a menu style.

8 Click **Slide Show**.

9 Select options as desired.

10 Click **Change Slide Show**.

11 Insert recordable DVD and click Burn.

12 Click **Close** when finished.

End

NOTE

When you close the DVD Maker, you are prompted to save your show. Click Yes and provide a file name when prompted so you can make more DVDs later. ∎

NOTE

In Step 12, click Make Another Copy... to burn another copy. Because the DVD is already encoded, burning a second copy is faster than starting over. ∎

IMPORTING PHOTOS FROM A CAMERA

Windows Live Photo Gallery makes importing photos from a camera very simple, while enabling you to add tags and place photos in folders as appropriate. Here's how to use it.

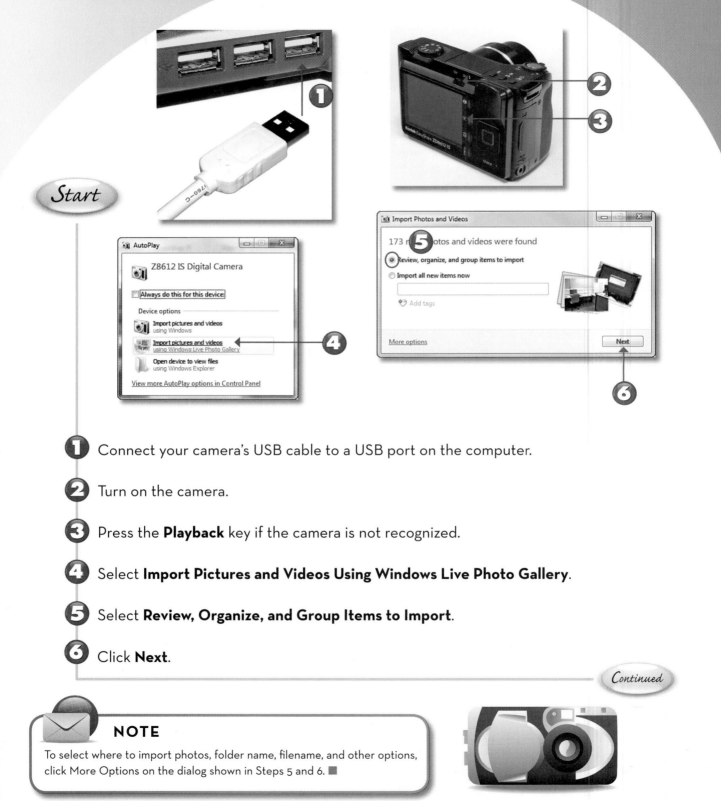

1. Connect your camera's USB cable to a USB port on the computer.

2. Turn on the camera.

3. Press the **Playback** key if the camera is not recognized.

4. Select **Import Pictures and Videos Using Windows Live Photo Gallery**.

5. Select **Review, Organize, and Group Items to Import**.

6. Click **Next**.

Continued

NOTE

To select where to import photos, folder name, filename, and other options, click More Options on the dialog shown in Steps 5 and 6. ■

7 Enter a name (optional); if you don't name the group, the date is used for the folder.

8 Enter tags as desired.

9 Clear checkboxes for groups you don't want to download.

10 Click **Import**.

11 Click to view newly-imported photos and videos.

End

NOTE

You can also import photos and videos with a card reader. You might prefer to use a card reader because you won't run down your camera's batteries and you won't have problems with your camera shutting down partway through a picture transfer. ■

PRINTING PHOTOS

You can print photos from Pictures Library or Windows Live Photo Gallery. In this example, we'll print photos from Windows Live Photo Gallery, but the process is the same for printing from Picture Library.

In this example, we select four pictures to print. By changing the number of copies of each picture, you can fill an entire sheet of photo paper with the same image.

Start

1 Select the pictures you want to print.

2 Click **Print, Print**.

Continued

NOTE

If you see photos you want to print, but they have color or exposure problems, use the Fix option to repair problems first before printing them. ▪

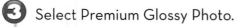

Select Premium Glossy Photo.

Select **Advanced Photo**.

Select **Layout**.

Click **Print**.

End

NOTE

To select multiple photos for printing, click the first photo. Then, hold down either Ctrl key and click the others. ■

NOTE

In this example, we used letter-sized paper. If your printer can use different paper sizes, select paper size before selecting a layout. ■

SETTING UP YOUR EMAIL ACCOUNT WITH WINDOWS LIVE MAIL

Windows Live Mail is an easy-to-use email client that works with almost all types of email accounts, including Hotmail. In this tutorial, you learn how to set it up for a Hotmail account. If you use an email service other than Hotmail, check with your email provider for the correct information to use for servers and other settings.

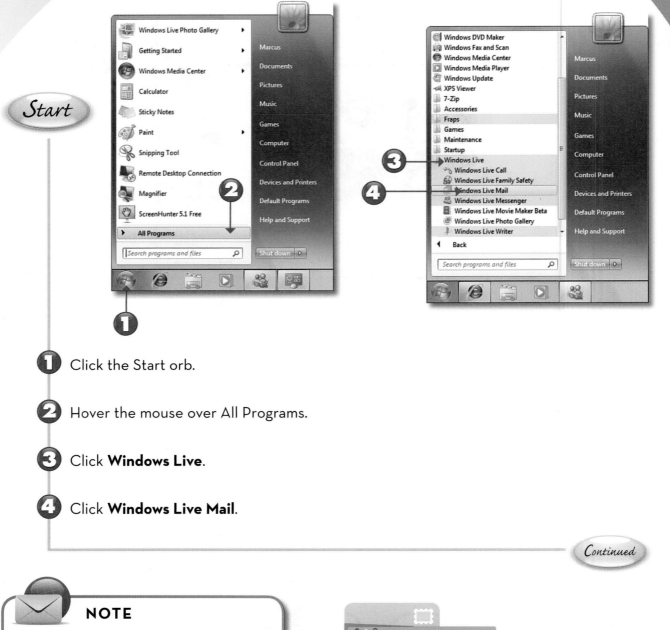

Start

① Click the Start orb.

② Hover the mouse over All Programs.

③ Click **Windows Live**.

④ Click **Windows Live Mail**.

Continued

NOTE

The gold highlighting across some programs in the menu is indicates programs that you haven't used yet. After you run a program for the first time, the highlighting is removed. ■

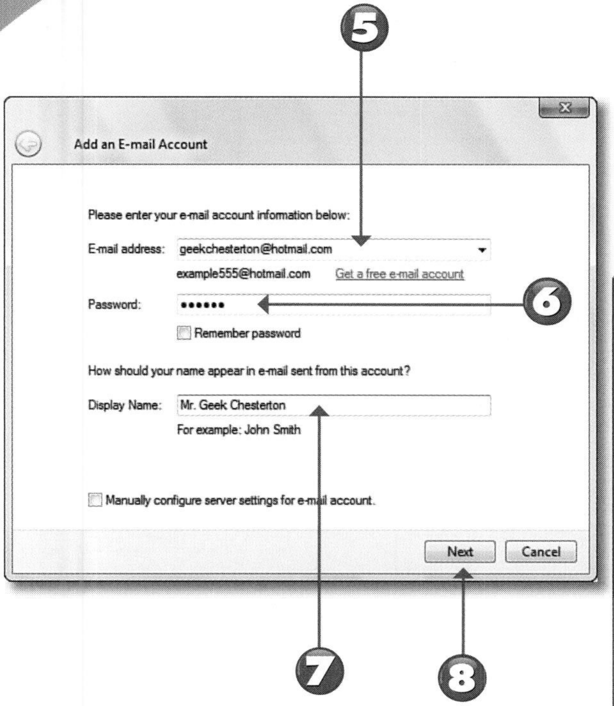

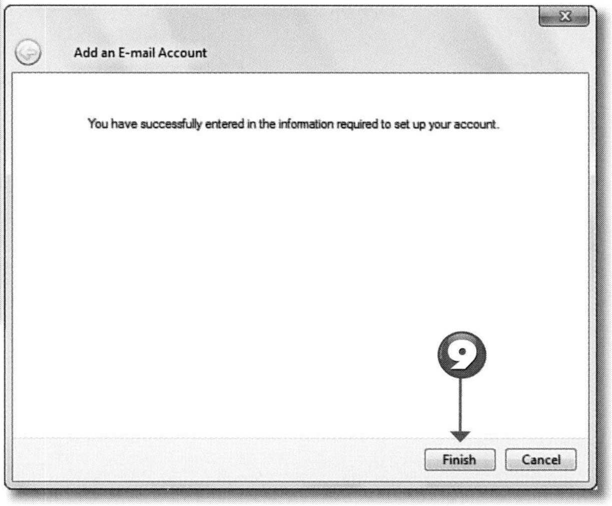

5 Enter your email address.

6 Enter your password.

7 Enter the display name for email you send.

8 Click **Next**.

9 Click **Finish**.

End

NOTE

You can use the Remember Password checkbox to save time when you check email, but don't use this option if you share your computer and don't use a password on your user account. ■

RECEIVING EMAIL

Windows Live Mail provides a convenient three-pane interface that helps you view your email. Here's how to receive and view your messages.

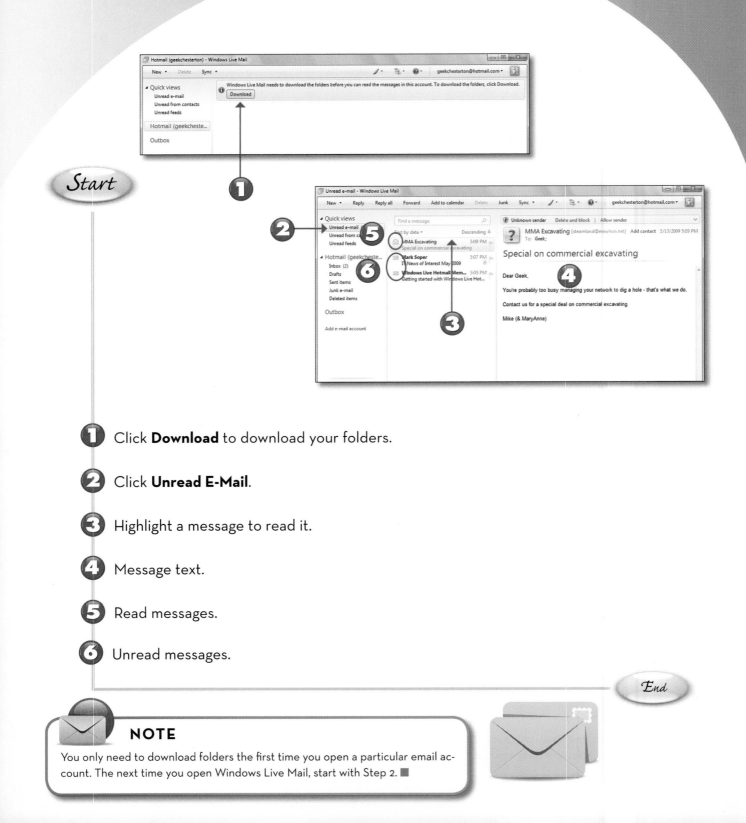

Start

1. Click **Download** to download your folders.

2. Click **Unread E-Mail**.

3. Highlight a message to read it.

4. Message text.

5. Read messages.

6. Unread messages.

End

NOTE

You only need to download folders the first time you open a particular email account. The next time you open Windows Live Mail, start with Step 2. ■

OPENING FILE ATTACHMENTS

Windows Live Mail uses the paper clip icon to indicate messages with attachments. This tutorial shows you how to open email attachments.

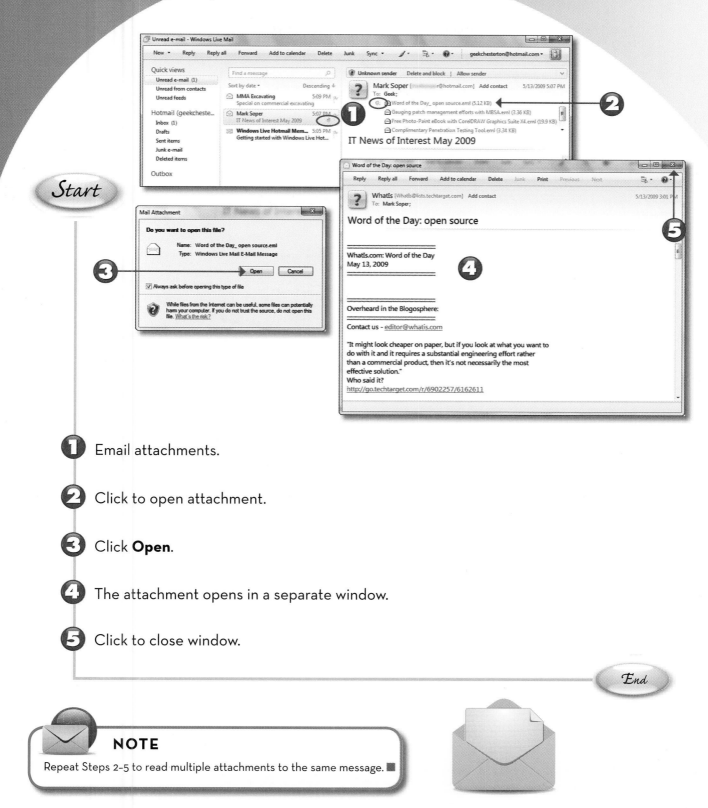

1 Email attachments.

2 Click to open attachment.

3 Click **Open**.

4 The attachment opens in a separate window.

5 Click to close window.

NOTE

Repeat Steps 2–5 to read multiple attachments to the same message. ■

REPLYING TO EMAIL

You can reply to an email from either the Inbox or from the message window itself. This tutorial shows you how to reply from the Inbox.

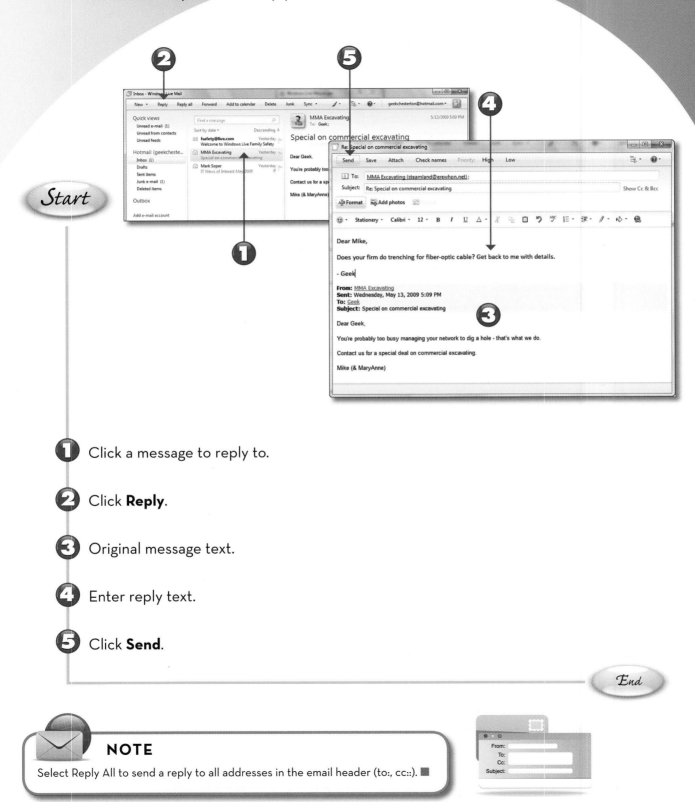

Start

1. Click a message to reply to.

2. Click **Reply**.

3. Original message text.

4. Enter reply text.

5. Click **Send**.

End

NOTE

Select Reply All to send a reply to all addresses in the email header (to:, cc::).

FORWARDING MESSAGES

Have a message you think will be of use to another user? Forward it. You can forward a message from the Inbox or from the message window.

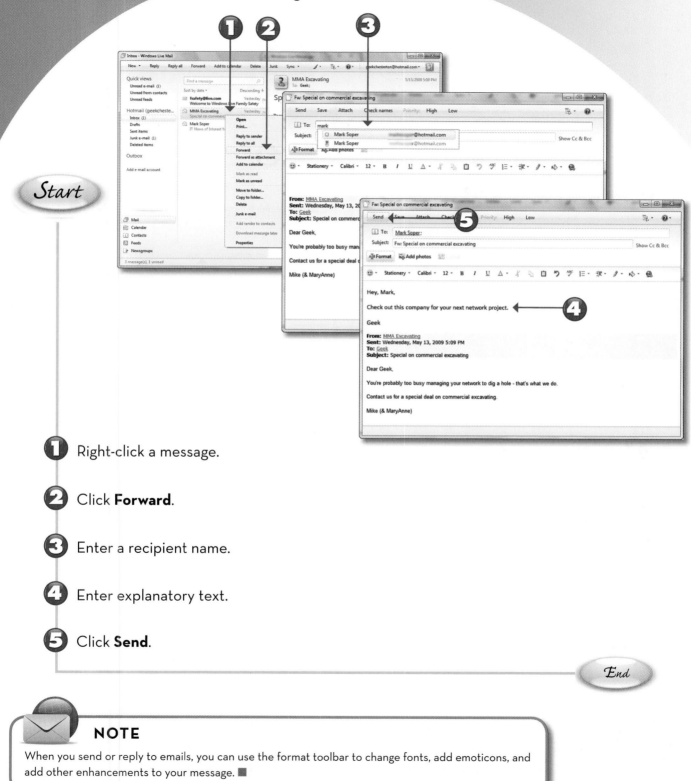

Start

1 Right-click a message.

2 Click **Forward**.

3 Enter a recipient name.

4 Enter explanatory text.

5 Click **Send**.

End

NOTE

When you send or reply to emails, you can use the format toolbar to change fonts, add emoticons, and add other enhancements to your message. ∎

DELETING MESSAGES

You can delete emails from either the Inbox or the reading window. In this example, you'll learn how to delete an email from the reading window.

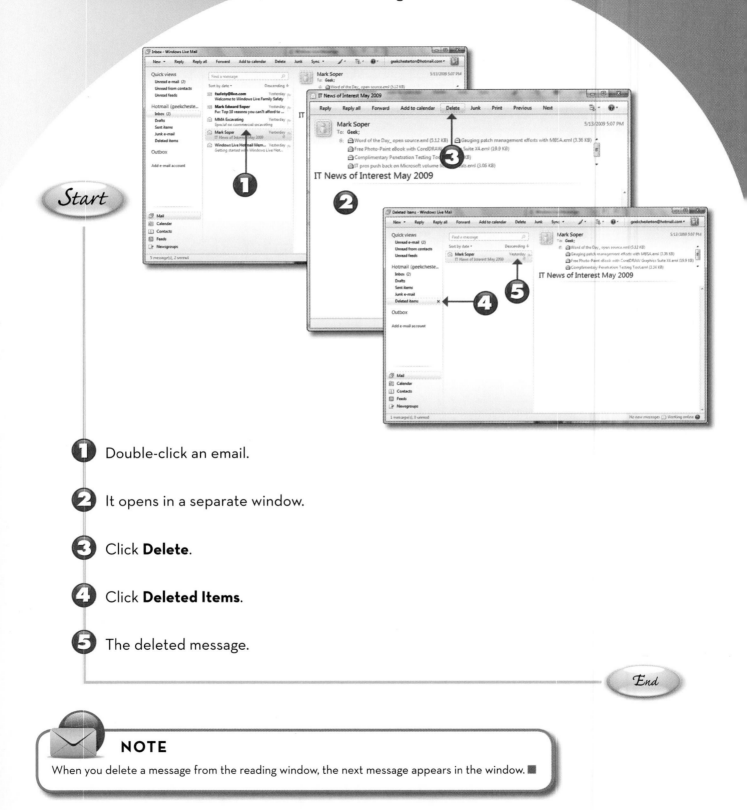

Start

1 Double-click an email.

2 It opens in a separate window.

3 Click **Delete**.

4 Click **Deleted Items**.

5 The deleted message.

End

NOTE

When you delete a message from the reading window, the next message appears in the window. ■

CREATING A CONTACT

Windows Live Mail also works as a contact manager. Here's how to add a contact from an email you've received.

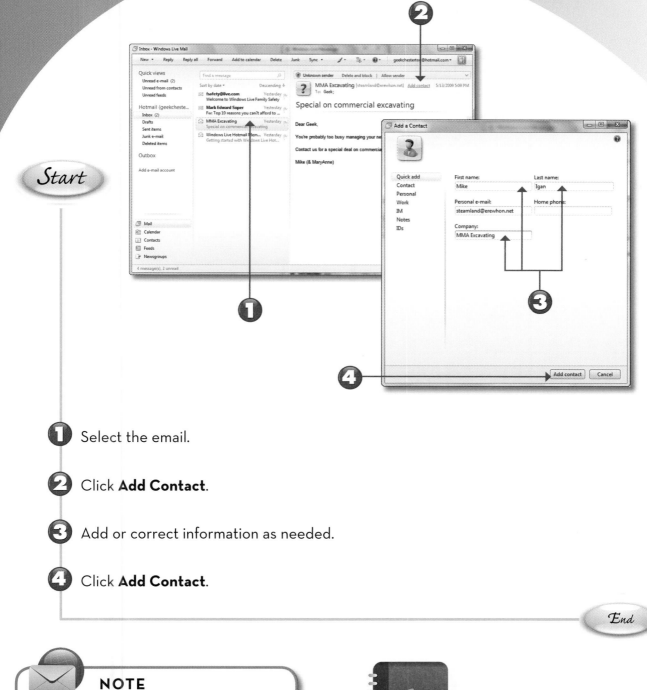

Start

1 Select the email.

2 Click **Add Contact**.

3 Add or correct information as needed.

4 Click **Add Contact**.

End

NOTE

By default, the Quick Add feature used here assumes all emails are personal emails. You can edit your contacts later to add or reclassify email addresses and other information. ■

STARTING AN EMAIL TO A CONTACT

In this exercise, you learn how to select a contact and start an email to that contact.

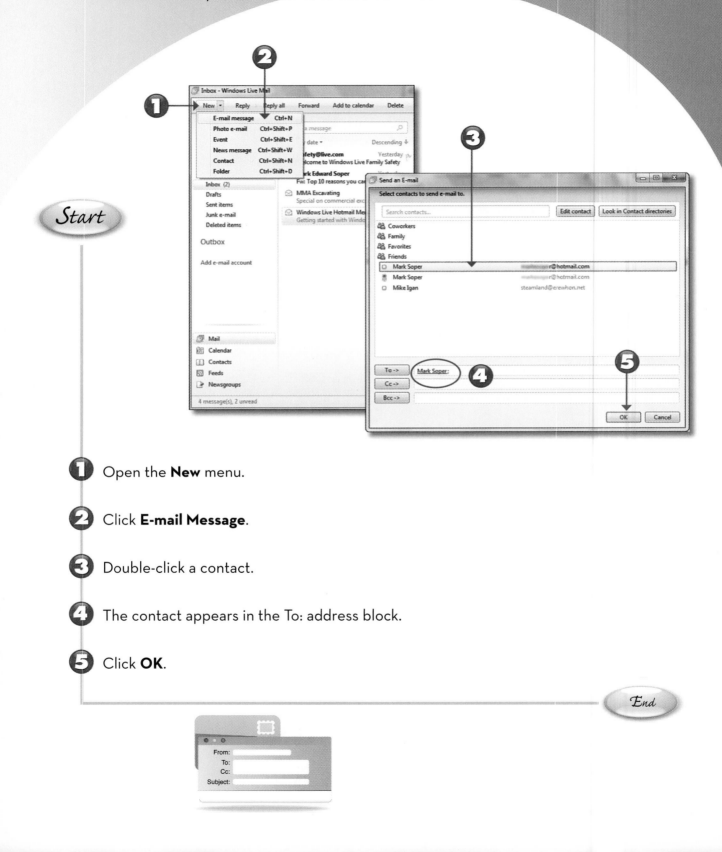

Start

1 Open the **New** menu.

2 Click **E-mail Message**.

3 Double-click a contact.

4 The contact appears in the To: address block.

5 Click **OK**.

End

ADDING TEXT FORMATTING TO AN EMAIL

You can add text formatting such as bold and italic, different fonts, different font sizes, and other enhancements to an email by using the formatting bar above the text entry window. Here's how.

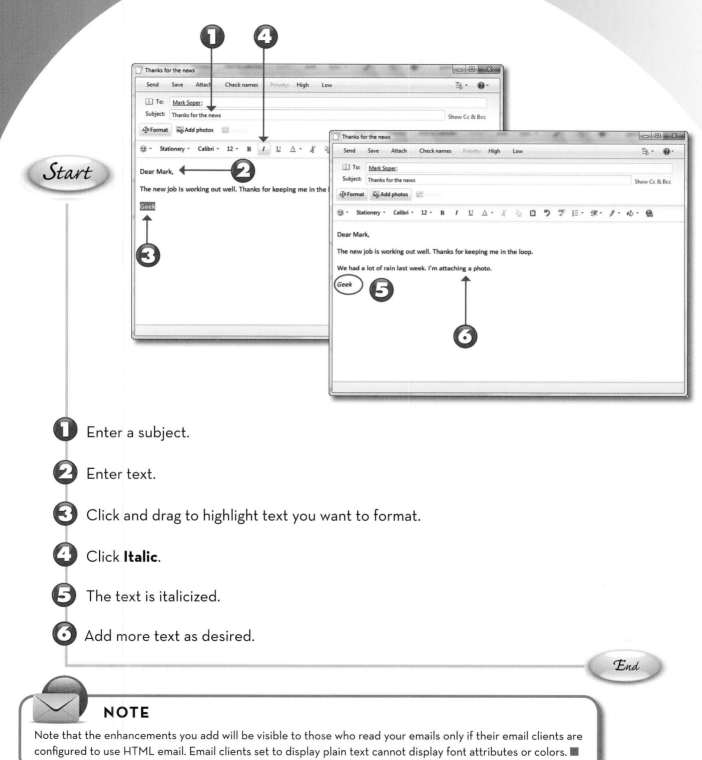

Start

1 Enter a subject.

2 Enter text.

3 Click and drag to highlight text you want to format.

4 Click **Italic**.

5 The text is italicized.

6 Add more text as desired.

End

NOTE

Note that the enhancements you add will be visible to those who read your emails only if their email clients are configured to use HTML email. Email clients set to display plain text cannot display font attributes or colors. ■

ADDING ATTACHMENTS

Email continues to be a popular way to share photographs. In this example, you learn how to add a photo to an email and caption it.

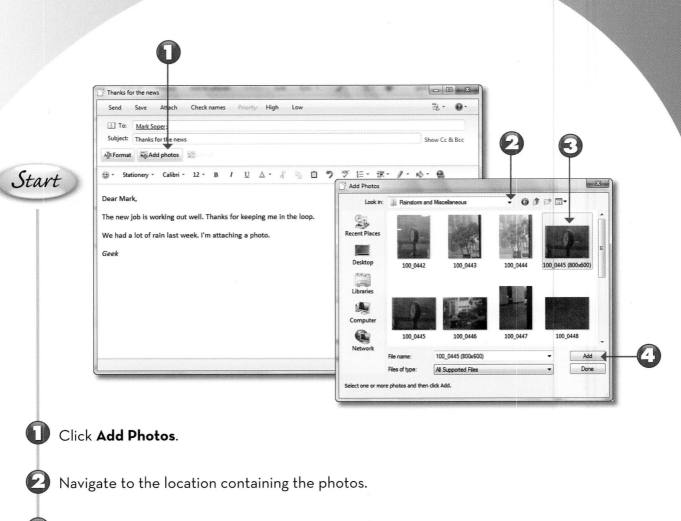

Start

1 Click **Add Photos**.

2 Navigate to the location containing the photos.

3 Select a photo.

4 Click **Add**.

Continued

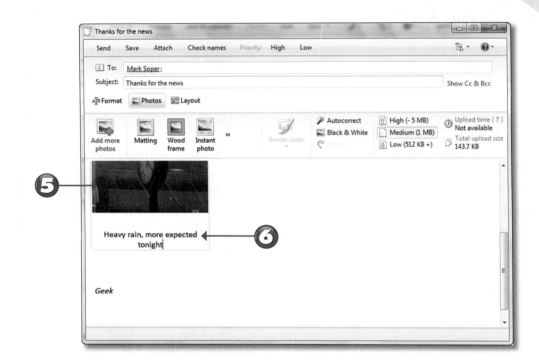

5 The photo is added to the email.

6 Click the frame below the photo and add a caption as desired.

End

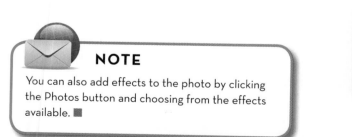

NOTE

You can also add effects to the photo by clicking the Photos button and choosing from the effects available. ■

Glossary

Use this section to bring yourself up to speed on important concepts and terms relating to Windows and to your computer. Terms in *italics* are also in the glossary.

10/100 Ethernet   Ethernet cards, hubs, and switches that support either 10Mbps (10BaseT Ethernet) or 100Mbps (Fast Ethernet) wired network standards.

10/100/1000 Ethernet   Ethernet cards, hubs, and switches that support 10Mbps (10BaseT Ethernet), 100Mbps (Fast Ethernet), and 1000Mbps (Gigabit Ethernet) wired network standards.

A

Accelerator   A feature of Internet Explorer 8 that enables you to highlight text in a web document and map, search, or perform other activities using that text without opening up a separate browser window.

access point   Device on a Wi-Fi network that provides a connection between computers on the network. Can be combined with a router and a switch.

ACPI   Advanced Configuration and Power Interface. It controls how peripherals, BIOS, and computers manage power and is supported by Windows 7.

active partition   Hard disk partition that can be used to boot the computer; only primary partitions can be active.

ActiveX   Microsoft technology for interactive web pages; used with Internet Explorer.

administrator   Windows term for the manager of a given computer or network; only users in the administrator's group can perform some management tasks. Other users must provide an administrator's name and password for tasks marked with the Windows security shield icon.

Aero Peek   Windows 7 feature that hides/reveals the contents of all desktop windows while leaving outlines on-screen when the contents are hidden. Requires Windows Aero graphics support.

Aero Snap   Windows 7 feature that enables user to move the active window to the left, right, and top of the desktop, maximize it, or minimize it by using keyboard shortcuts. Requires Windows Aero graphics support.

APIPA   Automatic Private Internet Protocol (IP) Addressing. IP addresses in the 169.254.x.x range are automatically assigned if the computer cannot receive an IP address from a router or gateway device.

application program   Program used to create, modify, and store information you create. Microsoft Word, Adobe Photoshop, and Corel-DRAW are all application programs.

archive attribute   Indicates file has not yet been backed up; automatically set when a file is created or modified.

B

backup   Making a copy of a file for safekeeping, especially with a special program that must be used to restore the backup when needed; backups may be compressed to save space. Full backup backs up the entire contents of the specified drive or system; a differential backup backs up only the files that have changed since the last full backup. Windows 7 uses the Backup and Restore center for system and file backups.

binary   Numbering system used to store computer data; 0 and 1 are the only digits.

binding   Configuring network hardware with protocols it will use.

blog   Short for weblog. A journal created by one or more writers and posted on the Web, a blog usually has short paragraphs added on a daily or weekly basis that discuss current topics of all types with links to other web sites for more information, such as similar or contrasting points of view on the topic.

blogger   Creator of a blog. See *blog*.

blogging   The process of creating a blog. See *blog*.

Bluetooth   A short-range wireless networking standard that supports non-PC devices such as mobile phones and PDAs, as well as PCs. Bluetooth uses frequencies ranging from 2.402 to 2.480GHz with a range up to about 30 feet. Data transmission runs at 1Mbps or 2Mbps, depending upon the version of the technology supported by the devices. Windows 7 includes Bluetooth support.

boot   Starting the computer. A *warm boot* is restarting the computer without a reset or shutdown. A *cold boot* is shutdown or reset before startup.

boot disk   Disk with operating system files needed to start the computer. Windows 7 DVDs are bootable.

boot sector   Starting location of operating system files on a floppy disk or hard disk.

boot sequence   Procedure followed by system during the startup process; also called bootstrapping.

Broadband Internet   Internet connections with rated download speeds in excess of 100Kbps. Most common types include cable modem and DSL, but ISDN, fixed wireless, FIOS, and satellite Internet services are also broadband services.

browser   Program that interprets HTML documents and allows hyperlinking to web sites. Windows 7 includes Internet Explorer 8 as its standard (default) web browser.

BSOD   Blue Screen of Death. This is a fatal system error in Windows that stops the system from starting; it is also called a stop error, and is named after the blue background and the white text error message.

C

cache hit   Data in cache.

cache miss   Data not in cache. It must be retrieved from next cache level, normal storage, or RAM location.

CardBus   32-bit version of PC Card/PCMCIA slot used for fast network interfacing, USB 2.0, and IEEE-1394 ports on some laptops.

carpal-tunnel syndrome   A common type of Repetitive Strain Injury (RSI) affecting the wrists.

CD   Compact Disc.

CDFS   Compact Disc File System.

CD-R   Recordable CD. Contents of CD-R can be added to but not changed.

CD-ROM   Compact Disc-Read-Only Memory. Standard optical drive. Most can read CD-R media, but drives require MultiRead capability and a UDF reader program to read CD-RW media.

CD-RW   Compact Disc-Rewritable. Rewritable CD. The contents can be changed. A CD-RW drive can also use CD-R media.

clean boot   Booting system without device drivers; Windows 7 uses Safe Mode boot options to boot with only essential drivers.

ClearType   A Windows feature used to provide better-looking text on LCD displays. Windows 7 includes a wizard to make this feature easier to use.

client Computer that uses shared resources on a network.

client/server network Network using dedicated servers such as Windows Server.

cluster size See *allocation unit size*.

CMYK Cyan, Magenta, Yellow, Black. Refers to a four-color model for graphics and printing; these are the ink colors used by most inkjet printers; compare to RGB (Red, Green, Blue), a three-color model used for on-screen graphics.

coast Time period that a computer's power supply can continue to run without AC power flowing to it; the coast time for typical PC power supplies is longer than the switchover time from AC to battery backup power.

cold boot Starting a system from power-down or with reset button; memory count and other hardware tests are performed.

Compact Flash Popular flash-memory storage standard used by digital cameras. It can be attached to desktop and portable PCs by means of a card reader or PC Card adapter.

consumables Collective term for paper, media, ink, and toner used by various types of printers. The true long-term cost of a given printer must take into account the cost per page of the consumables used by the printer.

continuous-tone Original photographs contain tones from blacks to white; laser printers convert these to digital form for printing.

Control Panel A Windows feature that sets Windows hardware options. It can be accessed from the Start menu in Windows 7.

cool-switching Windows use of Alt + Tab keys to move from one active program to another.

CPU Central Processing Unit. The computational "brains" of the computer, such as Core i7, Phenom, and so on.

CRT Cathode Ray Tube. A monitor's picture tube, a large vacuum tube that displays information. Largely replaced by LCD or other flat-panel technologies.

D

DAE Digital Audio Extraction. The process of converting tracks from a music CD to a digital format such as MP3 or WMA at faster than normal 1x analog speeds. Windows 7's Windows Media Player and Windows Media Center use DAE to rip (convert) audio into digital form.

dedicated server Computer used strictly to provide shared resources, such as a computer running Windows Server.

defragment Reorganizing the files on a drive to occupy contiguous sectors to improve retrieval speed; a defragmenting utility is included in Windows 7.

desktop Windows 7 uses the desktop for program shortcuts, access to components such as the Recycle Bin, for program windows, and for desktop gadgets.

desktop PC A computer that sits on the top of the desk, instead of on the floor (tower style). Usually has fewer drive bays and fewer expansion slots than a tower PC.

device driver Program used to enable an operating system to support new devices.

Device Manager Windows portion of system properties sheet used to view and control device configuration. These include IRQ, DMA, I/O port address, memory address, drivers, and other configuration options.

Device Stage A Windows 7 feature that enables you to see and manage multi-function devices, such as all-in-one devices, smart phones, and others from a single dialog.

Devices and Printers   A Windows 7 feature that displays all devices and printers on a single dialog for quick access to the management features for each device.

DHCP   Dynamic Host Configuration Protocol. Provides IP addresses as required; allows a limited number of IP addresses to service many devices that are not connected at the same time. Most routers include a DHCP function to provide IP addresses to connected computers.

digital rights management   Also known as DRM. This refers to storage devices such as Secure Digital flash memory cards or to file formats and programs such as WMA (created by Windows Media Player), which allow the creator of digital content to control how the content is used and where it is played back. MP3 digital audio does not support DRM.

DNS   Domain Name Service or Domain Name Server. Translates domain names into IP addresses.

dpi   Dots per inch. The resolutions of a printer, scanner, or monitor are commonly defined in dpi. Higher values provide sharper images and text, but use more memory or disk space to store.

driver   See *device driver*.

dual-boot   Operating system installation that enables you to run the previous operating system as an option.

DUN   Dial-Up Networking. Using an analog (phone line) modem to connect to other computers.

duplex   A communication method that enables data flow in both directions. Full-duplex allows simultaneous send and receive at the same speed. Half-duplex allows alternating send and receive.

DVD   Digital Video Disc. Also known as Digital Versatile Disk. High-capacity replacement for CD-ROM.

DVD±RW   Refers to drives that support both *DVD-R*/RW and *DVD+R*/RW media.

DVD+RW   A rewritable *DVD* standard supported by the DVD+RW Alliance, and sold by HP, Philips, Sony, and other vendors. Most of these drives also support DVD+R write-once media.

DVD-R   Digital Video Disc-Recordable.

DVD-RAM   Digital Versatile Disc-Random Access Memory. A rewritable *DVD* standard developed by Panasonic and supported by the DVD Forum. A few of these drives also support DVD-R write-once media.

DVD-ROM   Digital Video Disc-Read Only Memory. Retail and upgrade editions of Windows 7 are distributed on DVD-ROM media, as are many other application and utility programs from major publishers.

DVD-RW   Digital Video Disc-Rewritable. A rewritable *DVD* standard developed by Pioneer Electronics and supported by the DVD Forum. These drives also support *DVD-R* write-once media.

DVI   Digital Visual Interface. Replaced DFP as the standard for support of LCD displays on desktop computers. DVI-D is for digital displays only; DVI-I supports digital and analog displays.

E

EFS   Encrypting File System.

email   Electronic mail. The contents of email can include text, HTML, and binary files (such as photos or compressed archives). Email can be sent between computers via an internal computer network, a proprietary online service such as AOL or CompuServe, or via the Internet.

ergonomics The study of the usability of hardware and software products with an eye to comfort and efficiency.

Ethernet Network that uses an IEEE 802.3 access method.

executable file .exe file; a machine-readable program file that can be run in any area of memory or any type of program file, including .com and .bat files.

expansion board Also known as add-on card or add-on board.

expansion slot A motherboard connection used for add-on cards; ISA, PCI, PCI Express, and AGP are typical types.

extended partition A nonbootable hard disk partition that can contain one or more logical drives.

external command A command-prompt command that is actually a separate program.

F

Fast Ethernet A 100Mbps version of Ethernet that runs over Category 5 or better-quality UTP cables. Most Fast Ethernet hardware supports full-duplex operation for an effective speed of 200Mbps. Fast Ethernet hardware, which is also compatible with 10BaseT, is called 10/100 Ethernet.

FAT File Allocation Table. The part of the hard disk or floppy disk that contains pointers to the actual location of files on the disk.

FAT12 12-bit file allocation table. FAT method used for floppy disk drives only.

FAT16 16-bit file allocation table. FAT method used by MS-DOS and Windows 95; also supported by Windows 7 and earlier versions; allows 65,535 (2^{16}) files maximum per drive and drive sizes up to 2GB (4GB in Windows 7 and some other versions). Windows 7 supports FAT16 for data drives only.

FAT32 32-bit file allocation table. FAT method optionally available with Windows 7 and earlier versions. It allows 2^{32} files maximum per drive and drive sizes up to 2TB (terabytes). Windows 7 supports FAT32 for data drives only.

FDD Floppy Disk Drive.

fiber-optic Network cabling using photons rather than electrical signals to transfer information.

file attachment Text or binary data such as pictures, music files, and other types of data files that are sent along with an email message.

file attributes Controls how files are used and viewed and can be reset by the user. Typical file attributes include hidden, system, read-only, and archive; Windows 7 also supports compressed and encrypted file attributes when the NTFS file system is used.

file extension Up to three-character alphanumeric after the dot; indicates file type, such as .bat, .exe, .doc, and so on.

file system How files are organized on a drive; FAT16, FAT32, and NTFS are popular file systems supported by various versions of Windows.

Firewall A network device or software that blocks unauthorized access to a network from other users. Software firewalls such as Zone Alarm or Norton Internet Security are sometimes referred to as personal firewalls. Routers can also function as firewalls. Windows 7 includes a software firewall.

FireWire 400 Alternative name for IEEE-1394a high-speed serial connection (also known as i.Link).

FireWire 800 Alternative name for IEEE-1394b high-speed serial connection.

firmware Software on a chip, such as BIOS.

Flash memory   Memory device that uses electricity to change its contents, but does not require power to maintain its contents; widely used for BIOS chips and for digital camera and digital music storage. Sometimes referred to as Flash ROM.

floppy disk   Low-capacity removable media used by floppy drives. Some recent systems include
3.5-inch floppy drives.

font   A particular size, shape, and weight of a typeface. 12-point Times Roman Italic is a font; Times Roman is the typeface.

forced hardware   Hardware that is normally plug-and-play (allowing changes to the hardware configuration as needed) and has been manually set to use fixed resources; not recommended in most cases but might be necessary for compatibility with older programs, which expect a device such as a sound card to use a particular configuration.

format   Can refer to document layout or the process of preparing a disk drive for use.

FORMAT   Windows program to prepare a drive for use; hard disks must be partitioned first.

FQDN   Fully Qualified Domain Name. Similar to UNC naming, but uses the domain name or IP address of the server rather than its network name.

frame rate   How quickly still images are displayed on-screen to simulate movement, usually measured in FPS (frames per second). Values below 30fps will cause noticeable jerkiness in viewing streaming media. Much higher frame rates are desirable for gaming for more realistic and responsive gameplay.

FTP   File Transfer Protocol. File transfer to or from a special server site on the World Wide Web.

G

gadget   Small programs that can be placed anywhere on the desktop. The user can adjust the transparency of each gadget and move them from a primary to a secondary display. A new feature in Windows 7 that replaces the Windows Vista Sidebar Gadget feature.

gateway   Access point that allows a network (such as a LAN) to access another network (such as the Internet).

GB   Gigabyte. 1 billion bytes.

generic driver   Device driver that provides minimal functions for a hardware device.

GHz   Gigahertz.

Gigabit Ethernet   A 1000Mbps version of Ethernet that runs over fiber-optic cable and can also use Category 5 or better grades of UTP copper cable for short-distance runs. See also *10/100/1000 Ethernet*.

GUI   Graphical User Interface. User interface with features such as icons, fonts, and point-and-click commands; Windows and MacOS are popular GUIs.

H

hard drive   Storage device with rigid, nonremovable platters inside a case; also called hard disk or rigid disk.

hardware   Physical computing devices.

HCL   Hardware Compatibility List. A list of hardware that is compatible with a particular Windows version.

HDD   Hard Disk Drive. Windows 7 is typically installed to an HDD.

HDMI   High Definition Media Interface. HDMI cables and ports can carry HDTV video and audio signals.

head   Reads and writes data in a drive.

header   Beginning of a document, an email message, or a file.

hidden attribute   File attribute that makes a file invisible to the default Windows Explorer view or to the DIR command.

high-level format   Type of format performed by Windows Format program on hard drives and floppy drives; rewrites file allocation tables and root directory but doesn't overwrite existing data on the rest of the disk surface.

Hi-Speed USB   Another term for USB 2.0.

HomeGroup   A Windows 7 network feature that enables two or more Windows 7 systems to belong to a secure, easy-to-manage network.

hot-swappable   Devices that can be attached and removed while the computer is running. The most common hot-swappable devices for PCs use PC Card, CardBus, ExpressCard, USB, eSATA, and *IEEE-1394* connectors.

HTML   Hypertext Markup Language. A standard for markup symbols that allows hyperlinking, fonts, special text attributes, graphics, and other enhancements to be added to text files for display with web browsers, such as Microsoft Internet Explorer and Netscape Navigator. The official source for HTML standards is the World Wide Web Consortium (W3C).

HTTP   Hypertext Transfer Protocol. The basis for hyperlinking and the Internet; it is interpreted by a web browser program such as Internet Explorer 8.

HTTPS   Hypertext Transfer Protocol over Secure Sockets Layer. This type of connection is used in electronic banking and shopping.

hub   Central connecting point for UTP-based forms of Ethernet. A hub broadcasts messages to all computers connected to it, and subdivides the bandwidth of the network among the computers connected to it. See *switch*. Also refers to a device used to enable multiple USB devices to connect to a single USB port.

I

icon   Onscreen symbol used in Windows to link you to a program or routine.

IEEE   Institute of Electrical and Electronics Engineers. Sets standards for computer, electrical, and electronics devices.

IEEE-1394   A series of standards for high-speed serial interface, also known as FireWire or i.Link.

IEEE 587A   Standard for surge protection devices.

IEEE 802.11a   A wireless Ethernet standard that uses 5GHz radio signals and provides performance at rates from 6Mbps up to 54Mbps. It is not compatible with other 802.11-based wireless networks unless dual-band access points are used. It is also known as Wireless-A.

IEEE 802.11b   A wireless Ethernet standard that uses 2.4GHz radio signaling for performance from 2Mbps to 11Mbps. It is compatible with *802.11g*-based wireless networks, but not with 802.11a-based networks unless dual-band access points are used. It is also known as Wireless-B.

IEEE 802.11g   A wireless Ethernet standard that uses 2.4GHz radio signaling for performance up to 54Mbps. It is compatible with *802.11b*-based wireless networks, but not with *802.11a*-based networks unless dual-band access points are used. It is also known as Wireless-G.

IEEE 802.11n   A wireless Ethernet standard that uses 2.4GHz radio signaling (and optionally, 5GHz signaling) for performance up to 270Mbps and above. It is compatible with

802.11g-based wireless networks, and with *802.11a*-based networks if the device includes 5GHz support. It is also known as Wireless-N.

IEEE 802.x   Series of IEEE networking standards used as the basis for Ethernet, Token Ring, and other network types.

IIS   Internet Information Server. An optional feature of some Windows 7 versions, IIS enables a computer to act as a web server.

i.Link   Sony's term for *IEEE-1394a* or FireWire 400 ports. i.Link ports use the four-wire IEEE-1394a connector rather than the six-wire connector used by other implementations.

IMAP   Internet Mail Access Protocol. IMAP email supports email folders on the server, rather than on the email client.

in the wild   Term for viruses found outside virus labs.

INF file   Windows hardware installation file type.

inkjet printer   Popular non-impact printer type.

install   Process of making a computer program usable on a system, including expanding and copying program files to the correct locations, changing Windows configuration files, and registering file extensions used by the program.

Intel   Leading manufacturer of CPUs, chipsets, and other PC components. See Intel's web site at www.intel.com.

interface   Connection between two devices.

internal command   Command-prompt command that can be run from the command prompt without loading an additional program file; stored in Windows 7's Cmd program.

Internet   The world-wide "network of networks" that can be accessed through the World Wide Web and by Telnet, FTP, and other utilities.

I/O   Input/Output.

IP   Internet Protocol.

IPSec   Internet Protocol Security. Used for Virtual Private Network (VPN) connections.

IrDA   Infrared Data Association. Sets standards for infrared (IR) communications between computers and devices.

ISO   Industry Standards Organization. Sets standards for many types of technology, including computers, photography, and others.

ISP   Internet Service Provider. A company that provides individuals and businesses with access to the Internet through dial-up, DSL, cable modem, wireless, or LAN connections.

J

Java   A programming language developed by Sun Microsystems for use on a wide variety of computers; it is widely used in web browsers for animations and interactive features. It requires special files called Class Libraries to be added to the web server.

JavaScript   A programming language that can be embedded in HTML files for interactive features, such as those found in Web 2.0 social-networking websites.

jump list   A Windows 7 feature that enables programs and documents to be started from taskbar shortcuts.

K

Kb   Kilobit. 1,024 bits.

KB   Kilobyte. 1,024 bytes.

Kbps   Kilobits per second. Often used to rate modems and broadband Internet connections.

known-working Computer or component that has been tested and is known to work correctly; not the same as "new."

L

LAN Local Area Network. A network in which the components are connected through network cables or wirelessly; if a router is used, the network is a *WAN*. See also *WLAN*.

landscape mode Print mode that prints across the wider side of the paper; from the usual proportions of a landscape painting. Landscape mode is usually slower than the default portrait mode because the fonts and graphics must be rotated. This mode is controlled by the application performing the print job.

laser printer Type of nonimpact page printer.

LCD Liquid Crystal Display. Type of screen used on portable computers and on flat-panel desktop displays.

LED Light Emitting Diode.

legacy Technology that predates modern standards. ISA slots, PS/2, serial, and parallel ports are typical examples of legacy technologies.

legacy USB support BIOS option that enables USB keyboards to work outside of Windows in command-prompt and BIOS setup modes.

local drive A drive letter that is built into or directly attached to your own computer, such as hard, floppy, IDE, USB, SCSI, or IEEE-1394 drives. Network drives that have been assigned drive letters (mapped drives) appear as local drives in the My Computer view of the system in Windows.

logging Recording events during a process. Windows 7 creates logs for many types of events; they can be viewed through the Computer Management Console.

logical drive Drive letters that reside within a disk partition, especially within an extended partition; a single physical drive can contain two or more logical drives.

M

MAC Media Access Control. Each network adapter has a MAC address (also known as the physical address), and you can see the MAC addresses for the adapters in your computer by running the IPConfig /All command from the command prompt.

macro A series of commands that can be stored inside a spreadsheet or word-processing file to automate certain operations.

mapped drive Using a drive letter as a shortcut to a network resource.

mastering The process of creating a CD or DVD with a program such as Easy Media Creator or Nero. These programs and others write large amounts of data to the media with disk at once or track at once methods, instead of the packet-writing method used by UDF.

matrix Describes the arrangement of the nozzles in the printhead of an inkjet printer. The smaller the nozzles and the more closely they are positioned to each other, the better the print quality.

Mb Megabit. One million bits.

MB Megabyte. One million bytes.

Mbps Megabits per second. Often used to describe speeds of networks and broadband Internet connections.

MBps   Megabytes per second.

media   Anything used to carry information, such as network cables, paper, CD or DVD discs, and so on.

memory module   Memory chips on a small board.

MHz   Megahertz.

Microsoft Knowledge Base   Online collection of Microsoft technical articles used by Microsoft support personnel to diagnose system problems. Can also be searched by end-users by using the http://support.microsoft.com web site.

MMC   Microsoft Management Console. The Windows utility used to view and control the computer and its components. Disk Management and Device Manager are components of MMC.

modem   Short for Modulate-Demodulate, this device converts information into another form for transmission between computers over phone, cable, or DSL lines.

monitor   TV-like device that uses either a CRT or an LCD screen to display activity inside the computer. Attaches to the video card or video port on the system.

mouse   Pointing device that is moved across a flat surface; older models use a removable ball to track movement; most recent models use optical or laser sensors.

MP3   Moving Picture Experts Group Layer 3 Audio. A compressed digitized music file format widely used for storage of popular and classical music; quality varies with the sampling rate used to create the file. MP3 files can be stored on recordable or rewritable CD or DVD media for playback and are frequently exchanged online. The process of creating MP3 files is called *ripping*.

MPEG   Motion Picture Experts Group; creates standards for compression of video (such as MPEG 2) and audio (such as the popular MP3 file format).

MUI   Multilingual User Interface.

Multi-touch   A Windows 7 feature that enables icons and windows on touch-sensitive displays to be dragged, resized, and adjusted with two or more fingers.

NAS   Network-Attached Storage.

NAT   Network Address Translation.

netbook   A mobile computing device that is smaller than a laptop and has a folding keyboard and screen (usually no more than about 10-inches diagonal measurement). Netbooks have lower-performance processors, less RAM, and smaller hard disks (or solid state drives) than laptop or notebook computers. Windows 7 runs on netbooks as well as more powerful types of computers.

network   Two or more computers that are connected and share a resource, such as folders or printers.

network drive   Drive or folder available through the network; usually refers to a network resource that has been mapped to a local drive letter.

Network and Sharing Center   Windows control center for wired, wireless, and dial-up networking functions.

NIC   Network Interface Card.

NNTP   Network News Transfer Protocol. Used by newsgroups.

NOS Network Operating System. Software that allows a PC to access shared resources; might be part of a regular OS or might be an add-on.

NTFS New Technology File System. The native file system used by Windows 7 and some earlier versions of Windows. All NTFS versions feature smaller allocation unit sizes and superior security when compared to FAT16 or FAT32.

O

objects Items that can be viewed or configured with Windows Explorer, including drives, folders, computers, and so on.

OEM Original Equipment Manufacturer. OEM products are sold to system builders, not at retail. Might lack some features of the retail version, such as bundled software.

optical Storage such as CD and DVD drives, which use a laser to read data.

OS Operating system. Software that configures and manages hardware and connects hardware and applications. Windows 7, Linux, and MacOS are examples of operating systems.

overclocking Speeding up a computer by increasing the multiplier and/or bus speed used by a CPU or video card past its rated limits; can create faster systems but can also cause system crashes.

P

packet writing A method for writing data to an optical disc in small blocks (packets). This method is used by UDF programs. Packet-written media requires a UDF reader, unlike media created with a mastering program, which can be read without any additional software.

PAN Personal Area Network. Bluetooth is an example of a network technology that supports PANs.

paper path Route paper takes through a printer; straight-through paths have fewer jams.

partition Section of a hard disk set aside for use by an operating system.

partition table Area near the beginning of the hard disk storing disk geometry used to prepare the drive, operating system(s) in use on the drive, and partition start/end positions.

password A word or combination of letters and numbers that is matched to username or resource name to enable the user to access a computer or network resources or accounts.

path Series of drives and folders (subdirectories) that are checked for executable programs when a command-prompt command is issued or drive/network server and folders used to access a given file.

PC Card Newer name for PCMCIA technology; credit card-sized devices inserted into a notebook computer for networking, modem, memory, and I/O expansion.

PCMCIA Personal Computer Memory Card International Association. Original name for PC Card technology; see *PC Card*.

PDA Personal Digital Assistant. A hand-sized computer that provides datebook, notepad, and limited application software features. The Palm and Handspring series (which run PalmOS) and the PocketPCs (which run a version of Windows CE) are popular examples of PDAs.

peer server Client PC that also shares drives or other resources on a Windows network.

peer-to-peer network   Network in which some or all of the client PCs also act as peer servers.

personal firewall   Software that blocks unauthorized access to a computer with an Internet connection. Can also be configured to prevent unauthorized programs from connecting to the Internet. The free Shields Up! service at Gibson Research (http://grc.com) tests the protection provided by personal firewalls and recommends specific products. Windows 7 includes a personal (software) firewall.

photon   Light measurement corresponding to the electron; used by fiber-optic cables to transmit data.

PhotoViewer   Windows 7 utility for photo viewing and printing.

physical drive   Same as hard drive or hard disk; all physical drives must be partitioned and high-level formatted before they can be used by Windows.

piezo-electric   An inkjet printing technique in which ink is forced through the printhead by the activation of a piezo-electric crystal.

PIN   Personal Identification Number.

pinning   The act of locking a program or document to the Windows taskbar or Start menu. You can use this feature along with jump lists to put shortcuts to your most commonly-used programs in either location.

PnP   Plug and Play. A Windows technology for using the operating system to detect and configure add-on cards and external devices such as modems, monitors, scanners, and printers. PnP hardware can be moved to different resource settings as needed to make way for additional devices.

POP   Post Office Protocol.

POP3   Post Office Protocol 3.

portable   A computer you can carry around and use with battery power; the most popular type is the notebook computer.

portrait mode   The default print option that prints across the short side of the paper; it gets its name from the usual orientation of portrait paintings and photographs.

PostScript   Adobe's printer language optimized for elaborate graphics and text effects; used on many laser and inkjet printers used in graphics arts.

POTS   Plain Old Telephone System. Regular copper-wire telephone system that uses modems to connect one computer with another; distinguished from ISDN or DSL telephone systems.

power management   BIOS or OS techniques for reducing power usage by dropping CPU clock speed, turning off monitor or hard disk, and so on during periods of inactivity.

PowerShell   Windows utility for automating system tasks and creating system management tools. Included in some editions of Windows 7 as an optionally installed feature.

primary partition   Hard disk partition that will become the C: drive on a single-drive system.

print spooler   Program that stores and manages print jobs on disk and sends them to the printer; an integral part of Windows.

printer language   Rules for printer commands issued by the printer driver; popular languages include PostScript and HP PCL.

printhead   Printer component that places the image on paper using pins and ribbon or inkjet nozzles.

properties sheet   Windows method for modifying and viewing object properties. Accessible by right-clicking the object and selecting Properties.

proprietary   Opposite of standard; refers to technologies that are used only by a single vendor. For example, a particular proprietary memory module fits only a few models of notebook computers made by a particular vendor.

protocol   Common language used by different types of computers to communicate over a network.

proxy server   Web server that sits between the actual server and client PC and sends a copy of the actual content to the PC; used for filtering of content and security.

Q

QoS   Quality of Service. QoS is a feature of most recent networks. It provides priority to streaming video and audio for better video and audio playback and clearer VoIP telephone calls.

QWERTY   The standard arrangement of typewriter keys is also used by most English or Latin-alphabet computer keyboards; the name was derived from the first six letter keys under the
left hand.

R

RAM   Random Access Memory. Memory whose contents can be changed.

RAS   Remote Access Service.

read caching   A method of disk caching that uses RAM to hold data being read from disk; data being saved to disk goes straight to disk instead of being held in RAM. Windows uses read-caching for floppy, USB flash memory, and removable-media drives by default to avoid data loss from disk changes.

read-only   Storage that is protected from changes.

read-only attribute   File attribute used to protect a file from unauthorized changes; cannot be overridden or altered and can be deleted only by explicit user override.

read-write caching   A method of disk caching that uses RAM to hold data being saved to disk as well as data being read from disk for faster performance. Windows uses read-write caching for hard drives by default.

Recovery Environment   Special Windows 7 repair mode used for restoring damaged systems; can be launched at startup or from the Windows 7 DVD.

Recycle Bin   Windows holding area for deleted files, allowing them to be restored to their original locations; can be overridden to free up disk space.

registration   Windows process of matching file extensions with compatible programs.

Registry   Windows structure that stores information on programs and hardware installed on the system and user configuration settings.

removable-media   Any drive whose media can be interchanged; floppy disk, CD-ROM, optical, tape, and USB flash memory card drives.

replicate   Make a copy.

resolution   The number of dots per inch (dpi) supported by a display, scanner, or printer. Typical displays support resolutions of about 96dpi, whereas printers have resolutions of 600dpi to 2,400dpi (laser printers). Inkjet printers might have even higher resolutions. Bitmaps should be scanned or created to suit the different resolution requirements of the target device. A low-resolution bitmap works well on-screen but won't print well because printers have higher resolution than displays.

RF   Radio Frequency. Different versions of Wireless Ethernet use different radio frequencies.

RGB   Red, Green, Blue.

ribbon cable   Flat cable used to connect internal drives to interfaces.

ripping   The process of converting CD audio tracks into digital music formats such as MP3 or WMA.

ROM   Read Only Memory. Memory whose contents cannot be changed.

root directory   Top-level folder on a drive that stores all other directories (folders); the root directory of C: drive is C:\. Sometimes referred to as a root folder.

router   Device that routes data from one network to another. Often integrated with wireless access points and switches.

S

safe mode   Windows troubleshooting startup mode; runs the system using BIOS routines only. Can be selected at startup by pressing the F8 key repeatedly and then selecting it from the startup menu that appears.

sampling rate   Frequency at which analog sound data is stored for digital conversion; a higher sampling rate produces better quality but also larger .wav files.

SD card   Secure Digital card. Popular flash memory card format for digital cameras and other electronic devices. Maximum capacity is 2GB. See also *SDHC card*.

SDHC card   Secure Digital High Capacity card. Popular flash memory card format for digital cameras and other electronic devices. Devices that use SDHC cards can also use SD cards. However, devices made only for SD cards cannot use SDHC cards. SDHC cards are speed rated and have a capacity of 4GB to 32GB.

serial   Data-transmission technique that sends a single bit at a time at various rates; used by RS-232, USB, Serial ATA, and IEEE-1394 interfaces.

Serial ATA   Also known as SATA, this version of ATA uses thin data and power cables to transmit data serially at rates of 150MBps or 300MBps. SATA uses the same commands as ATA. Most recent motherboards have built-in SATA host adapters, but you can also add an SATA or ATA/SATA host adapter card to existing systems.

server   Computer that shares drives and other resources over a network. Peer servers can also be used as workstations; dedicated servers provide services to other computers such as file, print, email, and so on.

SETUP   Common name for installation programs.

shared resource   A drive, printer, or other resource available to more than one PC over a network.

shortcut   A Windows icon stored on the desktop or in the \Windows\Programs folder with an .lnk extension; double-click the icon to run the program or open the file.

single sheets   Individual sheets of paper such as copy, laser, inkjet paper; the most common form of printer paper used today.

SLI   Refers most commonly to an nVidia technology for speeding up 3D graphics by using multiple graphics chips to render a scene.

Smart Media   A type of flash memory used by some obsolete digital cameras; requires a card reader or PC Card adapter to be compatible with portable and desktop computers.

SMB   Server Message Block.

SMTP   Simple Mail Transport Protocol.

SNMP   Simple Network Management Protocol.

software   Instructions that create or modify information and control hardware; must be read into RAM before use.

SOHO   Small Office/Home Office.

solid state drive   A hard disk equivalent that uses non-volatile memory for storage instead of a disk mechanism. Used in many netbooks and some laptops. Windows 7 includes support for solid state drives.

SP   Service Pack. A service pack is used to add features or fix problems with an operating system or application program.

spam   Unsolicited email. Named after (but not endorsed by) the famous Hormel lunch meat. Many email clients and utilities can be configured to help filter, sort, and block spam.

SPDIF   Sony-Philips digital interface format. A coaxial or fiber-optic cable used to connect some types of sound cards with home theater systems.

SPS   Standby Power Supply. Correct term for so-called UPS battery backup systems that switch from AC power to DC power when the AC power fails.

SSD   See *solid state drive*.

SSID   Service Set Identifier. The name for a wireless network. When you buy a wireless router, the vendor has assigned it a standard SSID, but you should change it to a different name as part of setting up a secure network.

SSL   Secure Sockets Layer. Technology used for secure web browsing.

standby   Power-saving mode in which the CPU drops to a reduced clock speed and other components wait for activity.

start page   The web page that is first displayed when you open a web browser; can be customized to view any web page available online or stored on your hard disk.

startup event   File loading and other activities during the startup of Windows.

storage   Any device that holds programs or data for use, including hard disks, USB drives, DVD drives, and so on.

straight-through paper path   Paper path available as an option with most laser printers to allow labels and heavier stock to go straight through the printer without being curved around rollers.

subsystem   Portion of a computer that performs a particular task; the printer subsystem, for example, contains the printer, cable, port, printer driver, and BIOS configuration settings.

surge protector   Device that absorbs high-voltage events to protect equipment from damage.

suspend   Power-saving mode that shuts down monitor and other devices; saves more power than standby.

S-Video   Analog video standard used in many VCR and DVD products for input and output of video signals. Many recent video cards use S-video for their TV output. Can be downconverted to composite video by using an adapter.

swapfile   Area of a hard disk used for virtual memory; Windows uses a dynamic swapfile (called a paging file in Windows 7) that can grow or shrink as required.

switch   Network device that sets a direct path for data to run from one system to another; can be combined with a router or wireless access point; faster than a hub because it supports the full bandwidth of the network at each port, rather than subdividing the bandwidth among active ports as a hub does.

system attribute   File attribute used to indicate if a file or folder is part of the operating system; boot files are normally set as system and hidden.

System Restore   A feature built into Windows 7 that enables the user to revert the system back to a previous state in case of a crash or other system problem. System Restore points can be created by the user and are created automatically by Windows when new hardware and software is installed or by a predefined schedule. When you restore the computer to a previous state, no data or program files are erased, but registry entries for drivers, hardware, or programs created after the restore point are lost. Thus, you might need to reinstall a device or program after you use a system restore point. When you use System Restore in Windows 7, it checks to determine what programs and drivers might need to be reinstalled.

T

TAPI   Telephony Application Programming Interface. Windows method for interfacing with modems and other telephony devices; allows the system to interface with POTS, PBX, videophones, and others by interfacing with their TAPI drivers.

taskbar   Windows feature that displays icons for running programs, generally at the bottom of the primary display. In Windows 7, the taskbar also contains jump list shortcuts to frequently-used programs.

TB   Terabyte. 1 trillion bytes.

TCP/IP   Transmission Control Protocol/Internet Protocol. The Internet's standard network protocol that is also the standard for most networks.

temp file   Temporary file. A file created to store temporary information such as a print job or an application work file. It may be stored in the default Temp folder (such as \Windows\Temp) or in a folder designated by the application. Temp files may use the .tmp extension or start with a ~ (tilde).

toner cartridge   A one-piece unit containing toner, developer, and an imaging drum. It is used in many laser printer models and is sometimes referred to as an EP cartridge.

topology   The arrangement of cables in a network.

touchpad   A pressure-sensitive pad that is used as a mouse replacement in some portable computers and keyboards.

Tracert   The Windows version of the Traceroute command; used to track the routing between your computer and a specified IP address or server.

TrackPoint   An IBM-designed pointing device that is integrated into the keyboards of portable computers made by IBM and Lenovo and is licensed by Toshiba and other firms. Also referred to as a pointing stick, it resembles a pencil eraser that is located between the G and H keys; the buttons are located beneath the spacebar.

Trojan horse   Program that attaches itself secretly to other programs that usually has a harmful action when triggered. It is similar to a computer virus but cannot spread itself to other computers, although some Trojan horses can be used to install a remote control program that allows an unauthorized user to take over your computer. Antivirus programs can block Trojan horses as well as true viruses.

TWAIN   Technology developed by the TWAIN Working Group to provide a standard interface between scanners and digital cameras and imaging programs. Launch the TWAIN driver for your imaging device in your program, acquire (scan or download) the image, and the image is retrieved into your application. TWAIN is not an acronym.

Type I slot   Thinnest PC Card slot; seldom used for devices.

Type II slot   Medium-thickness and most common PC Card slot; Type II slots can be used as a single Type III slot. Common Type II devices include modems, network interface cards, combo cards, SCSI and USB cards, and newer ATA-compatible hard drives.

Type III slot   Thickest PC Card slot. Common Type III devices include older ATA-compatible hard disk drives; a Type III slot can also be used as two Type II slots.

typeface   A set of fonts in different sizes (or a single scalable outline) and weights; Times New Roman Bold, Bold Italic, Regular, and Italic are all part of the Times New Roman scalable typeface.

Typical installation   Application software installation option that should install the features needed by most users.

U

UDF   Universal Disk Format. A standard for CD and DVD media to drag and drop files to compatible media using a method called packet writing. Windows 7 supports various UDF versions.

UDP   User Datagram Protocol. Some network applications require that a firewall permit traffic on specified UDP ports.

UL-1449   Underwriter's Laboratory standard for surge protectors.

UMA   Unified Memory Architecture. Memory is shared between the system and video circuit; reduces video cost but reduces performance.

UNC   Universal Naming Convention. Allows network clients to access shared resources without the use of mapped drive letters or port redirection.

uninstall   Process to remove Windows programs from the system.

Universal Disk Format   See *UDF*.

upgrade   Replacing an old version of software or hardware with a new version.

upgrade version   A version of a program (such as Windows 7) that requires proof of ownership of a previous version before it can be installed.

UPS   Uninterruptible Power Supply. Term for battery backup that uses a battery at all times to power the system; sometimes referred to as true UPS to distinguish them from SPS units (also employer of friendly driver in brown outfit who delivers computer products).

URL   Uniform Resource Locator. The full path to any given web page or graphic on the Internet. A full URL contains the server type (such as http://, ftp://, or others), the site name (such as www.markesoper.com), and the name of the folder and name of the page or graphic you want to view (such as /blog/?page_id=38). Thus, the URL http://www.markesoper.com/blog/?page_id=38 displays the "About Mark" page on the author's web site.

USB　Universal Serial Bus. High-speed replacement for older I/O ports; USB 1.1 has a peak speed of 12Mbps. USB 2.0 has a peak speed of 480Mbps; USB 2.0 ports also support USB 1.1 devices. USB 2.0 devices can be plugged into USB 1.1 devices, but run at only USB 1.1 speeds.

user-level　Network security used server versions of Microsoft Windows; server keeps a list of users and rights/permissions; a single password provides access to all resources the user is allowed to access.

username　Used with a password to gain access to network resources.

utility program　Program that enhances day-to-day computer operations but doesn't create data.

UTP　Unshielded Twisted Pair. Most common type of network cable; uses RJ-45 connectors.

V

VA　Volt-Amps. A common way to rate battery backup units.

VESA　Video Electronic Standards Association. Trade group of monitor and video card makers that sets video standards for resolution, color depth, and digital displays.

VGA　Video Graphics Array. First popular analog video standard; basis for all current video cards.

virtual domain　A portion of a physical web server; appears as a separate web server to the user and is accessed with a unique domain name.

virtual memory　Hard disk space used as a supplement to RAM; also known as swapfile or paging file.

virus　Computer program that resembles a Trojan horse that can also replicate itself to other computers.

VMM　Virtual Machine Manager. Windows 9x and later versions use VMM to provide multi-tasked services known as virtual machines to each running program, making each program think it has the entire computer at its disposal.

VoIP　Voice over Internet Protocol. Enables telephone calls to be transmitted or received over an IP network.

volt　Measurement of AC or DC electrical power.

voltmeter　Device that measures AC or DC electrical power; often integrated into a digital multimeter (DMM).

VPN　Virtual Private Network. Creates a secure "tunnel" over the Internet between a client PC and a corporate or other network.

W

WAN　Wide Area Network. Network that spans multiple cities, countries, or continents. Network sections may be linked by leased line, Internet backbone, or satellite feed; routers connect LANs to WANs and WAN segments to each other.

warm boot　Restarting computer with software command; no memory or hardware testing.

watt   Measure of heat used to rate power supplies.

WAV   A non-compressed standard for digital audio. Some recording programs for Windows can create and playback WAV files. However, WAV files are very large, and are usually converted into other formats for use online or for creating digital music archives.

wavetable   Method of playing back MIDI files with digitized samples of actual musical instruments.

Web Slice   An Internet Explorer 8 feature that displays content from other web sites while you view a web site in the main window.

WEP   Wired Equivalent Privacy. Now-obsolete standard for wireless security. Replaced by *WPA*.

Wi-Fi   The name for *IEEE-802.11a, IEEE-802.11b, IEEE-802.11g,* or *IEEE-802.11n* Wireless Ethernet devices that meet the standards set forth by the Wi-Fi Alliance.

wildcard   Character used to replace one or more characters as a variable in DIR, Windows Find/Search, and Windows Explorer. * = multiple characters; ? = single character.

Windows Action Center   Windows 7 feature that combines security and system warnings and notifications into a single interface.

Windows Live Essentials   Optional addition to Windows 7 that provides support for photo management and light editing, blogging, family safety, instant messaging, email, video editing, and a web browser toolbar.

Winmodem   US Robotics term for modems that lack a UART chip and use Windows for data handling.

WINS   Windows Internet Name Service. Method used by server versions of Windows to dynamically match NetBIOS computer names to their IP addresses (NetBIOS name resolution).

Wireless network   General term for any radio-frequency network, including *Wi-Fi*. Most wireless networks can be interconnected to conventional networks.

WLAN   Wireless local area network. Instead of wires, stations on a WLAN connect to each other through radio waves. The IEEE 802.11 family of standards guide the development of WLANs.

WMA   Windows Media Audio. This is the native compressed audio format created by Windows Media Player. Unlike *MP3*, WMA files support digital rights management.

word length   Number of bits in characters sent via serial port. 8-bit word length is used in PC-to-PC communications; 7-bit word length is used to communicate with mainframe computers.

WordBasic   Microsoft Word's macro language.

WPA   Wireless Protected Access. Replaced WEP as the standard for secure wireless networks. Original WPA uses TKIP encryption. An improved version known as WPA2 uses the even more secure AES encryption standard.

write-protect   Storage area that cannot be changed. Sliders on floppy disks, SD and SDHC flash memory cards are used to write-protect the contents, and motherboard options are used to write-protect many FlashROM BIOS chips to protect them from unauthorized upgrades.

WWW   World Wide Web. The portion of the Internet that uses the Hypertext Transfer Protocol (http://) and can thus be accessed via a web browser, such as Microsoft Internet Explorer, Netscape Navigator, and others.

X

XCOPY Windows command-line utility that copies groups of files into RAM and then to disk for faster transfers than COPY. This utility can also create folders during the copying process; when run with the Windows GUI in memory, it offers many additional features.

Z

Zip Iomega Zip is a removable-media drive using 100MB, 250MB, or 750MB proprietary media; also refers to the PKZIP format for compressed archive files.

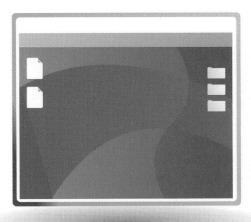

Index

Symbols

C

S

T

XP mode - 266